don't look back in anger

The Manchester City Fans' Story

To Lewis,

"Once a Blue, Always a Blue!"

Hope you enjoy the book!

All the best from

Sean & Don

C.T.W.D.!

By Don Price & Sean Riley

EMPIRE PUBLICATIONS

First published in 2019

This book is copyright under the Berne Convention. All rights are reserved. Apart from any fair dealing for the purpose of private study, research, criticism or review, as permitted under the Copyright Act, 1956, no part of this publication may be reproduced, stored in a retrieval system, or transmitted, in any form or by any means, electronic, electrical, chemical, mechanical, optical, photocopying, recording or otherwise, without the prior permission of the copyright owner. Enquiries should be sent to the publishers at the undermentioned address:

EMPIRE PUBLICATIONS
1 Newton Street, Manchester M1 1HW
© Don Price & Sean Riley 2019

ISBN: 978-1-909360-69-3

contents

PREFACE	5
FOREWORD	10
UNTYPICAL CITY	15
A WORD FROM THE AUTHORS	17
1: BACK IN THE DAY	23
2: THE ROYAL NAVY AND ME	30
3: MAINE ROAD	49
4: YOU'LL NEVER TAKE THE KIPPAX	54
5: WEMBERLEEE WEMBERLEEE	66
6: WE ALL HATE LEEDS AND LEEDS AND LEEDS	73
7: CAPTAINS	81
8: A CALL TO ARMS	97
9: CITY 'TIL I DIE	102
10: A NORWEGIAN BLUE	112
11: AWAY DAY BLUES	125
12: THE FALL AND RISE OF CITY	147
13: 25 YEARS AND WERE STILL HERE	153
14: THE GINGER WIG	157
15: HEED OVER HEELS WITH CITY	163
16: TYPICAL CITY	168

SEAN RILEY

PROLOGUE	179
1: SWEET SUBURBIA	183
2: TOTAL FOOTBALL IN TROUBLED TIMES	187
3: THE MOSS SIDE ACADEMY	195
4: FROM THE TWIN TOWERS TO HAMPDEN	203
5: SO NEAR, YET SO FAR	211

6: A KICK UP THE EIGHTIES 221
7: BACK IN THE BIG TIME 237
8: THE YO-YO YEARS 250
9: BALL, LEE AND DIVISION THREE 256
10: END OF AN ERA 272
11: THIRTY NOT OUT 276
AFTERWORD 282

preface

WHEN DON AND SEAN sent me the picture of the front cover to this book, I was immediately struck by the contrasting fortunes of Alan Ball and Pep Guardiola in relation to managing Manchester City and how their time at the club had a quirky relationship with my own experience of following the Blues with my daughters and then grandchildren.

Alan Ball's last league game as manager of City was away at Stoke City on 24th August 1996 - Pep's first league game in charge was at home against Sunderland on 13th August 2016, there were just eleven days short of twenty years in between. Ball's appointment was very underwhelming after Chairman Francis Lee had promised that one of Europe's top managers would be appointed to lead the Blues. Then one by one managers such as Franz Beckenbauer and George Graham ruled themselves out of a move to Moss Side and as the weeks went on Lee hinted at taking pre season training himself before unveiling his World Cup winning pal as City boss. Nine months later we were relegated on the final game of the 1995/96 season and if fans thought Ball leaving after just three games of the following season would signal a rebirth and charge back into the Premier League, well, two years down the line things had got even worse with relegation into the third tier of English football for the first time in the club's history.

By contrast, Pep Guardiola's arrival was greeted with immense joy. The announcement midway through the 2015/16 season that he would be arriving in the summer had Blues fans licking their lips in anticipation, meanwhile United fans (back peddling from championing Pep when the rumours suggested he was going to Old Trafford) coined the term 'Fraudiola' and 'Potless' within a year of Pep's arrival as City ended the season empty-handed - and Reds happily told anyone who would listen that they were much happier with Jose Mourinho having won three trophies in his first season. Yet two years down the line City had been crowned the 'Centurions' (whilst seemingly breaking every record ever set) and then last season the 'Fourmidables' as all four domestic trophies ended up in the trophy cabinet. Mourinho didn't even survive his third season as the fans turned on The Special One, the one they had predicted would chase Pep out of town.

Strangely Ball and Guardiola have one thing in common – they found their nemesis in the shape of Liverpool FC. Three games against the Merseyside giants defined Alan Ball's tenure; on 25th October 1995 City were knocked out of the League Cup 4-0 at Anfield. The team then returned down the East Lancs Road three days later for a Premier League game – presumably with a different game plan and a good idea of what to expect and how to counter it… only for Liverpool to pile on the agony winning 6-0, prompting the travelling Blues to mockingly chant "Alan Ball is a football genius" and sing a reworking of "Wonderwall" by Oasis into "…you're my Alan Ball" later changed to "fu*k off Alan Ball". As if to add pain to embarrassment Ball stated in the post-match interview that he "enjoyed" Liverpool's six-goal performance! It got even more ridiculous on the final day of the season. City, joint third from bottom with Southampton and Coventry City on goal difference, needed to better the result of one of those two clubs against Liverpool at Maine Road. With minutes to go and the game heading for a 2-2 draw, Ball (believing one of City's relegation rivals was losing) instructed Steve Lomas to head for the corner flag and see the game out. Ball was the only person inside Maine Road who thought City were safe! Everyone else knew that both Southampton and Coventry were also drawing – so the time ran down and City were relegated.

Pep's encounters with Liverpool have been just as dramatic. City were beaten in the Champions League Quarter Final in 2018, both games were littered with controversial decisions that went Liverpool's way. Pep was even 'sent to the stands' at half time during the second leg at the Etihad and let's not forget the little incident involving City's team bus being attacked outside Anfield during a widely publicised 'welcome party' that the police and home club did very little to prevent turning into a riot. This stoked a rivalry between the clubs and that intensity was increased further last season but this time with the tide turning in City's favour as the blues took four points off Liverpool (it would have been six had a last minute penalty by Riyad Mahrez at Anfield not bothered orbiting satellites). City's 2-1 win at home in January came courtesy of a remarkable goal line clearance by John Stones and those four points when added up in May saw City clinch the title by a point ahead of Liverpool, irritating Kop boss Klopp, Liverpool fans and the large and vocal scouse-loving media. And so it continues this season, with City beating Liverpool on penalties at Wembley to win the 2019 Community Shield, courtesy of a remarkable 93rd minute goal line clearance by Kyle Walker. So it appears that Pep may now be a thorn in Klopp's side.

Anyway, back to Alan Ball. In 1996 I was taking my daughters, then aged four and two, to home games, wondering if they would be up for a lifetime of suffering serial failures as our neighbours across town swept all before them. It was tough being a City fan at that time and an even tougher growing up as one. We parents had become immune to disappointment after disappointment, but would the next generation of Blues be so forgiving? In December 2018 I took my two grandchildren – aged 9 and 6 - to their first home game against Bournemouth and six months later I took them to the open top bus parade along Deansgate to witness the four pieces of silverware on show and the players and management receiving the acclaim they richly deserved from thousands of Blues lining the streets. I now wonder how they would cope should City not win a trophy this coming season or next season! I perversely want them to experience a bit of "Typical City" failure so they can truly appreciate the great times we have now and not become spoilt by success. How great it must be to be a Blue at school now compared to twenty years ago!

Of course a lot happened between Alan Ball leaving and Pep Guardiola joining. The club has had nine managers (and three caretaker managers - Asa Hartford, Phil Neal and Brian Kidd.) Of the nine managers, well first up after Ball was Steve Coppell, who lasted just six games and thirty-three days before he asked to get off the roller coaster, Frank Clark lasted just over a year as the old Division Three pulled City ever nearer. Joe Royle couldn't stop the rot but steered the Blues back into the second tier after an unforgettable play off final win over Gillingham at Wembley. At one point, after the infamous defeat at York City, the Blues were in 12th place in the third tier of English football, the lowest league placing in the club's history. Yet the fans never deserted the club – it almost appeared that the worse the team became, the more of us turned up. We were Grief Hunters! We really were there when we were shit, a point that away fans constantly seem to ignore.

After 'Sir Joe' (two promotions and two relegations in three and a quarter seasons!) Kevin Keegan arrived in 2001 introducing a swashbuckling style of play centred around Ali Benarbia, Eyal Berkovic, Darren Huckerby and a young, exciting Shaun Wright-Phillips, helping to fill the now ageing and dated Maine Road stadium. City bade farewell to Moss Side in 2003 after eighty years, moving from South to East Manchester and when Keegan left the club his assistant Stuart Pearce took over, employing his daughter's small, stuffed pony as a 'lucky mascot' and electing to play goalkeeper David James up front for the final minutes of a hugely important game (and he would have gotten away with it too if it hadn't have been for that pesky Middlesbrough goalkeeper saving Robbie Fowler's 92nd minute penalty).

Psycho's final season was a desperately poor affair that reflected in the lowest average attendance figures at the Etihad to date. Many fans have stated that season as the one that might have broken the camel's back and support wavered as a result, but the vast majority carried on as usual. What else would we do over the weekend? Just ten goals were scored at home all season and the last home goal came in a 2-1 defeat on New Years Day! By May Pearce was out and the following season City had both a new owner and a new manager. Former Thailand Prime Minister Thaksin Shinawatra gave away free noodles to fans in Albert Square and brought with him former England manager Sven Göran Eriksson. The Swede made a bright start but that soon faded and he only lasted a season and City's owner (affectionately known as 'Frank') lasted only a few months longer amid on going legal action in Thailand. With his assets overseas being frozen, City were on the brink of going into administration. Ex-United player Mark Hughes left Blackburn Rovers for City (a decision that was about as popular as Alan Ball's appointment among rank and file supporters). Hughes only lasted 18 months by which time City had acquired their current owners. They appointed the stylish Italian Roberto Mancini who promised to 'bring down that banner' at Old Trafford that counted the years since the club had last won a major trophy. Within twelve months of that historic FA Cup win City nearly blew the title on the final day before the most amazing end to a Premier League season of all time. However Mancini left in the aftermath of an FA Cup final defeat by Wigan Athletic, following player unrest.

In came Manuel Pellegrini, a quiet, charming man who in three seasons gave the club one Premier League title, two League Cups and a Champions League semi final. Halfway through his final season it was announced that Pep Guardiola would be joining the club in time for the following season, a decision the club had paved the way for by recruiting many of Pep's coaching and talent spotting team from Barcelona, where he had won three La Liga titles and two European Cups. Pellegrini got a great send off from the appreciative fans at his final game but we were all looking forward to seeing Guardiola's team. Three seasons on and it's safe to say we've not been disappointed and the question we ask ourselves is "Can we top the Centurions and Fourmidables?" Twenty years ago we wondered if it could get any worse, now we ask can it really get any better? I suppose the Champions League is the only pot missing...

So to get back to the book - should we look back in anger at the Peter Swales and Francis Lee eras, the bewildering signings such as Roque Santa Cruz and Jo to name but two; or the players seemingly 'downing tools' in shocking defeats to Middlesbrough (8-1) and already relegated Wigan Athletic in the 2013 FA Cup Final or the huge cast of dubious chancers we can point to in the club's history, be they players or owners!

Anyone who knows me will appreciate that, as usual, my answer comes from a line not from Oasis but The Smiths and their single "Shakespeare's Sister":

"I can laugh about it now, but at the time it was terrible..."

Phill Gatenby

foreword

I CAN'T REMEMBER EXACTLY when I decided I was a City fan. The evidence shows it must have been mid-1950s because I clearly felt devoted enough to ask for a particular present for my birthday. My dad, a Salford fan, grudgingly obliged. All these years later I am sure people will say such an item never existed, but I know it did. It was a Manchester City replica kit, endorsed by Roy Clarke. I can picture it now in a cellophane packet with Roy's autograph on the cardboard stiffener. A sky blue and white short sleeved jersey, hooped socks and a pair of what I was disappointed to see described as "white knickers"

And so I began going to matches with school mates; a Cup replay against Blackpool, a division above us, with 53.000 at Maine Road, then promotion at Rotherham. At seventeen I saw them win the League, at eighteen the FA Cup, at nineteen the League Cup and European Cup Winners' Cup. Blimey, I thought, this will go on forever. It didn't. If you are not old enough to remember what happened next please ask someone who is. If you are, then I am sure you will agree it was one of the more justified examples of the use of the phrase "roller coaster" in a sporting context.

But even when City were nearer to the Conference than the Champions League, the humour and passion of the fanatical City fans never went away. We always found ways of coping. When Don was running the Prestwich & Whitefield Supporters Club, he used a mixture of perverse determination, a highly developed sense of the absurd, ruthless cunning and an ability to get where water can't, to organise meetings, Sportmans' dinners, charity events, family fun days and some legendary away trips.

I have been in attendance at some of his alcohol-related events and therefore can see no reason to doubt the veracity of the stories you will be reading, though at times you will find yourself shaking your head at some of the things Don and his fellow contributors have put in the book. The passion, loyalty and the bizarre stand out. I can't think of anyone else but Don who would arrange for a pub to open in Prestwich at 9.30 am so a coach could take them to Oldham, which is 10 miles away, for a 3pm kick off. The reason given was to allow for "lunch" in Middleton, four and a half miles away! Many on the coach, however, still managed to miss kick off.

I was on the coach from Cardiff and it took about twelve hours to get to Manchester as we seemed to stop at a pub every half hour or so. The things you do for the love of City.

Life as a City fan is rather different nowadays, on and off the pitch, it's been a long journey. As you will see as you read on, there is much truth in the Chinese saying, "the journey itself is the reward".

James H. Reeve

we lived the dream

Manchester City is definitely a special club. It has that infectious ability to lose, has the feeling that it is going to go wrong, but we will end up smiling in the end. There were times in the club's history when we thought we were confined to mediocrity, going down the divisions we almost accepted it, and started to enjoy it because that is what we do, if we are not enjoying it then what is the point? We didn't dare to dream as it would hurt too much. The times we are in now seemed unimaginable back then. In our dreams, the thought that today might one day be reality would have been considered far-fetched. So now we cherish every moment, every minute and every day because we are living in a time we never thought possible. You can't knock us down, because we have been further down than you could ever imagine and guess what? We got out of it and most importantly we enjoyed it. (I pinched this from City Watch but I can't argue with the sentiment!)

untypical city

THIS BOOK IS ABOUT ordinary Manchester City fans, who have spent their lives following the club through the rocky years that haunted them, but they never lost their sense of humour and togetherness. From the 1950s to date, the fans of Manchester City never gave up, even though their team lunged from one crisis to another. Although City achieved some notable success in the late 1960s and early 1970s it always seemed we were teetering on the edge of a cliff waiting for the next big fall, and it wasn't usually long in coming. "Typical City" was the usual reaction from fans after a game we should have won easily but somehow managed to lose. Don never forgets taking his two lads to an away game at Birmingham. It looked like it was going to end up 0-0 until City scored in the 89th minute. While the fans were still celebrating, Birmingham went up the other end and equalised. Then the unthinkable happened and Birmingham went on to score another to claim victory. Why oh why did it always seem to happen to us?

Then there was the time we played Halifax in the FA Cup, you would have put your mortgage on a City win, good job we never did otherwise the streets of Manchester would have had a substantial amount of homeless people sleeping rough that January night as we somehow contrived a 1-0 defeat to one of the worst teams in the league. City fans are no different from those of long suffering fans of teams such as Bury, Rochdale or Blackpool or indeed any other fans up and down the country who have seen their club fall through the cracks. Like them we followed our team through the bad times hoping our time would come. Well ours did come with the new owners and massive investment, and from the moment we were taken over we've hardly looked back.

One question we keep getting asked is "where would the club

be now without that investment?" The only truthful answer I can give is probably up shit creek without a paddle but whatever the fortunes of the club the fans would still be there supporting the club through thick and thin. Sunderland, Leeds United and Nottingham Forest are just three teams out of many I could mention who were up there with the best but suffered a dip in fortune but their fans stuck loyally by their club just as we did when we dropped into the old Third division and only got out by the skin of our teeth following a play off final at Wembley against Gillingham. And this is what the book is about, the ordinary loyal fan who has followed City no matter what obstacles are put in their way.

a word from the authors

WELL LET'S START BY explaining why Sean and I joined forces to write this book. First of all we both have a love for football in general and for Manchester City in particular. We've have followed City through the generations. Over the years, like all football fans, they have seen many changes in the game ranging from rule changes on the field, all-seater grounds, alcohol restrictions at the ground, draconian and degrading treatment of fans in old decrepit stadiums that weren't fit for purpose, to the state of the art stadiums with top notch facilities that fans now enjoy.

They have seen sponsors, TV companies and wealthy owners invest heavily in football clubs and football culture has changed significantly over the last 30 years. The ordinary football fan has had to adapt to these changes. No longer can you wake up on a Saturday morning with a bit of a hangover having had a late night and decide you want to follow your team away from home. There are a couple of reasons for that little scenario not happening now, first there is an excellent chance your team won't be playing on a Saturday afternoon, as we all know by now that football kick-off times are now dictated by TV companies so a fixture can be played at almost time or day of the week. The second reason is that it is extremely hard to get your hands on an away ticket as they are in relatively short supply considering the number of fans wishing to attend away games. Clubs have adopted their own policies for distributing tickets for away games ranging from a loyalty point system to fans putting their name in a ballot, so not all the fans can be pleased all the time. It is like a military operation now to see if you are lucky enough to get a ticket, only then can you start to plan how you will get to the game and then wait with baited breath to see if the TV companies pull the plug on you and change the day and or time of the game.

Back in the day it was much easier just wake up with a sore head, get down to Piccadilly train station and pay on the "Football Special" have a few beers then pay to get in the ground. One downside to the changes is it is very hard to go as a family to away games now as it hard enough to get one away ticket never mind four or five, plus the cost is restrictive as tickets on top of travel can end up costing a tidy sum. It is usually easier to get tickets for Cup games as the away club usually receives a bigger allocation, so all is not lost for a budding away fan. We've both been following City through all these changes and all the comings and goings at Maine Road and the Etihad and write about our experiences in this book.

We first became mates in the 1990s when Sean started attending the Prestwich & Whitefield Branch of the City Supporters' club of which I was the founder and for ten years the Chairman. We had some epic times together and Sean has a belting chapter in the book about the time they celebrated their birthdays together in the Platt Lane stand at Maine Road. Sean first started going as a kid in the 70s and in the last 30 years has only missed one competitive match. It wasn't his fault though as the away game in Russia was supposed to be played behind closed doors and City didn't receive any tickets for their fans, so I suppose we can let him off on that one.

For many years Sean has been a regular contributor to Manchester City's only surviving fanzine *King of The Kippax* and has written articles for other football magazines and he also contributed a chapter in Don's previous book, *"We Never Win at Home We Never Win Away"* which received excellent reviews on Amazon and won rave reviews from football fans up and down the country and around the world (well my mate in Australia liked it!).

I started following City in the late 1960s and loved the hustle and bustle of standing on the Kippax but as I grew older opted for the gentler surroundings of the Family Stand when his two sons Steven and Sean started to go with him. I've also had some articles published in *King of The Kippax* and was a regular contributor to the Prestwich and Whitefield supporters' club newsletter. Apart from the previous book I have also written, *"A Football Fans Story, The Royal Navy, Manchester City & Me"*.

So why did we decide to team up for this one? Sean has always fancied writing a book and in fact a few years ago wrote a few chapters which remained in his computer but he never seemed to find the time to take the final step and give it a go whereas I've got loads of time on my hands as I'm retired; it seemed like destiny that we'd co-author a book on City.

We sincerely hope you enjoy reading the book as much as we enjoyed writing it. So, with no more ado either get yourself a brew or a can of lager or glass of wine, put your feet up while we take you through what has been an unforgettable journey for us as Blues.

Don Price

dedication

This book is dedicated to all City fans, former players and officials who are sadly no longer with us

acknowledgements

So many have helped in getting this book together and I am humbled by their sterling efforts. To protect the guilty, the innocent and the shy, one or two names have been changed. Many thanks to Sean Riley for his massive contribution, Empire Publications for putting the book together, Dave & Sue Wallace and Phill Gatenby for doing the proof reading and my wife Cath for sorting out all my spelling mistakes. For their contributions: James H Reeve, Anthony Rawson, Craig Simpson, Tor Sonsteby, Phill Gatenby (again) and Susan Bookbinder who have told their stories. Also a big shout to my mate Brian Searson, a Leeds fan, who added his own take on our club.

To all the fans who have contributed to the Memorial Chapter, thank you but the biggest thanks goes to all who have bought and read the book, we hope you enjoy it!

Yours truly has written the first few chapters, then Anthony, Craig and Tor add chapters before Sean tells the story of his 45 year love affair with Manchester City.

1: back in the day

I was born on the day City were beaten at Preston North End (6th March 1954) things could only get better, at least that's what his parents hoped! Well it wasn't a complete disaster of a season as City didn't get relegated but finished a disappointing 17th in Division One. Over the years City managed to disappoint and excite their fans many times in equal doses but our love for the club never wavered and fans of all ages are now reaping the rewards for our patience and playing the sort of football we could only dream of back then.

I WAS BORN AT CRUMPSALL HOSPITAL, which was a grim place back then, it is now called North Manchester General Hospital, but locals still call it by its original name, it's the same as we call Manchester Airport, Ringway and HMP Manchester, Strangeways. I am only just getting used to calling our ground the Etihad, but I think that is only because the other names, The Commonwealth Stadium, City of Manchester Stadium and Eastlands never had a ring to them. It took years for some fans to stop referring to our new ground as Maine Road! The name of the area around the stadium became known as Eastlands, about the time the stadium was being built for the Commonwealth Games and soon became popular with residents. Well it does sound more upmarket than Beswick, Bradford and Ancoats and for similar reasons why the Trafford Centre wasn't called Dumplington, and for the same reason Manchester United are not called Stretford Rangers. Whilst we are at it, parts of Ancoats are now known as New Islington. The world's gone mad!

Anyway, after entering this world to a Manchester City defeat, I suppose it was destiny that I spent my formative years watching City from the Kippax at Maine Road and spent many grim Saturday afternoons following them up and down the country. It wasn't necessarily that watching City was grim but just getting to some of the grounds was at times a logistical nightmare. Some of the grounds back then would make the average slum look five star. Our house was only about a mile from Prestwich Village and backed on to St. Mary's Park which was a magnet for the local youngsters to spend time on the tennis courts, swing park or play cricket and football. George Smith, the late great City player, was often in the park walking his dog and used to give us tips when he watched us play. Needless, to say his advice went right over my head.

Many areas of Inner City Manchester were still recovering from the war years with many slum areas getting demolished and families were being moved to different areas of Manchester. As a kid though, none of the stress that concerned and worried the adults bothered us as we didn't know any better and we were happy as long as we had a football to have a kick about in the park with and we would stay there all day long.

Besides my appearance, the next best thing to happen in 1954 was the end of rationing which was in place just after the outbreak of the Second World War being in place for 14 years. All sorts of essential food, supplies and household goods were rationed, as well as furniture, clothing and petrol for any lucky sods who could afford a car back then. We relied on so much imported stuff during the war, but the Germans were determined to deprive us, by having a strangle hold on the UK. The German U Boats (Submarines) did their best to starve us of much needed supplies and equipment by trying to sink the convoys bringing the essential items across the Atlantic to our shores. Before the war started, we imported about 56 million tons of products a year from America, soon after the war started this figure was dramatically slashed as the U Boats were causing havoc with the convoys and many brave Royal Navy and Merchant Navy sailors were lost in the battles of the Atlantic. The ration book was the key to survival, being issued to ensure that every household was treated equally and that everyone had the minimum required to survive.

The one thing I do remember when growing up was the term

that we use now "community spirit", which was alive and well back then. I think the main reason was that on the council estates the same families had lived there for donkeys' years and had grown up with each other, so everyone knew and respected each other. This togetherness really kicked in if you needed advice, help or assistance. Most families, especially during rationing, lived never mind from week to week, but for many it was day by day. It was very common for kids to be sent to their neighbours to borrow a couple of eggs or a cup of sugar, a few ounces of flour or half a pint of milk, or some tea leaves or a bit of margarine. Unlike now, no-one had credit or debit cards but with a bit of luck the corner shop might let you have some stuff "on tick" but woe betide if you never "settled up" on time. Also, most shops shut for a lunch hour every day and only opened half day on a Wednesday. Some also shut early on Saturdays and everything was shut all day Sunday, so it was a godsend to have nice understanding neighbours, as it was very easy to run out of essential food stuff. Another thing about having good neighbours is that most people never locked their back doors, which isn't some urban myth or a bit of exaggerated nostalgia on my part, it was just the way it was. Having said that the majority of people didn't have anything to nick! Most people, if they had a TV it was a black and white one; there were no iPads, smart phones, Laptops or the hundreds of other gadgets people have today and I couldn't see any thief trying to run off with your grannies mangle!

One highlight for us kids was helping the milkman at the weekends, before we went playing or watching football, we would help him deliver milk to the neighbours in our Avenue and would get a glass of orange juice for helping. Once the milk float ran over my foot, but I don't remember it being too painful as I never went to hospital and I don't think it stopped me playing football. Another regular feature was the rag and bone man with his horse (which we'd feed) and cart. The horse could have been a him, her or a donkey for all I know but the adults used to love it if he or she had a shit in the Avenue as they would be out with a shovel to put the muck on their roses!

At the time Prestwich had, and still has, a huge Jewish

population which were at the forefront of mass demonstrations when the legendary Bert Trautmann signed for Manchester City. Bert served in the German army during the war and was captured and interned as a Prisoner of War in England. City players who had themselves served in the war or who had friends and family that did, rallied round and supported him, and his brilliant displays in goals soon won the demonstrators round. It is hard to imagine the horrors, hardships and sacrifices the sailors, army, air force and indeed the civilians that were around during the war had to put up with. To be honest, I think most of the younger generation just take it for granted now, but I can't blame them really, as what happened seems like a lifetime away. One legacy of the war were the air raid shelters which were built in many places all over Manchester and there were loads in Prestwich. Whilst many were demolished soon after the war to make way for new buildings, many remained intact in Prestwich Clough (a Clough is a large woodland). Whilst the one in Prestwich might not be as famous as Boggart Hole Clough in Blackley it was where we, as kids, used to go to play and muck about in the air raid shelters.

The Clough was as far removed from the grime, smog and the slums of inner-city Manchester as could be, and many people would go there for their Sunday Walks. In the Clough there were many different sorts of trees, a variety of wild flowers and different species of birds who loved the habitat and there was also a free-flowing stream plus at one time a great little cafe. In the 1970s just after I started going out with Cath, we took her dog Sabre for a walk through the Clough. In my wisdom I was encouraging him to go into the stream, when I slipped and went arse over tit into the water and got covered in some horrible brown substance. God knows what else was in the water but needless to say you wouldn't find any fish in the stream.

The Clough backed onto St Mary's Church which featured in the many weddings and funerals in the popular soap Coronation Street. It's a fantastic church with a great heritage and a cracking pub next door which, surprise surprise, is called The Church Inn, but that's not the reason we got married there, honest!

Bonfire night, and the days leading up, was always something we looked forward to as kids. The older lads used to let us youngsters go with them to collect firewood and if we felt a bit daring would "raid" other gangs stash of wood and nick it for our own bonfire. Everyone from the Avenue used to turn out on bonfire night but a couple of times the fire was so high the flames burnt down the telephone wires, not that it mattered that much as most houses didn't have a telephone back then, but the council were none to pleased. As kids we got up to all the usual mischief like going hedgehopping, playing knock and run, and scrumping from gardens with fruit trees. Looking back, we really must have pissed off some people but as we had an unwritten policy of not shitting on our own doorstep, we rarely got into trouble with our parents. For a few years they held a Gymkhana (Horse Show) in St Mary's Park. To enable the show to run smoothly, besides the main entrances, they took the fence down in Rectory Grove to let the wagons taking the horses to get in smoothly. To help the drivers with directions, the council erected signs showing them where to go. We couldn't help ourselves and changed the signs and sent the wagons up Rectory Avenue instead which was a dead end! We thought it was funny as fuck but I don't think anyone else appreciated our sense of humour. The adults had a field day with all the horse muck that was left behind, they must have had the best roses in Manchester.

We must have spent most of our childhood in the park and would play football morning, noon, and night in all weather and conditions. The only problem we had was the amount of dog shit in the park but apart from that, only a burst football or tea time would stop us from playing. Apart from playing football we used to love to watch football but unlike today, apart from Match of the Day on a Saturday night and the FA Cup Final, that was the only football we could watch on the box. That is why going to watch a live football game was so popular. We also had the bonus of having a good local amateur side on our doorstep Prestwich Heys (Formally Heys Old Boys) named after the school where they used to study plus many players were ex pupils and "our mate"

George Smith used to manage them for a while. Unfortunately some of the lads we used to knock about with were from the dark side, but on occasions we would put our allegiances to one side and go together and watch Bury FC play as it was only 4 miles up the road. It was dead easy to get to, plus quite often the club gave our school vouchers so we could get in for nothing. Going to Maine Road was dead easy as well as a special bus used to go from the Woodthorpe Hotel on the corner of Bury Old Road and Sheepfoot Lane near Heaton Park. If we missed that we could either get a bus or the train to Victoria train station and jump on the number 123 bus straight to the ground.

Looking back now you can just see how times have changed and how quickly technology has moved on. Five-year olds these days can do things with mobile phones that their grandparents could only dream about. The nostalgic Red Telephone Box has all but disappeared as it seems everyone on the planet has a mobile phone or two. Supermarkets are open 24/7 and you don't even have to leave the house as you can order online, and the stuff will get delivered to your door.

Football is on television morning, noon and night and the local milkman and rag and bone man is all but confined to the history books. You must be extremely careful what you say now as the politically correct world has gone bonkers and I don't think we can even say The Three Wise Men now can we? Oh well if we can't that's me in the shit again!

We all owe a great debt of gratitude for what our parents, grandparents and great grandparents went through. Many that came back from the war never spoke about their experiences and just carried on in the best way they could. Many people show their gratitude by remembering our fallen in all wars and conflicts by attending the Remembrance Day parade at local cenotaphs. It is very pleasing that many youngsters not only attend the events but are involved as well, as boy scouts, girl guides, local brass bands, St John's Ambulance Brigade and cadets from the Navy, Army and air force also attend and many children go with their parents. Football clubs around the country also hold a minute's silence which is impeccably honoured and all the clubs have a poppy printed on their football shirts during that weekend's games which is then auctioned off for charity.

One thing that is sad in this day and age are the amount of veterans from recent conflicts that are living on the streets or in hostels as there is not enough "social housing" to place them in, but at the same time investors are buying luxury apartments by the dozen to make a profit, which you might say is fair enough but is it right they then leave them empty until the house market rises while ex-veterans are on the street? My days as a Trade Union Official are long gone but there is something wrong somewhere with a system that allows ex-service men and women to sleep on the streets while apartments all over the place remain empty. Okay, I will get off my soap box now before Cath kicks me off it. I hope you enjoyed my little trip down memory lane and hope people of a certain age group can relate to it. I can't believe I remembered half that stuff, it might be because I am doing sober November and not had a drink for weeks. For readers who weren't around back then, I am certainly not looking through rose-tinted glasses and I'm not saying they were the good old days or that we had it better or tougher than the youngsters of today. The kids of today still have problems just like we did, it is just part of life and of growing up.

The one thing that has definitely changed for the better are the fortunes of Manchester City FC. Since I first started watching City, we seemed at various times to have more downs than ups but now all that has changed. The roller coaster years are a thing of the past, so let's all continue looking forward to a bright future. No one deserves the success more than the loyal Manchester City Fans.

2: the royal navy and me

LOOKING BACK, I must have been stark raving bonkers to sign on to join The Royal Navy as a chef for twelve years at the tender age of fifteen. Seeing as I had never been away from home before, I had never set foot on a ship and I certainly didn't know how to cook (what do you mean I still don't?) as my culinary skills were zilch, what possessed me to join up will remain one of life's little mysteries, oh well someone had to join up, so it might as well have been me.

I will get the well-worn Navy joke out of the way first. I heard it numerous times whilst in the Navy by dissatisfied sailors, "The chef's exam" in the Royal Navy is the hardest of all the exams as no one has ever passed it yet? Ha-ha flipping Ha. Well at least I got that out of the way before some smart arse told it me again.

Although I had swam in the sea at Blackpool and been on the rowing boats and skiffs on Heaton Park Boating Lake, it hardly qualified me for a life on the ocean waves in the Navy. I was not academically minded at school but that doesn't mean I was totally thick; I just wasn't interested in any of the lessons except sport but unfortunately wasn't much good at that either. I wasn't into fixing things or making things and surprise, surprise I still can't do either! Give me a plug to fix and there is a good chance we would have a power cut, I was useless at woodwork and metal work. Music wasn't a strong point either, I was alright playing the tambourine but there was never any call for a full-time tambourine player in Prestwich. So with my choices severely limited and having the misguided belief being a chef would be an easy option, I applied to join both Radcliffe Catering College and the Royal Navy, as luck would have it I was successful in both applications but as the letter from the Navy landed through the letter box first I decided to let the Royal Navy make the most out of my hidden talents. Now before we go any further this is a warning to remind people who read my first book *A Football Fans Story. The Royal Navy, Manchester City & Me*. It had loads of stuff about my time in the Royal Navy in it. I suppose the title gave it away. Anyway I will do my best not to bore you to death by repeating what you have already read, instead I will just give a quick recap and stick loads of new stuff in, so please don't jump ship and put the book down and watch the TV and for those who haven't read the book, the warning doesn't apply to you lot, so grab another beer or a tot of rum and I will carry on.

In 1969 when I joined up Britain had interests and Naval bases all over the world and the prospects of being paid to visit some countries I hadn't heard of and others that I didn't have a clue where they were appealed to me as I had never been abroad and the only time I had been out of Manchester was to go to Blackpool or to watch City play. At that time the country had a Navy to be proud of and it was a match for any in the world. The pride of the fleet were the Aircraft, Helicopter and Troop Carriers; we had the Eagle, Albion, Bulwark, Ark Royal, Hermes and Illustrious as well as powerful Destroyers, Frigates, Mine sweepers and we also had a huge submarine fleet. Nowadays the Navy is a shadow of its former self and while we have just launched a new Aircraft Carrier, we don't have the right type of planes for them, hopefully by the time you are reading this masterpiece that situation will have been rectified. Sailing into Plymouth or Portsmouth harbour was a site to behold as the ships moored up would look first class in all their splendour with the white ensign flying majestically in the wind. We had many ships to be proud of back in the day. Across the water from Portsmouth is Gosport which was home to HMS Dolphin the Navy's Submarine base and where I spent twelve months trying out my culinary skills on many unsuspecting sailors while continuing my training. Unfortunately, our conventional submarine fleet has all but disappeared and HMS Dolphin is now a submarine museum so if you're ever in that neck of the woods pop down and have a look as I am sure you won't be disappointed. It is on my to do list to go back again as my last visit to the base was in 1998. I will, just for research purposes only, pop round to see if the old submariners watering hole The George and Dragon is still going. When I started going in there I wasn't even seventeen years old but always got served. The place was always full of characters, it never seemed to operate the same opening and closing time as the rest of the United Kingdom as it seemed whatever time you went it was always open, well the side door in the yard was, even if the main door wasn't. Even though HMS Dolphin doesn't have any operational submarines, the Navy still has a submarine fleet but they are all nuclear powered and based in Scotland.

Before I started going on about the fleet and submarines, I meant to tell you about HMS Ganges, as that is where I was first sent in 1969 to start my Navy training, but I jumped the gun never mind, I am back on track again now… HMS Ganges was a sprawling training establishment set in acres of land in Shotley Gate in Suffolk, not too far from Ipswich and also not too far from Harwich where many of you may or may not have boarded the ferry to Holland. I remember shitting myself when I first arrived (not literally I hasten to add, just a figure of speech) It was all so new and strange to me. There were thirty people sleeping in the Mess, when I say mess it wasn't a mess as such it was clean and tidy, the equivalent word for non-seafaring folk would be a large room with beds or for students living away from home a dormitory, but anyway it was where we slept. The first night was horrendous with people shouting, snoring, farting and two or three were crying, the mattress and pillows were not from Slumberland, I can assure you of that. For someone who had his own bedroom back home it was a bit of a culture shock but all I could do was grin and bear it, and over the next days and weeks it started to become the norm as everyone was in the same boat and we just got on with it. The third week we were there City were playing Ipswich at Portman Road but as luck would have it as new trainees, we had no leave for the first few weeks not even at on a weekend. What a sickener as Ipswich was only down the road. There was no chance of sneaking out either as there were more guards on duty than at Strangeways plus we only had Navy issue clothes and

Don't Look Back In Anger

uniform as all our civilian clothes were boxed up and sent back home. As it happened one of the instructors was a City fan from Gorton and he got me the matchday programme which was good of him as most of the instructors treated us like shit especially for the first few weeks. We drew 1-1 with Franny Lee scoring for City and even though I wasn't at the match I was there in spirit. I kept that programme for years until I moved to a new house and gave it away with the rest of my programme collection. The team that day consisted of all English players with most of them local coming from Manchester, Winsford and Bolton. Tony Book was an outsider from Bath (signed from Plymouth Argyle) and although we bought Colin Bell from nearby Bury FC, he was originally from County Durham. What a team that was!

Joining the Navy took me way out of my comfort zone. It was a very hard regime from day one especially for the first few months and wasn't for the faint hearted as there never seemed to be any light at the end of the tunnel. Many lads applied to buy themselves out which you could do after you had served three months. If you decided you wanted out after the three months were up there was another opportunity after six months. After six months you were snookered as there was no further opportunities as a trainee to buy yourself out. Surprisingly, even though the training was extremely tough, only a small percentage of people bought themselves out. We must have all been gluttons for punishment or wanted to prove a point, deep down we knew things would get better. One thing that kept me going through that period was having a laugh with other City fans who I met there plus my brother and my mum sent me the *Football Pink* every week and now and again I would be sent some programmes.

The biggest gripe for me and many of the young recruits was the training, it was so repetitive it became boring and only a couple of hours a week were set aside to learn any catering skills. Instead we spent most of the time marching, running, doing cross country, swimming, cleaning the mess deck, getting shouted at, learning how to sew, polishing anything that needed polishing, washing and ironing clothes. Also going to school to attain a better standard of Maths and English, going on the assault course, training with rifles, which is all well and good but seriously there was no need to do it for twelve months, especially when we found out if you joined up over sixteen years of age you went to HMS Raleigh at Tor Point near Plymouth for training and were only there for about eight weeks, work that one out if you can because I still can't. That meant there was hardly any leisure time for us, you couldn't just pop out of the main gates and go for a walk when you felt like it. We were only allowed out at certain times on some weekends and that was just for a few hours and we all had to go out in our "Number Ones" which was our best uniform and even though I say so myself we all looked dead smart and were very proud of wearing the uniform. While at times I thought the regime at Ganges bordered on the sadistic and extreme, at other times I found it exhilarating, exciting and great fun, maybe making it fun was my way of coping with it.

While under training it is exactly the same for everyone and no matter how hard or tough, it is it isn't long until it becomes the norm and it somehow became acceptable as we were all in the same boat (no pun intended) and we just used to all grin and bear it together and help each other out when we could. While at the time we used to all moan like fuck about what we were experiencing we used to just count the months, weeks and days until we passed out of Ganges and were no longer trainees but proper sailors and an integral part of the Royal Navy.

I always seemed to be hungry, especially during the first couple of months I was there. Don't get me wrong we were all well fed and the food was very good but we were always on the move, whether it was marching, running, swimming, doing the assault course or playing football, being in the gym or out on the water sailing. I must have been burning off more calories than I was taking in even though I hadn't even heard of calories back then. Luckily we had a NAAFI and there were vending machines full of sweets and chocolates, that's if we had any money left as I always seemed to be skint, Just reading this back I seem like a right moaning old fart, but for the first six weeks our pay was only £1 a week and we had to make sure we had enough soap and toothpaste before we could buy any toffees and chocolates or cigarettes. Luckily most of us were sent "goodie boxes" from our families and it was great when letters arrived especially if the goodie boxes were full of chocolate bars and sweets,

Although we were all under 16 when we joined, we were allowed to smoke fags back then, as it would have probably been more hassle than it was worth to try and stop us as at that point. All of us would turn 16 while we were there and back then the vast majority of people in the UK seemed to smoke as there were no 'stop smoking' campaigns back then. However the opposite was in full swing as there were smoking adverts on television, in the newspapers, in magazines and on billboards. You could smoke on the bus, on trains, in pubs and clubs, in restaurants in the cinema and even on aeroplanes and football grounds. How bizarre that seems now.

The thing that did piss me and other lads off big time was when we had to have a kit muster which meant all our kit had to be laid out perfectly ready for inspection. It just depended on who was doing the inspection whether it got passed or not or whether it was launched all over the mess or even out of the window. Remember we were still only kids just out of school and away from friends and family for the first time, most had hardly if ever used an iron, if they washed any clothes it would have been done in a launderette and not by hand. None of us would have polished our shoes to the standard expected by the instructors, so we were still on a learning curve. Once we had our kit laid out we were all really proud of what we had achieved and how far we had come in such a short space of time, so for some jumped up little Hitler to rip your efforts to shreds and dump your kit on the floor so you had to do it all again was pretty heart breaking and humiliating. We quickly realised it was nothing personal and the instructors were just pushing us to our limits, but you still felt pig sick at the time. The longer we were there, the more we got used to it and some of the shit they threw at us became like water off a duck's back after a while. It wasn't all doom and gloom though as you could have a good laugh with some of the lads. I enjoyed the swimming and sailing and playing football, it was good fun on the rifle range and now and again it would be our turn to watch a movie at the Cinema. When we got a bit of free time we could also play snooker and ten pin bowling but as I was shit at snooker and never had the money for ten pin bowling I never bothered. I did for some strange reason enjoy going over the assault course, but I could never understand why.

After a while we could apply for weekend end leave but as it would take too long to get to Manchester after finishing our duties on Friday we would then have to leave Manchester early on the Sunday about lunchtime, it didn't seem to be worth the expense or the hassle, so I never bothered. When we got time off on a Sunday, we went into Harwich which was on our doorstep and Felixstowe wasn't too far away and as they had a big funfair, we went there a couple of times. We couldn't do much when we were on leave as we were usually skint, but it was great just to get off the base with no one bawling and shouting at us and giving us grief.

When I first left school I had to wait a couple of months before I went to HMS Ganges so I worked at Pauldens in Manchester (now Debenhams) where my wage was £5 a week. When I joined the Navy my wage was dropped to £1 a week for 6 weeks then increased to £1 and 10 shillings then after 3 months it went to £2 a week and stayed at that for the rest of my time at Ganges. In 1969 a packet of 10 fags would have cost the equivalent of 10p, fish & chips 15p, a pint of beer under 20p and a litre of petrol around 30p. Since then the tax man has really gone to town on fags, beer and petrol so the moral of the story is don't smoke, drink, or drive a car and you will be loaded.

Over the years until it shut in the mid-1970s thousands of young, nervous, frightened kids fresh out of school joined HMS Ganges then a year later passed out as fit young men ready to carry on their training either at another shore base or on a sea going ship anywhere in the world. I, along with all the other Junior chefs, joined HMS Pembroke at Chatham in Kent which was the home of the Royal Navy Catering College. We were there for 6 weeks where I was taught and I learnt so many more catering skills in that time than I did in the twelve months at Ganges. We were put in the same mess and cookery class as some of the lads who had spent only a couple of months at HMS Raleigh and I couldn't help but wonder what the previous twelve months was all about.

After my stint there I spent 12 months at HMS Dolphin where my claim to fame was being on duty when one of the submarines, the Artemis, which had just gone through a very expensive refit, sank alongside the harbour while being refuelled, I kid you not! A combination of errors led to three hatches being left open which should have been shut and the submarine sunk with three of the crew being trapped onboard. Thanks to the skill, training and professionalism of the crew and rescuers they were all rescued alive and well, a little over twelve hours after it had sunk. I worked through the night making and serving hot food and drinks for the rescuers and the vast amount of TV crews, journalists, and reporters that were covering the event. The sinking of the submarine alongside the harbour of the submarine base was a huge embarrassment for the Royal Navy, heads did roll, and three crew members were court-martialled, luckily lessons were learnt and thankfully there has not been a similar accident involving our submarines. I have huge respect to all past and serving submariners as the conditions they work under are not ideal to say the least. Although I never went to sea in one, I have been on several when they were moored up, as often I would go onboard to deliver supplies to the crew and would stay for a brew and a chat.

My first trip abroad was to Brest in France as part of the advance party as several submarines were going there to have joint exercises with the French Navy and Air Force. My main job was brewing up for the officers and taking mail on board for the crew. I really felt I was taking part and doing something worthwhile, whilst getting paid to go abroad was an added bonus and a fantastic experience. I really enjoyed my time at HMS Dolphin as I learnt a hell of a lot from the other chefs and people were a lot more friendly and helpful, it was just like chalk and cheese compared to being at Ganges. It wasn't a holiday camp and there was a lot of discipline and hard work involved but at least we all felt valued and part of a team, plus we all got a pay rise which certainly boosted my morale. Being based in Gosport meant it was dead easy to get to London whenever City played there. One season I saw City play Chelsea at Stamford Bridge three times, once in the League, once in the FA Cup and once in the European Cup Winners' Cup. As we didn't have to work every weekend, sometimes I went to my mates in Swindon and even went with them to Bristol to watch Swindon play. Once I went to Southampton to watch Saints and Chelsea play and many times I went to Fratton Park to watch Portsmouth. I used to shoot off all over the place to watch City play as well. We used to get three free travel passes a year, but I saved them for when I went on my two weeks leave and we used to get that three times a year. The rest of the time if there were no cheap deals on the train or on the coach, I just used to hitch hike. Another one of life's little mysteries is why I never went to the Isle of Wight. It is so easy to get to from Portsmouth and the Ferries run several times a day so it would have been a great place to visit on a weekend when I was off duty. Cath reckons it's because City never played there, and she is probably not far wrong!

After twelve months at HMS Dolphin and a total of two years since I joined the Royal Navy, I finally joined my first sea going ship. When I joined HMS Achilles I was still only seventeen and I had to fly from the Royal Air Force base in Brize Norton in Oxfordshire to join my ship as the Achilles was in Singapore as part of an eighteen-month deployment. In my first six months on board I visited places that back then most people could only dream about. Besides Singapore I visited Cape Town, Cochin, Karachi, Bahrain, Mombasa and Gibraltar. We also visited St Helena in the Southern Ocean and to this day I don't know why. St Helena is where Napoleon Bonaparte was exiled by the British and is a couple of thousand miles from the nearest land and the fact that we were only there for six hours and the ship's company who were on duty were not allowed ashore. Yep you guessed it, I was one of the duty chefs and wasn't allowed ashore. The visit was clouded in a bit of mystery, but anyway 'ours was not to reason why' and all that claptrap, we just got on with it and did as we were told.

While we were on that deployment, we took part in the Beria Patrol which was to oversee a total blockade of oil shipments to Rhodesia (now Zimbabwe) through Beria in Mozambique in accordance with a United Nations Resolution. The first time we did the patrol we were at sea for six weeks including Christmas and the New Year. We then went to Mombasa for a couple of weeks, so we could catch up on some general ship's maintenance and repairs, also to give the ship's company a bit of well earned rest. The sea at Mombasa was the clearest I have ever seen in my life and in all the places I have been since, it still ranks as one of the best.

After the welcome break it was back on patrol but this time it was only for four weeks. Our job was to stop and board any tankers trying to beat the blockade, unfortunately the blockade wasn't successful as the oil got through by other means. In the ten years the sanctions were in place seventy-six Royal Navy ships at one time or another took part in the patrol. Although the outcome wasn't very successful three good things came out of it; I managed to save some money, I got a brilliant suntan in the winter, I swam in the Indian Ocean and sunbathed on spotless sandy beaches. Okay four things then. We were also allowed to use the beach hotel facilities but I'm not sure what the paying guests must have thought of us lot just turning up and having a ball. This is the life I thought, and the reason why I joined the Navy, and all thoughts of the tough regime and the sadistic instructors launching my kit everywhere at HMS Ganges quickly vanished.

I was a pretty good swimmer at the time and loved to go snorkelling which is a wonderful experience and that is when I regretted not going on the diver's course at HMS Ganges. Because I was a decent swimmer back then I had been asked if I wanted to go on it. I reluctantly declined as going in the freezing cold waters around Harwich and Felixstowe in January and February didn't really appeal to me and secondly, I needed all my focus and concentration just to get me through the twelve months training, as it was very demanding both physically and mentally so I didn't need any further distractions.

After I had been away for six months from the UK (Achilles and most of the crew had been away eighteen months) we stopped in Gibraltar on the way back to Plymouth to get the ship spruced up and looking good for the grand arrival into Plymouth. While in Gibraltar I celebrated my eighteenth birthday but before I went ashore I had to help with the cocktail party as many important guests and dignitaries from Gibraltar were invited onboard. I always enjoyed working the cocktail parties, whichever port we were at, and even though it was extra work, it was a great chance to get a few free drinks before heading off to the bright lights to see what lay in store for the rest of the night.

The arrival back into Plymouth was basked in tradition with small boats escorting us in. The Royal Marine Band was on the quayside blasting out music, other ships were giving us a blast from their sirens and wives, girlfriends and families were lined up on the dockside and we were all in our No 1 uniforms looking splendid lining the upper deck of the ship. Some of the crew that had been away for eighteen months had received visits from their family while we were in Singapore as the Navy had arranged subsidised flights from the RAF to fly them out, but many hadn't seen their families for eighteen months. While everyone was catching up and playing happy families I went on two weeks leave to Manchester and went on my first ever visit to Goodison Park where lo and behold City beat a pretty decent Everton side 2-1. While on leave I also watched City beat an excellent Chelsea side 1-0 at Maine Road stood on my favourite spot on the Kippax. Chelsea had a brilliant team in the early 1970s with the likes of Peter Bonetti, Charlie Cooke, Chopper Harris, Peter Osgood and John Hollins and when they played well they were a joy to watch and City had to be at their very best to beat them. The two weeks leave was soon over, and it was back to Plymouth for more exercises and patrols of the English coast. While serving on the ship we won the Fleet Cooking Competition which is held every year and was a great achievement and something all the chefs were rightly proud of.

After a couple of months back in the UK we were tasked with visiting Iceland as part of a goodwill exercise as tensions were building up about territorial rights to the Icelandic fishing grounds. Needless to say, the visit was not a success and while we were in Iceland's capital Reykjavik the "Cod Wars" kicked off again. Our presence was no longer welcome and we didn't stay long. The Cod War wasn't a war in the conventional sense but a term the media used to describe the long running conflict between the UK and Iceland. Basically, Iceland wanted to stop the UK fishing in what they believed were their fishing grounds and issued an exclusion zone of fifty miles. The crews of Britain's fishing fleet disagreed and challenged the exclusion zone and once again the Royal Navy were called in to support the trawler men. Our primary role was to assist the trawlers and stop them getting rammed and their nets cut by Icelandic tugs and the coastguard and to go to the aid of any damaged trawlers and to administer first aid to any injured trawler men. It wasn't the first time the two countries had clashed and as there had never been a satisfactory outcome it was always on the cards it would kick off again.

Unfortunately ships like HMS Achilles, which was a Leander Class Frigate capable of hunting and sinking enemy submarines as well as shooting down airplanes and destroying enemy surface ships, were just not designed for fishery protection and many Navy ships as well as the trawlers were damaged as they were repeatedly rammed by the Icelandic tug boats. It was another long drawn out affair but once it became clear neither side were going to back down and it was rumoured that Iceland would shut down the American Air Force base at Keflavik, pressure was put on the United Kingdom by America and the United Nations (and possibly NATO) to come to some sort of agreement. An agreement was eventually forced upon the fishermen, which resulted in a massive reduction of the UK trawler fleet and hundreds of fishermen lost their jobs. Many Royal Navy ships were badly damaged either by being rammed or by ramming the Icelandic tug boats, and many serious incidents were recorded.

Of course the Navy ships could have just opened fire and inflicted serious damage on the Icelandic vessels but that course of action would certainly not have gone down well in the world of public opinion. There were many hairy moments on both sides and at times the crews were very concerned for not only the safety of their ship but for the safety of themselves and their crewmates, as if any one ended up overboard the chances of survival were slim in the atrocious waters of the North Atlantic. You couldn't help but admire the skill, bravery and determination of the Tug crews and the crews of the Coastguard as the seas were treacherous enough without taking on the might of the Royal Navy as they were fighting for something they passionately believed in. It goes without saying their skills and bravery were matched by both sets of trawlermen. For the crews of the Royal Navy ships we had no choice but to go where we were sent, but whilst it was an adventure and very exciting to be doing something we all thought was worthwhile, I would much rather have been swimming in the seas of Mombasa than freezing my nuts off near Iceland. The weather was particularly bad when we were there but for all our troubles the fishermen in much smaller vessels must have been worse off than us. Dozens of Navy ships at one time or another were used during that period and just like when we were on Beira Patrol the skill, courage, commitment and professionalism of the crews of the Royal Navy were not matched by the politicians of the day (nothing new there then!), So next time you get stuck into your fish, chips and mushy peas I hope you say a quick thank you to the brave fishermen who caught them for you.

Being on patrol for so long up and around Iceland took its toll not only on the ship but on the ship's crew as well. We were always on the go, sometimes working six hours on and six hours off for days at a time and that in itself is both physically and mentally draining. It therefore came as a welcome relief when the ships were relieved and we could return to our home port of Plymouth for the ship to receive general maintenance, to repair any damage that was caused and for the crew to wind down and go on some home leave. While on the patrol the bonus was, we could save some money, but the downside was we weren't getting a suntan! Oh well that's life.

The Falklands War was the next big test for the Navy and whilst

Don't Look Back In Anger

I had completed my service by then and was working as a chef at Prestwich Hospital, I, like the majority of the country was fascinated by the news reports and daily briefings about what was happening, and what was being beamed back to television in the UK, plus I was still in touch with mates who were in the Navy. Cath's cousin William was in the Navy at the time serving on HMS Hermes which was the number one target for the Argentine airplanes. It was rammed home how serious this conflict was and that we were not going to have it all our own way when the Destroyer HMS Sheffield was hit by an Exocet missile and destroyed with many lives were lost including a lad who used to play football with us in St. Mary's Park. He had joined the Navy a year before me. What made it even more heart breaking was that his dad was having a drink in the Social Club at Prestwich Hospital at the next table to us when the news came on the television that the Sheffield had been hit, although it said lives were lost it never said who. Everyone stopped drinking and offered him support and encouragement, needless to say none of us fancied finishing our pints and we went home soon after wishing him all the best. We were devastated the next day when we found out his son was one of those lost. A lot has been made of the Falklands War and the rights and wrongs of it but if you have ever read any books on the subject or watch any of the numerous documentaries, the conclusion is that we were only successful by the skin of our teeth and if it had gone on much longer the outcome could have been very different, such is the reality of war. It must have been an absolutely terrifying experience for all the servicemen and merchant seamen and women that took part and I salute each and everyone of them.

Nowadays the Royal Navy has seen many cuts to the service it would be impossible to sustain operations like the Beira Patrol, the Cod War and the Falklands War, in fact we would be hard pressed to retake the Isle of Wight if that was ever invaded! One thing that kept up the moral of the ship's company was receiving regular supplies of mail and gifts and parcels from back home. While at sea, when appropriate, the Royal Air Force would literally drop sack loads of mail in to the sea near the ships and the ships boat or dingy would be launched to pick it up. I always looked forward to receiving the *Football Pink* and match day programmes to get the latest news about City. The other morale booster was to get the football results piped through the ship's Tannoy on a Saturday afternoon or evening, depending on the time difference, where ever we were. There was plenty of mickey taking from the rival fans when the results came through, and it was just amazing that little stuff like that can give you a big boost when you are away from home.

Just before Christmas 1974, after spending many months on exercises and having visited South Africa, Pakistan and India on a goodwill visit (more cocktail parties) we were back in my old stomping ground of Mombasa ready for another great suntan. After Mombasa the ship was due to sail to Thailand, Singapore, Hong Kong, China, and Japan. The ship did sail but unfortunately I didn't as I broke my leg playing football. After spending a few days in hospital, I was discharged to a dead posh hotel while waiting for repatriation to the UK. While once again I had a great winter suntan, I was gutted at missing out on the trip of a lifetime.

After recovering at HMS Nelson, which was a big shore base in Portsmouth, I was posted to HMS Osprey, a Royal Navy Helicopter air station in Portland near Weymouth in Dorset. The helicopter pilots specialised in Air Sea Rescue and often the base was on high alert as the helicopters were scrambled for rescue missions both on land and at sea. Being based there once again made it dead easy to get to London to watch City play and once when we were playing United at Maine Road, I hitch hiked to Manchester in record time. I still remember that game well as Jimmy Nicholl scored a brilliant own goal to make sure we got a share of the points.

Being a chef at a Naval Base was a lot less pressure and less demanding than being on a sea going ship. On a ship, besides normal galley duties, we took part in fire fighting drills and during live firing exercises I was in the gun turret passing shells up to be fired as it wasn't fully automated back then. Trying to cook and serve food to over 230 hungry sailors from a small galley in rough seas is not an easy task, also you don't have any time off when you are away from the UK. The first six months I served away on HMS Achilles I didn't get one day off and sometimes I was working sixteen hours a day, but strangely it was just accepted as normal and we just got on with it. Besides doing the cooking the chefs did all the cleaning in the kitchen as we didn't have the luxury of kitchen porters like chefs in hotels do. As an older chef once said to me "if you can cook on a sea going ship in a force nine gale you can cook any where". The hard work though was a small price to pay for visiting all the countries we went to. There was lots of tension on the ships at times, as living in cramped conditions and being away from families and loved ones brought its own unique problems but I loved it at the time and wouldn't have swapped the chance of that experience for anything. In comparison cooking at Naval Bases on dry land was very cushy compared to being on board as once you finished duties you could just go to the bar for a pint or get the bus from HMS Osprey into Weymouth and in the summer go on the beach or just stroll about and many of the married men had their families in the married quarters. Apart from being allowed out of the base once we finished our duties we had regular weekend leave. There was also a lot less tension as the living conditions were so much better as the galleys were much bigger and better equipped, and there were more chefs working in the galleys. As a result of my experience working in the Officers galley, the NCOs (Chief Petty Officers and Petty Officers) and also in the ship's company galleys, I passed my City & Guilds qualifications which gave me good preparation for a life as a chef back in civvy street. After working for a year in a bakery I worked as a chef for thirty years in the NHS getting promoted to Assistant Head Chef, so although at times life in the Navy was hard, you won't find me knocking it.

Although many sailors enjoyed their time onshore bases I didn't, I just didn't want to be there I just wanted to be back at sea visiting different places and seeing the world. To be honest I was a bit of a pain in the arse at HMS Osprey as I was supposed to be there for two years and I kept mithering to leave and eventually I got my way.

After twelve months there I was back on the high seas again as

I joined the type 21 Destroyer HMS Devonshire. There were some great lads on board who were really into football and we always had some great banter. I went up to Sunderland with Woody and stayed at his mum's house when City played up there. I also went to Liverpool for the weekend and stayed at Dingers when we played Everton, and pitched up unannounced at Pete's house in Staffordshire when City played at Stoke. Pete wasn't in but his mum and dad looked after me. Dinger helped me out once when I was Duty Chef in Hamburg and I'd been ashore all night and was in no fit state to cook the breakfast so he ended up frying loads of eggs for me.

While on board the Devonshire we did goodwill visits to Middlesbrough, Newcastle and Fishguard in Wales and thousands of people went on a guided tour of the ship and the feedback we got was very positive. The real reason I wanted to go back on a sea going ship was to once again go abroad and whilst on the Devonshire we visited some brilliant places including Hamburg. Haifa, Messenia. Lisbon, Gibraltar and Malta to name just a few. The most interesting place was Odessa which at that time was part of the USSR and we were the first British War ship to visit the Soviet Union for around thirty years. One bit of sad news though was after that visit we were patrolling off the coast of the Scilly Isles, when there was an accident with one of the ship's helicopters which resulted in a loss of life which always hits a ships company hard as everyone knows each other.

As sad and as tough as that incident was, as sailors on a Navy Ship we just had to knuckle down and carry on with our duties.

In 1976, after a mini refit we set sail for a tour of the Far East and I was certainly looking forward to visiting the countries I missed out on when I broke my leg, but my luck was jinxed again and a few miles off the coast of Portugal one of the ship's boilers blew up. That's probably not the technical term but it sounded like a bomb had gone off and did a lot of damage so the emergency alarm was sounded and we all had to muster at emergency stations. We had to wait for hours on the upper deck in the pitch-black wondering if the damage control parties and fire-fighting teams could get the situation under control or would we have to abandon ship. We were all trained in damage control and fire-fighting but many of us were hoping our skills were not going to be put to the test, and as luck would have it the lads got it under control before it was my turn to give it a go. They all did a brilliant job in extremely difficult circumstances and each and everyone of them got a well deserved pat on the back and a few cans of beer as well for their trouble.

So that was the end of another trip to the Far East but every cloud has a silver lining as eventually, under escort, the Devonshire limped into dock in Malta where we stayed for about eight weeks undergoing emergency repairs before heading back to Portsmouth. I could think of a lot of worse places to pitch up to than Malta and I teamed up again with my old mate 'Flash Gordon' from the Achilles who was stationed at the Naval Base. I also met up with a long-lost mate from Whitefield called Ammo who was at the RAF base on the Island.

It wasn't many weeks after we arrived back from Malta that I left the Navy and commenced life back in civvy street. One thing I will always be grateful to the Navy for is the training I received, the places I visited and the people I met. Although it is over forty years since I left the Navy, I am still in touch with some of the lads I met whilst I served. Cath and I went to Devon for one of my mate's weddings recently and we stayed with Keith and Kath for a lovely couple of days. I am still in contact with Flash and even though I have not seen him since Malta, we message each other on Facebook and send emails as he lives in Thailand, but you never know we might bump into each other again one of these days. Gilly, who was a City fan I served with on the Devonshire, is another one we message to each other now and again and the other year we met up in Liverpool along with Dinger, Rattler and Steve "John" Lennon and had a few good drinks together. All was going well until Gilly got up and knocked a table full of drinks over, oh well some things don't change! It is on the cards we will be meeting up again in the not too distance future, but I definitely won't be sitting next to him. There have been a few documentaries over the years about the Royal Navy and there have been massive changes since I left. Women are now allowed to serve on sea going ships and some have even had their own commands as Captains. I remember there was massive resistance for women to serve at sea, not least from wives and girlfriends of the sailors who thought their loved ones might get up to a bit of hanky panky. Not much chance of that happening in my day as we were too busy at sea and too pissed up on land. Being a homosexual is no longer an offence which again caused a lot of controversy at the time but no one bats an eye lid any more.

Anyway that's my lot about the Royal Navy and I hope you've had an insight into what happens in the Senior Service. It certainly brought back some memories while I was writing this, so I might go and get a tot of rum. Talking of rum, up until 1970 all sailors in the Navy who were over the age of twenty were given a daily issue of rum, it got abolished because at long last the 'powers that be' must have thought it wasn't a good idea to let half-pissed up sailors loose on Her Majesty's ships and submarines, what could possibly go wrong? If you want any more info on the stuff in this chapter or about the Navy please get in touch with me or check it out on Google. If everything goes according to plan this book is being published in October 2019 exactly fifty years since I joined up.

3: maine road

JUST MENTION MAINE ROAD to any City fan of a certain age and their mind will quickly revert to a nostalgic time and great memories will be revived. We have all suffered highs and lows at the ground and witnessed the slow decline of a once proud stadium that was ahead of its time when it was first built. Just walking to the ground for an evening kick off and seeing the floodlights on and smelling the whiff of onions from the burger vans always gave me a spring in my step as I hurried to the ground. From the rickety wooden seats in the old Platt Lane stand to the open Scoreboard end where the away fans would get soaked to the skin, to the hustle and bustle of the Kippax, and the posh seats of the Main Stand. City fans would pack themselves into the ground to roar the team on. Hang on did I say posh seats! Well most people, including myself, thought that the seats were where only the well-off could afford to go. Well they were probably posh when the stand was first opened but when I first went in there in the late 1980s as my weary legs couldn't keep me upright for ninety minutes, especially if I had been having a few drinks in the Clarence, Sherwood or the Parkside beforehand, the seats were a bit of a disappointment as the Main Stand had been neglected over the years. Now there has been tons of stuff written about Maine Road and I doubt from a City fans perspective I could add anything new. So, I have canvassed the thoughts of a few visiting fans mainly through social media as my budget didn't stretch to carting myself the length and breadth of the country to interview them! So, let's see what the fans of other clubs thought about entering our sacred domain.

Ian an Arsenal fan who now lives in Watford went to Maine Road three times. He told me he thought it was a proper old school ground, he laughed and didn't answer when I asked him if he was being kind and thought it was a dump. He also thought it strange how no two stands were the same but thought the ground had lots of character. He was once there for a night game with his mates and he couldn't find their car and got a bit concerned as there were large groups of youths lurking nearby so it was a great relief for him when he found the car and the bonus was it was still in one piece.

Norman and his cousin James are Sunderland fans who loved coming to Maine Road and usually stayed for the weekend. They came down the year they got relegated and Sunderland brought between twelve and eighteen thousand fans, depending who you listen to over the years. Even though they got relegated they had a great time mixing with City fans before and after the game and ended up drinking with loads of City fans in the pubs round Piccadilly. Although they thought the ground had seen better days, they always thought the atmosphere was good.

Paul a Luton fan has only been to the ground the once and that was when Luton relegated City. He thought the atmosphere was electric that day and many City fans he saw were "off their heads" - nowt new there Paul. After the game he thought it was a bit intimidating as he encountered a lot of angry City fans, but he didn't witness any trouble.

Micky, although being a Leeds fan spent quite a bit of time in Manchester when he was at university for eighteen months. He remembers having some scary moments when watching Leeds play and like other fans he thought the back alleys round the back of the ground were awful to walk through as you had a feeling you could get ambushed at any moment. He thought the ground was okay, but the toilets were ten times worse than Elland Road, but the pies were better. He saw a couple of bands play there and thought it a lot less stressful watching the bands than watching football.

Alan a Spurs fan didn't have good memories of the ground when he went for the first time. Spurs were beaten but he was near the "Gobby Mancs" who were giving him loads of abuse and he reckoned it was the worst away trip he had been on. To make it worse he and his mates got involved in a fight with some City fans and one of his mates had to go to hospital with a broken wrist and his cousin got a "proper kicking." To top it off, a few of their coach windows were put through. He went a few more times after that bad experience and never had any other problems. He thought the atmosphere was usually decent and the Etihad is not a patch on what Maine Road was like. Can't argue that one with you mate.

Mike from Southampton isn't the only one who thought whoever designed the layout of the ground must have been on acid or something as he thought "fuck all" matched and it all looked very odd. He liked the fact that the ground was slap bang in the community with great pubs and shops nearby. He thought it a big pity that City never stayed and just redeveloped the ground as the Etihad might look great, but it just doesn't feel like a football ground especially with all the corporate boxes all over the place

Paul from Reading went in the late 60s to an FA Cup game and thought it was brilliant as there were loads of Reading fans and it was a great atmosphere.

Michael, another Arsenal fan, thought it was a brilliant ground with a cracking set of fans and it was the first time he had proper mushy peas on his chips. He was there for an evening game and Arsenal went 4-0 up after about twenty minutes and was amazed that the City fans didn't walk out in disgust but the fact that the majority stayed until the end really impressed him.

John a Sheffield United fan said most of the time he enjoyed going as the atmosphere was usually decent and most of the fans were sound but the walk back to the train station even with a police escort was a bit scary, He also mentioned that the bogs were disgusting and most people just pissed on the wall outside.

Phill from Plymouth never actually went to Maine Road to watch a football game but has been a few times to watch bands and was there when Oasis played and thought it was magic. He thought the chippies nearby were great and the curry sauce he had on them was the best he'd ever had.

June from Liverpool actually worked for a contract catering firm that supplied food and drink to the fans on match days. She laughs about it now but recalls the first time she arrived to start work. They arrived near the ground early and parked up. Three young lads seemed to come out of nowhere and asked the eternal question "can we mind your car mister." The male driver said they would pay when they got back. Oops obviously he didn't know the rules. When they got back, the windscreen wipers had been ripped off and the rear light had been kicked in. June only worked for the company four times at Maine Road as she was fed up with her and the other staff getting abuse from the City fans for being Scousers.

George a lifelong West Bromwich Albion fan went to Maine Road for his first ever away game and in total went six times. He thinks all the hype about having a great atmosphere is a big myth as he didn't think it was anything special and he went as far to say it was pretty crap.

Arny a die-hard Millwall fan was at our ground back in the old Third Division when City won 3-0. He remembers it kicking off before, during and after the game and a chair thrown by a City fan hit his mate on the head. He said that he and his mate had never been as scared at a football match as they were that day, plus their coach had two windows smashed.

Jack from the Midlands went a few times to watch Aston Villa and although he was never caught up in any violence he was always on his guard as he thought the area the ground was in was very shifty. He was another who liked the curry sauce, but thought the toilets were not the best. He got to know a couple of City fans and used to have a pint with them when City played at Villa Park but lost touch with them.

Don't Look Back In Anger

Billy went there to watch Leeds United when City beat them 6-1 in the Full Members Cup in the 1980s and thought the atmosphere was very poor and I can't argue with that but there weren't many fans at the ground that day and I always remembered it was usually a great atmosphere when Leeds came to town.

Karl a Liverpool fan went many times and thought the City fans always made a lot of noise and he always enjoyed going even though he got thrown out once for shouting abuse at some City fans. He remembers though there was usually a lot of trouble with the rival fans and he used to avoid the backstreets in case any City fans were lying in wait.

Ralph from Portsmouth loved it at Maine Road and thought it was the best away ground he had been to as it reminded him of Fratton Park in how close to the pitch you were plus the shops, pubs and houses were on the doorstep. He was there the year Liam Gallagher and Noel were introduced to the fans on the pitch when Liam went over to the Portsmouth fans and started giving it the "big I am". He got a lot of stick back from the Pompey fans that day and could have caused a riot.

Well that was a pretty mixed review, some liked the ground, some didn't, some got caught up in crowd violence while others didn't witness any and some enjoyed a drink with the City fans. Most thought the atmosphere was okay and much better than the Etihad. We all have our own views but it great to get an outsider's point of view, Think most of us can accept it was time to move on and while the Etihad is an excellent stadium there is still room for improvement in a lot of aspects including the stewarding, ticket office and the web site. The biggest problem though is getting away from the ground at full time as the road layout and the bus and metro service is not the best, but that is something possibly out of the control of the club, more's the pity. There is a group of supporters called City Matters which were elected by fellow fans who meet with the club pretty regularly to hopefully resolve these and other issues. Let's hope improvements can be made so fans can be as happy off the pitch as they can be on it .

4: you'll never take the kippax

THE KIPPAX STREET STAND at Maine Road was a huge terrace that ran the length of the ground opposite to where the players came out onto the pitch. It was where City's most vocal and passionate fans congregated and when the fans were in full voice is was a sight and sound to behold. The Kippax was unique in the fact that most other clubs had there "ends" behind one of the goals like the Shed at Chelsea or the Kop at Liverpool. It was originally just called the "Popular Side" but became known as the Kippax, after the street it was on. It went all posh and got a roof put on top in 1957.

To keep fit, Colin Bell used to run up the steps of the Kippax as it was a good test of stamina. Most City fans couldn't walk up it without getting out of breath never mind run up it. Looking back, it wasn't a place for the faint-hearted and it helped if you were quite big otherwise your view could be pretty shit especially if it was packed and you were standing near the back. When it was packed fans used to climb onto the rafters at the top of the Kippax as well as climbing up the floodlights. When the crowd surged forward or when City scored if you didn't have a barrier in front of you there was a good chance you would end up on your backside or about twenty yards from where you started. At the front of the terrace there was a small wall separating the fans from the pitch and it was here where many youngsters would sit to watch the game, but you had to get in the ground early as the places were much sought after and very limited. The only downside was that you could be hit by a wayward pass and it could be pretty painful if you got hit by one of those balls especially back in the day when they used those big heavy leather caseys, not like the dead soft ones of today. After saying that, I wouldn't want to be hit by a ball if Kevin de Bruyne kicked it as he can't half whack them.

Don't Look Back In Anger

It wasn't only the ball that could hurt you. Now my memory of years gone by has never been brilliant due to the fact that my brain cells have been bombarded by vast amounts of alcohol over the years, but some things just stick out and no amount of alcohol will allow some memories to fade. I was only about eleven or twelve years old and still very much a short arse as I took up a prime position on the wall. Out of the blue I got such a whack in the face, not from a football or another kid but from a fully-grown six-foot policeman, I had never been hit like that by anyone in my life before and it was such a shock as I never saw it coming. My crime was that, like all the other kids, my feet were dangling pitch side so we could get a better view and apparently, I didn't respond quick enough to his shouted request to put my legs the other side of the wall. What an absolute bastard, I nearly burst into tears, but back then I was such a stubborn little sod I wasn't going to give him the pleasure of him seeing me in pain and discomfort. Over the years I sometimes wondered whatever happened to him as you would have to be a right shithead to hit a kid in the face with the force he did. Just like bullies the world over he would gladly pick on the weak and the vulnerable, but he would probably shit himself if he had to get involved in a scrap with fans or anyone his own age.

Now you can call me unlucky or whatever but about ten years later something similar happened again to yours truly and I got another whack from a policeman, this time in the middle of the Kippax. I thought fucking hell it can't be him again can it? This time it was at the end of a testimonial game and there were still a couple of thousand City fans on the Kippax singing away and showing support for Johnny Hart whose testimonial I had gone to watch. Now that was the first testimonial game I had been to and after being attacked by a policeman I swore to myself, I wouldn't go to another. None of my mates fancied going and it was only because I was on leave from the Navy and wouldn't be able to get to another City game while I was at home that I decided to go, plus the fact that City's legendary goalkeeper Bert Trautmann was going to take part in the game as well. The game had only been finished for a few minutes and fans were still showing their appreciation and everyone was in a jovial and happy mood when I noticed a police sergeant moving from the bottom of the Kippax to the top telling people to leave, and as he was passing me, out of the blue he just punched me hard in the stomach. I don't know if I have just got one of those faces (or stomachs) the police just can't resist punching, but I don't know what motivated him into doing so but I keeled over and nearly threw up such was the force of the punch. That was the arrogance of some policemen in those days, they thought they could do what they liked and get away with it. A lad who had seen what happened helped me up from the floor and said he would be a witness if I reported it as he had taken the policeman's number, I didn't think anything would happen to him and decided it wasn't worth the hassle. Apart from those two encounters I thought the police at Maine Road were much better than at a lot of grounds up and down the country, as there were some right bastards knocking about in the 1970s and 1980s, who seemed to view all football fans as hooligans.

There have been some brilliant games played at Maine Road and the atmosphere has been electric especially watching from a packed Kippax. At times fans would get on their mate's shoulders to lead the singing and to start the songs off and when you get 20.000 plus fans all in one terrace singing and cheering at the same time it's enough to make the hairs on the back of your neck, and everywhere else for that matter, to stand up. The facilities in the Kippax were poor back then especially compared to the Main Stand and as the toilet facilities for the blokes were a health hazard, I would dread to think what the ladies were like. Many City fans' first experience of watching a game was from the Kippax and it was like an addiction, just speak to City fans who went in the 60s 70s and 80s and they will all say the same .The whole experience could overwhelm you.

This is Phil Hilton's experience: *On Saturday 18th October 1980 four fourteen year-olds went from our little village near Wigan went to Hurley's sport shop for new designer tracksuits and trainers. I'd had no real football influence in my life by then but sometimes went with my uncle to Wigan or Bolton. That day happened to be one of John Bond's early games in charge, so me and one of the lads left the others to the shopping and jumped on the bus to the ground to see what all the fuss was about, as there was loads of publicity about the game as it was against Crystal Palace who were managed by the man Bond had replaced as City boss, Malcolm Allison. Going on the Kippax for the first time was like stepping into a different world. The noise, the smell and the atmosphere got me hooked and I then realised that me and City were meant to be. The Kippax played a big part in my life as after that first experience and I was there every week. For the next 20 years I hardly missed a game home and away experiencing the highs and many lows. Through my love for the club I met many amazing people and made friends for life with people I met on the Kippax.*

Now I don't want to confuse you or anyone else really, but in the Main Stand you sat down. When the Scoreboard End was converted to the North Stand you stood, when they put seats in you sat. Now is it only me that got confused calling an area of the ground a "stand" even though you sit. Okay, time for my medication again so I can get back on track. The doctor warned me to take it on time and if you never listen to any one else, always listen to the Doctor.

Whenever we played the rags at Maine Road in the 1970s and 1980s there were usually pitched battles between rival fans before, during and after the games and it was usually centred around the Kippax. Whenever we played them, we used to sing this little ditty

"If I die in the Kippax Street whoa, whoa. If I die in the Kippax Street whoa, whoa.
If I die in the Kippax Street there'll be ten Red bastards at my feet whoa, whoa, wha, wha".

Now obviously I didn't perish in the Kippax Street as you have no doubt deduced otherwise I wouldn't be writing this masterpiece and to the best of my knowledge, fortunately, no one else did either. Now the rags have never been original in much that they do and even less when it comes to songs, so it never came as a big shock to us when they copied the song from us but changed the word from red to blue. Ah bless them, anything to make them feel better. Before we had proper segregation, the United fans used to be put in a section of the Kippax near to the Platt Lane stand to watch the game. The police really had their work cut out on Derby day and especially in the Kippax, and in the authority's wisdom they separated the fans with a thick rope running from the top to the bottom of the Kippax. I am not sure which bright spark really expected that master plan to work and needless to say it didn't. Nearer to kick off time the pubs round the ground were emptying of City fans and once they were all in the Kippax, they kept pushing the United fans closer and closer to the Platt Lane stand with the chant of "YOU'LL NEVER TAKE THE KIPPAX" ringing in their ears.

Although at times there were some serious outbreaks of violence and the hardcore would throw coins, the occasional bottle, brick and sometimes darts at each other, for the majority it was just chanting songs sticking two fingers up and a bit of huffing, puffing and shouting a bit of abuse. After the game many City and United fans who were probably squaring up to each other in the afternoon were back in their local pubs having a drink together.

One year a mate of mine Jimmy, a United fan, didn't have a ticket, so I said I would go to the ground early with him to see if we could get him one without paying silly money from the touts, and I was sure we would be able to get one. As we were walking down Claremont Road towards the Sherwood pub, I saw a large mob of fans walking up the road towards us. As we got closer, I recognised a lot of them as it was a big City firm known locally as the Cool Cats. I knew loads of them to let on to as I had seen them at games many times especially away games and there was a couple I knew quite well as I had a pint or two with them in one pub or another. The game against the rags was not long after we had played at Shrewsbury in the Cup and they had been scrapping with other City fans and I had a chat with some of them afterwards to find out what it was all about. They weren't really sure themselves but they said "shit happens". Anyway, as we approached, they parted to let us walk through the middle of them and whilst the ones I knew let on to me they were giving Jimmy right dirty looks. That's when I

Don't Look Back In Anger

looked and realised the dick still had his United badge on. Fuck me I stopped breathing for a few seconds which felt like minutes at the time as it would have only taken one of them to say something and it could have all gone a bit pear shaped. Fortunately they were all decent lads and it was not their style for a mob of them to attack one United fan. As soon as we'd passed, Jimmy took his badge off sharpish. I was so pleased I knew some of them otherwise it could have gone tits up. Anyway we had a few pints and I managed to sort Jimmy a ticket out. Once in the ground we went our separate ways but arranged to meet in a pub after the game. After the match when I met him, his face looked a right mess and, as it turned out, he had a broken nose. Oh no, I shouldn't laugh, ha-ha, oh go on I will then. What happened was after the game there was a group of United fans gathered outside the ground looking for trouble, and after seeing Jimmy, thinking he was a City fan, one of them head-butted him, then the City fans who thought Jimmy was a Blue attacked the United fans. You just couldn't make it up. It was the last time Jimmy came to a derby with me!

Hooliganism still exists nowadays but nothing remotely on the scale of the 1970s and 1980s. I think these days people spend their time abusing opposition fans rather than fighting them and if people do square up, they tend to jump up and down for a few minutes before a punch is thrown. It must be terrifying if you get caught up in violence as people on drink or drugs can be so unpredictable and you can never tell what they will do next. But unlike back then, the police and authorities by and large seem to have the situation under control and people can travel to and from the game most of the time trouble free. But there is always a chance of some violent disorder breaking out when you least expect it

The first major outbreak of violence I witnessed at City was in about 1969 at home to Everton. It was an evening game and as fans were leaving the Kippax they went to the Scoreboard End to confront the Everton fans. There was probably more pushing, shoving and shouting than serious punches being thrown but anyone who fell or got pushed to the floor was in danger of getting kicked in the head. There was only a couple of police about when the trouble first broke out and they were getting attacked as well. For a fifteen-year-old who hadn't witnessed anything like that before I suppose I felt a bit of excitement merged in with a lot of nervousness, I think because it was dark as well that made it a bit of a surreal experience. The attack on the Everton fans I found out later was supposed to be in revenge for City fans being attacked at Everton the previous time we had played them. Whether that was bullshitting to justify the attack or if it was true, who knows? Nowadays, because of the segregation and the number of stewards and police on duty that situation rarely happens these days at the Etihad.

One game that always stood out for me was when we played Reading in the FA Cup in 1968. They were in a lower league than us at the time but brought a big following and they were all in the Scoreboard End. Loads of City fans mingled in with them but instead of fighting with them they nicked their bobble hats and scarves. Although we had an off day and the score was 0-0, we went back to their place and won 7-0. Throughout the late 1960s and early 1970s, many fans could be seen with "trophy scarves" attached to their wrists, and some fans spent more time trying to pinch opposing fans' scarves than they did watching the match. Watching City from the Kippax was always brilliant because apart from watching the game from a great vantage point, you were standing with your mates singing and chanting. It was always a great buzz when the players ran on to the pitch in front of a packed Kippax roaring the players on. Nowadays there are only Liverpool fans in the Premier League who hold their scarves up and sing "You Will Never Walk Alone" back in the day it was sung by many different sets of supporters and there was never a better sight than 20,000 fans in the Kippax in full voice singing it with their scarves held aloft, and it was another 'hair on the back of your neck' moment. Leeds United fans used to sing it a lot as well. Why other fans stopped singing it and Liverpool alone in England adopted it for themselves is anyone's guess, but it was probably due in part to the fact that Gerry and the Pacemakers, who were part of the Merseybeat scene in the 1960s, released it in 1963 and also possibly because it was re-released after the Hillsborough tragedy.

The song was originally released in America in 1944 for the hit musical Carousel and Frank Sinatra was the first artist to record it followed by many more artists including Ray Charles. In 1956 Carousel was made into a film. Celtic and clubs on the continent also sing it regularly as well but in England Liverpool have well and truly made it their own. There have been some memorable games against Liverpool at Maine Road and none more so when we played them in the League Cup Semi Final in 1981 - the noise that night was deafening from start to finish and we were robbed by having a good goal by Kevin Reeves disallowed.

Thrashing or even just beating United always brought the best out of the fans on the Kippax and who will ever forget the 5-1? It was just a pity most United fans had left by the final whistle as those that stayed would have been green with envy. When City fans started the inflatable craze it was great to see thousands of inflatable bananas being waved in the Kippax, you just couldn't replicate that these days. For me though, one of the stand out nights of the 1970s was when we played Middlesbrough in the League Cup Semi Final. The buzz and intensity of noise was just incredible and although we were trailing 1-0 from the first leg, as soon as the players came onto the pitch there was no way we were going to lose that game. Graeme Souness, who went on to manage a few top clubs including Liverpool, was a Boro player at the time and here is a bit of inside information that not many people know - his wife and her family are staunch City fans. How about that then?

Most City fans of a certain age, and it has been well documented, so I won't bore you to death, will probably tell you the best atmosphere ever was when Colin Bell made his comeback against Newcastle on Boxing Day 1977. Colin had fought a long battle for fitness after suffering a serious injury and came on at half time to a truly sensational once in a lifetime wall of noise that never seemed to stop and to top it all we won the game as well which was always a bonus. The game was marred by serious violence with fans fighting each other just inside the entrance to the Kippax and City fans were throwing bricks from the top of the hill which were hitting City fans as well as Newcastle fans and many had to receive medical treatment. If you ever get the chance to speak to Colin, he will tell you that was the most emotional game he ever played in for a variety of reasons, not least it was his comeback game and he was, and still is, grateful for the magnificent support the City fans gave him that day.

Fans who weren't in their teens then will probably have the promotion game against Charlton as their number one game for atmosphere and again, the noise levels were off the scale. The official attendance was around 45.000 fans but anyone who was at the game or stood in the Kippax knows there were many more in there that day. The FA Cup quarter final replay against Everton in 1981 was up there as well and when the third goal for City went in the whole of the Kippax went mental.

A bit of a weird one was when we played Coventry in January 1974. It was a League Cup Quarter Final replay but because of the oil crisis at the time, which affected every industry including football, clubs had to conserve energy, so instead of playing in the evening with the floodlights switched on the game was played earlier in the afternoon. I am not sure how so many people managed to get time off work to get to the game, but the crowd was recorded at about 25,000 and with the racket they made it sounded like double that amount as City won 4-2. Not long after that the country had to endure yet another crisis with workers being put on a three-day week and people were stocking up with candles in fear of the lights going out again, so it was a welcome relief to go and watch the football.

Although Schalke in 1970 didn't bring many fans when we played them in the semi-final of the European Cup Winners' Cup, the ground and Kippax was rocking long before kick-off. The noise level never subsided as we won 5-1 to qualify for the final which we won in Vienna against Polish team Gornik Zabrze.

Sunderland fans used to always come in big numbers and none more so than when they drew us in the FA Cup 5th round in 1973. They were in the old Second Division at the time so were the underdogs but got a draw at Maine Road in front of 54,000 before beating us back at their ground in the replay in front of a similar size crowd! They went on to beat a great Leeds United team at Wembley in the final. There were probably twelve to fifteen thousand Sunderland fans in Manchester that day and I don't recall any trouble but just a great atmosphere. Loads of their fans were mixing and mingling with City fans in the pubs and clubs after the game. We had a drink with many of them near Piccadilly as their coaches were picking them up at midnight.

Before one game against Middlesbrough, I was walking through the car park to go in the ground when I saw hundreds of Boro fans fleeing from the Kippax. What had happened? In either a deluded or drunken state or a bit of both, the away fans thought they would get in the Kippax early to stake a claim in the home of the City fans in the mistaken belief they would be able to "Take The Kippax." They must have felt cocky getting in there just after 2pm with no opposition from pensioners and kids, while all City's lads were in the pubs. It was a different kettle of fish just before 3pm when thousands of City fans made their way into the ground. I wondered at the time when exactly did the Boro fans decide it was a bad idea to even consider going in the Kippax that day because as soon as it kicked off they couldn't get out quick enough.

With little or no segregation that situation was played out at football grounds every week all over the country, as apart from Cup games and the local Derby it was just pay on the gate. It is one thing though giving it the big 'un and going in the home supporters end at 2pm thinking you are the dog's bollocks. It is a whole different ball game when the ground fills up getting on for three o'clock and you realise if you don't get out you are going to get kicked out and will probably get a few slaps on the way for good measure!

It is hard to imagine that any of the incidents I have highlighted could happen today because away fans are segregated, it would be very difficult for a group of away fans to gain access to the home end in any great numbers as access is by ticket only and most clubs run a membership card system. More and more fans tend to be season ticket holders with a designated seat, so if fans did want to cause trouble they would be easily identified. There is also plenty of CCTV cameras as well as police and stewards on duty both inside and outside the ground. Plus, the mindset of the football supporter is totally different nowadays as is the demographic of fans. Most who were involved in trouble in the 1970s and 1980s will be in their fifties and sixties now and are probably taking their kids and grandkids to the games. If fans are treated decently, and have nice facilities there is less reason for them to want to go and punch someone's lights out.

Now as you have been reading this chapter I guess some of you are thinking "why hasn't he mentioned this or that game? I remember that game, the atmosphere wasn't that great, or that incident didn't happen like that". Over the passage of time people's minds can play tricks, especially drinking the amount City fans drank on a regular basis and things aren't always how we remember them. But the games I mentioned are firmly etched in my memory and some of them I can recall like yesterday. I can't remember where I went last week or what I had for my tea at the weekend but I can remember the fine details of a football game from over forty years ago. I don't know whether that is good or bad sign but I'll ask my doctor when he next does his rounds before he locks up for the night.

Now to put the balance right there were loads of games for whatever reason the atmosphere was poor, and it would be wrong to say any different. It might have been because it was not a good attendance, or it was a bad game, or the weather was crap. It didn't help when teams like Bury from down the road came and beat us at Maine Road, but for the majority of games, being in the Kippax was a fantastic experience, except if the guy behind you fell forward and spilt his pint over you It could have been worse though and you could have spilt your pint over the bloke in front of you. Quite often, one side of the Kippax would bizarrely start chanting Rangers, then equally bizarre, the other half would respond with the chant of Celtic. Even though I did join in, I never got the reason behind the chant. It was explained to me but it never sank in, although I do seem to remember it was only chanted during a boring bit of the game, so maybe that had something to do with it, but it was anybody's guess what the players made of it all.

One sight that will stick in people's minds is the giant banner that was sponsored by the fanzine *Blueprint* being passed from one side of the Kippax to the other.

Well I hope this has sparked a memory or two for the older fan and for fans too young to remember the Kippax I hope it has given you a bit of an idea into what it was like back then. I won't mention how bad the bogs were and that there was nowt to dry your hands on, and I won't mention how flat the beer was or the fact that the hot dogs and burgers that were not sold before the game were the same ones being sold afterwards. Please feel free to contact me with your experience from when you used to go on the Kippax, as I love listening to what other people thought of it back then, especially if you had a burger then had to use the toilet, that would have been an experience not to have been repeated.

5: wemberleee wemberleee

TO MOST FOOTBALL FANS Wembley is the home of English football, but it is also known for being a right pain in the arse to get to and from if you are going by coach or car. The original Wembley stadium, which was demolished in 2000 to be replaced by the new stadium, was built in time for the 1923 FA Cup final and was originally called the Empire Stadium and built in about one year at a cost of three quarter of a million pounds. The Cup Final that year was between Bolton Wanderers and West Ham United and became known as the "White Horse Final" and, as it was not all ticket, the 127.000 capacity was exceeded and some estimates reckon there were around 225,000 packed into the ground and many for their own safety spilled onto the pitch.

The white horse was called Billy and he and his rider along with other mounted police nudged and guided the fans back to pitch side and onto the terraces, so the game could eventually start. From that year until the year 2000 every Cup Final was played at Wembley and City v Spurs in 1981 saw the first ever Wembley replay (if you were concentrating in a previous chapter you would know that). The first League Cup Final to be played there was between Queens Park Rangers and West Bromwich Albion. QPR were in the old Third Division at the time pulling off a shock victory. The first Charity Shield game played there was not until 1974. City also played there against Chelsea in the ill-fated Full Members cup. These days they try to host as many games and events as possible at the stadium including semi finals of the FA Cup as well as the play off finals from the lower divisions, The FA Vase and American football and pop concerts. Pope John Paul II held a mass there as did American Evangelist Billy Graham. American stuntman Evil Knievel crashed his motor bike while trying to clear thirteen buses there and the term unlucky thirteen was certainly appropriate in his case. In 1985 Bob Geldof organised the huge Live Aid Concert which raised money for starving people in Ethiopia. So many things have gone on there over the years but arguably the greatest game for English Football was when Geoff Hurst scored a hat-trick against West Germany in the 1966 World Cup Final and to date that is the only time England have won it. The most shocking crowd scenes though were after a game against Scotland when the Jocks got on the pitch and proceeded to rip up the turf and destroy the goal posts.

For many reasons I didn't see City play at Wembley on February 28th 1976 against Newcastle and I bet you're thinking he's either got a brilliant memory or he looked the date up. I don't want to disappoint you but it's my brother's birthday, so it was dead easy. In 1955 and 1956 when we played Newcastle United and Birmingham City respectively, I was still in nappies so that's a bit of a decent excuse. In 1969 when we played Leicester in the FA Cup final, I didn't leave school until the end of May so didn't have any money to buy a ticket and to get to London and most importantly get back again. My parents thought I was too young to go and wouldn't give me any money. Bleeding hell I was joining the Royal Navy in the October. When we played West Bromwich in the League Cup 1970, I couldn't get any leave from HMS Ganges as it was "Open Day" on the Sunday and all leave had been cancelled on the Saturday (which was the day after my sixteenth birthday) as we had to clean and polish everything, plus I was in the Navy's window ladder display team and was training for the display on the Sunday. Even if I could have got time off, I still had the problem of no money, no ticket and no civilian clothes but it would not have been a problem for me to go in my Navy uniform.

Come the next final against Wolves in 1974, I had money, I had civilian clothes, but I was on board the Royal Navy Frigate HMS Achilles which was docked in Lubeck in Germany, if you have never heard of the place, well neither had I or most of the crew until we arrived. Good job the navigator knew where he was going. Lubeck is about an hour away from Hamburg. The ship was due to sail the evening of the game so that was yet another

Wembley trip I missed out on. Why the hell did we have to be in Germany that particular weekend? Unlike the previous two Wembley appearances we were on the wrong end of a 2-1 score line in a game we should have won comfortably but although we dominated the game, especially the second half, we didn't take our chances. I have spoken to Wolves fans over the years and they are at a loss as to how they won. The referee on the day was called Dave Wallace, pity it wasn't the Dave Wallace who is editor of the City fanzine *King of the Kippax* as we would have won hands down. Our goal scorer Colin Bell saw a shot hit the bar and bounce down but unlike the famous goal scored by Geoff Hurst, Colin's effort didn't cross the line. With the clock ticking away it looked like the game would end in a draw until John Richards hit the winner with about five minutes left. To say the City players and fans were gutted was a bit of an understatement to say the least.

We didn't have to wait too long for our next Wembley appearance and the first one for yours truly. I had bought a season ticket in case we ever got to Wembley as in those days you were guaranteed a Wembley ticket with a season ticket. The season ticket was only about eight pounds and if I couldn't go to a game one of my mates would use it. I was home on leave in Manchester before the game and although some of my mates were going on the train, I decided to go with some others in the back of a transit van leaving Manchester after the pubs shut on the night before the game. We hadn't gone long when I regretted my decision as it was cold, dark, and cramped, beer was getting spilt, so the floor was all wet and there was no chance of getting much kip as people were farting and snoring all night, which reminded me of being back on-board ship. We arrived in London in the early hours of the morning and must have looked a right sight. We parked up went and got some breakfast and had a quick clean up before going to Euston train station to meet up with some other lads who were due to arrive on one of the trains from Manchester. There were a few scuffles on the train station as there were a load of "cockney reds" waiting to get the train to Manchester as they were playing at home that day. I still can't understand why so many of them would want to support a team two hundred odd miles away when there are so many great teams in London. I appreciate some might originally have come from Manchester or their parents or grandparents might have done but not that bleeding many surely. Many Newcastle fans were also on the train station so I thought it was only going to be a matter of time before it kicked off big time. While most of the Newcastle fans we came across were pretty sound there were a few who were more interested in winding City fans up and trying to start fights than they were in having a pint and a laugh. We had a huge Royal Navy ensign (flag) with the words "Dennis Tueart Walks on Water" printed on it, some Newcastle fans took it upon themselves to try and nick it off us and made a grab for it. It was never going to happen so begrudgingly they conceded defeat and left us alone.

I must admit after all my expectations of Wembley my first impression was that it was a bit of a shit hole, especially in the end we were in. The toilets were nearly as bad as the ones at Maine Road and many took to having a piss up the wall and the food and drink was very expensive. None of that bothered us lot as we were at Wembley and that was all that mattered. Mike Doyle was the captain and including the sub there were seven local lads in the team. Ten of the squad were English with Willie Donachie and Asa Hartford making up the Scottish contingent. Nowadays most Premiership clubs are lucky to have three or four English players' in their team and it is a huge bonus if any of them are locals. Like everything else in life football has evolved and the top players in the world want to come and play in England. What a pity Messi never played in the Premiership as he would have made a great addition, especially if he played for City. There was endless speculation and rumours about him coming but it was never to be.

The atmosphere in the ground was amazing with both sets of supporters trying to out sing each other. Newcastle fans were stung into silence when a young Peter Barnes put City 1-0 up when he scored in the twelfth minute, but they were soon back in full voice when Alan Gowling equalised ten minutes before half time. Normally at a game I would go for a pint at half time, but as it was my first time at Wembley, I didn't want to miss any of the game queuing up as it was a bit of a trek to the bar from where I was standing. As it happened it was a good shout on my part as many fans were still in the bar area when Dennis Tueart scored his famous overhead goal to make it 2-1 for us and that is the score the game ended on. For the fans and players alike, it made up for the disappointment two years earlier against Wolves. After the game we had a few beers in London then went on to Oxford to carry on our celebrations.

My next Wembley visit was in 1981 against Spurs and although we played really well the game ended in a 1-1 draw. For the first game I stayed the weekend in London but for the replay it was straight there and back in a car. Although it was another cracking game, we ended up losing 3-2. So, my first three visits to Wembley saw me win one, draw one and lose one. My next visit was not until 1999 and that ended in a victorious penalty shootout against Gillingham.

When the powers that be decided Wembley was on its last legs and a new stadium had to be built, there was plenty of speculation about it being built in Birmingham which would have made more sense as it would have been easier for most supporters to get to. As the opinions of ordinary fans don't matter it was decided to be rebuilt on the same site while an alternative and much cheaper plan would have been to build a stadium with a "tenant" in place and roundabout the same time Arsenal were building a new stadium so it would have made much more sense to make Arsenal's ground a bit bigger and use that as the National stadium, if indeed we needed one at all. Most national teams in Europe and around the world don't have their own stadium instead they just play at different club grounds and that way more fans can see their national team play without spending a fortune in travel costs

As the cost of rebuilding Wembley went over a mind-boggling three quarters of a billion pounds, we have to ask was if was right to spend that money on a national football stadium when at the same time in London there is a record number of children living in poverty, record homelessness, record number of people sleeping rough and record numbers of foodbanks. After saying that if

Don't Look Back In Anger

Wembley wasn't rebuilt, I have no doubt the money would not have been spent to help the more vulnerable of our society. You are probably wondering why I am raising the issue of the homeless and of poverty again, the reason is as a society sometimes we just have to question the wisdom of what the 'powers that be' do that affect us all. Okay, that's me off my soapbox again but Wembley is still a pain in the backside to get to and from plus the FA are actively looking to sell the stadium, lock stock and barrel so someone somewhere doesn't think it's a good idea to keep it as the National stadium, so by the time you read this Wembley could have been sold off.

Although we had to wait many years from the Full Members Cup final against Chelsea to the play off against Gillingham to get to Wembley again, nowadays it is like our second home as we have played in many FA Cup semi-finals and Finals, League Cup Finals and the Community Shield, so we are back there nearly every year for one reason or another. Because of the added expense of going to Wembley and due to the fact we are going so regularly, some fans are prioritising which games they will attend, so City fans who normally wouldn't fit the criteria to get a ticket for say the FA Cup Final will have more chance of getting a ticket for the semi-final or Community Shield. For all its faults Wembley is still seen as an iconic stadium and a place where all players want to play, and all football fans want to go to even if it is just to say "Been there done that and worn the Tee shirt".

Charlie from Rusholme had a good point to make when I was having a pint with him in Wetherspoons in Piccadilly. He was saying that after nearly thirty years of wishing he could go back to Wembley to watch City, it has for him becoming repetitive and an expensive 'do' as he will have been fourteen times since 2011. He has also been there when Spurs played City, as Spurs for a couple of seasons were using Wembley for its home games. Getting time off work is also an issue for him, not only for getting down to London but other away games as well as we seem to play most days of the week now, but that is the price of success and he wouldn't have it any other way. He has noticed that City's away support is getting on in age a bit and some of the hard-core fans that used to go to

Don't Look Back In Anger

most away games are now starting to pick and choose which games to go so, hopefully younger fans can experience the laughs we had visiting different grounds. Anyone who has been to Wembley even if their team lost will have, I hope, some great memories, I know I certainly do. When we played Gillingham in the play offs my two lads and my wife also came and we stayed in Hemel Hempstead for the weekend. What with limited availability of tickets plus the price of them, no way would we be able to go as a family again but it's those sort of memories I will cherish.

Our recent win against Chelsea in the League Cup final saw the Chelsea goalkeeper refusing to be substituted and Sarri the Chelsea manager having a dicky fit. That was a talking point for the next week instead of focusing on yet another trophy for City. My youngest lad Sean and his mate Joe both went to the game and they thought the whole episode funny as fuck and a huge embarrassment for Chelsea. One thing is certain though, the City fans that do go to Wembley always have a brilliant time before, during and after the game. The best time for most though, I should imagine was when we beat United in the semi final. Well done Yaya! I just had to mention that one. I must heap praise on the Watford fans who all stayed to the end cheering their team on despite getting beat 6-0 in the 2019 Final and I will also pay tribute to all the City fans that went and for many it was their fifth trip in less than twelve months. Well that's my lot about Wembley and you never know I might bump into you the next time we play there if even if it does get sold off, I should imagine the FA will try and get an agreement so some Cup finals can still be played there. You just never know what is around the corner, but one thing is certain and that is money talks.

6: we all hate leeds and leeds and leeds...

THAT WAS THE CHANT of football fans up and down the country whenever their team played Leeds United. There is a bit more to the song, but I promised the publisher I would keep the swearing to a minimum. I'm sure you can get the gist of it.

There were two main reasons fans sang that song. One reason was that Leeds had a fantastic team in the early 1970s under the management of the late Don Revie and most fans were envious of their success. They had a reputation for being a hard team who asked for and gave no quarter. Leeds fans also had a banner for their hero, Norman Hunter, which read 'Norman Bites yer Legs'. As well as being a great player, Hunter was hard as nails and had a 'never say die' attitude which rubbed off on the rest of the team. He was involved once in a serious incident which both shamed and shocked the football world. It was a game between Leeds and Derby, probably the top two teams in English football at that time, at Derby's famous old Baseball ground. It was a scrappy game, and no one really knows what triggered the incident, but Norman launched an attack on ex-City favourite Franny Lee. Franny was a short arse compared to Norman, but he fought back, and a full-blown scrap took place on the pitch.

Leeds trainer and Derby's physio grabbed a player each in an attempt to break up the fight and escort them off the pitch. Well you would have thought that would be the end of it and the red mist would have gone away but both players continued to threaten and abuse each other. There was a turn up for the books as Billy Bremner, another player who was as hard as nails and known for putting it about, was acting as a peacemaker at the same time as other players were getting involved. While Derby won that game

3-2, most people of that generation remember it not for the result but for the players kicking off. Don't forget they were fans' heroes and as role models were supposed to set an example.

While I would describe most Leeds players of the 70s and 80s as a bit thuggish, two I did like were Tony Currie and Duncan McKenzie as they were both very skilful and exciting to watch. I always remember Joe Jordan and Gordon McQueen getting tremendous amounts of abuse when they played at Maine Road and the atmosphere on the Kippax always seemed to go up a notch whenever we played Leeds. It was a bit of a surprise when both players were sold to the rags and obviously the abuse continued and if anything got even worse. I think both players, especially Joe Jordan, thrived on the stick he got, and he could dish it out as well.

Leeds won the old First division title three times altogether. Once in the 60s, once in the 70s, and they became the last team to win it in 1992 before the Premier League was formed. They have never won the Premiership and as they spent so many years out of it, I can't see them winning it in the foreseeable future. They were also runners up in the League five times, but no one ever remembers who came second (apart from Liverpool perhaps last season!). It was the same with the FA Cup, whilst they only won it once they were beaten finalists 3 times. They have a large fanatical fanbase so how they got into a financial mess which saw them having to flog their best players year after year and led them to being relegated in 2004 is any one's guess. If it was a big surprise they got relegated it's an even bigger surprise how long it is taking them to get back into the top flight. They have been knocking on the door for a while so they could be back soon. Some fans have a bit of sympathy when another club gets relegated but not many outside of Yorkshire shed a tear when the once mighty Leeds took the plunge.

The second reason people sang "we all hate Leeds etc etc" was because of the behaviour of a sizeable majority of their fans. They spent many years trying to terrorise and fight opposing fans not only in England but abroad as well. A journalist wrote a book about the Leeds Service Crew which was a notorious hooligan firm who followed Leeds home and away. She was very much deluded in some of the stuff she wrote, especially when she says that the fans from other clubs who took part in the violence were willing participants and ordinary football fans were never deliberately targeted. Tell that to the shoppers who cowered in terror in various towns and cities up and down the country when Leeds fans went on the rampage. Or to the German fans of Bayern Munich when Leeds fans ripped up the seats and threw them at fans, police and stewards during the 1975 European Cup Final. Then after the game they were attacking any German fans they came across. An innocent Leeds fan was tragically killed when violence broke out between Leeds and Birmingham fans when he was crushed to death, on the same day as the Bradford fire. That accident came at the last game of the 1985 season at St Andrews, and there was pitched battles before, during and after the game. Leeds fans reportedly attacked a coach carrying guests from an Indian wedding party smashing the coach windows. The Shadow Sports Minister Dennis Howell was at the game and alluded to the hard-line hooligan element on the day of the riot and mentioned the Trendies as well as The Service Crew. The Birmingham hooligans, the Zulus, were also very active that day and many, many police as well as fans were attacked and ended up in hospital. In 1990 up to 10 thousand Leeds fans turned up in Bournemouth for a bank holiday game. Violence broke out all weekend, windows were smashed, motorbikes were set on fire and Leeds fans fought running battles with riot police while terrified residents were too scared to go into town. But the author of that book must have had rose tinted glasses on as she claimed that the damage was done by "scarfers" who were nothing to do with the firm. Should imagine the author would have us believe that the Leeds Service Crew were all tucked up in bed drinking hot chocolate while this mayhem was taking place. Some people must think we're all nuts and will believe anything. I don't know who invents the names of these hooligan gangs but I imagine some were made up by journalists and authors as I never heard of half of the names until the hooligan books came out. How do you join anyway? Bet you don't get a membership form with your photo on the back of it as it won't be the same as joining the Boy Scouts that's for sure.

Anyway, who gives a shit what they called themselves? If your business is being wrecked or your coach is being smashed up or someone is kicking the crap out of you do you really give a monkey's if they are an organised firm or just some hangers on?

I went to watch City play at Elland Road many times in the 70s and 80s and witnessed Leeds fans attacking City fans on many occasions and at the time it was also widely reported in the local press when a group of Leeds fans attacked a City fan who was with his young son and the young lad got hit as well. City always took a massive following to Leeds and those games produced not only some of the best atmospheres I have witnessed at a football game but also the worst out breaks of football violence as well. When City knocked Leeds out of the FA Cup in 1978, Leeds fans invaded the pitch in the misguided belief that they could get the match abandoned. No such luck for them that day, although the players had to be led back in the changing rooms while order was restored on the pitch. The ref came back out with a microphone and told the crowd that the game would not be abandoned even if they had to stay until midnight. Eventually the morons left the pitch and even though they managed to score from the penalty spot they still got knocked out of the cup 2-1. The Leeds fans continued their unruly behaviour outside the ground and attacked the City fans with bricks, bottles and anything else they could get their hands on and were involved in running battles with City fans all the way back to the coach and car parks as well as the train station and again many innocent fans from both sides were caught up in the mayhem. Now you may think witnessing that sort of stuff would put people off from going to a match ever again but as a 23-year-old in the 70s I thought that was pretty much the norm and the following season thousands of City fans once again descended on Elland Road as we had sadly seen it all before and it would take more than a riot and a bit of violence to put us off from attending a game.

Now not all Leeds fans were crackers and many I spoke to were ashamed of the hooligan's behaviour. One time I was watching City at Leeds for some reason that eludes me I was sat in the stands which was a rarity for me but in them days you could have a drink while watching the game and although I can't remember the result I recall it was a very pleasant afternoon having a drink and watching the game with some great Leeds fans without any fear of getting my head kicked in. A couple of the lads admitted they thought Maine Road was one of the scariest grounds they had been to, especially if they took a wrong turn down the back streets. Now all football fans back then had a hooligan following and City fans were no angels either. To a lesser extent some clubs still have a hooligan following but thankfully the days when thousands of away fans converged on towns and cities intent on mayhem are long gone. After saying that it was not so long ago that Glasgow Rangers fans did their best to wreck Manchester after getting beat in the UEFA Cup final and there is the odd bit of trouble on European nights, especially when Liverpool fans were allowed to attack the City players' coach with impunity. Violence before, during and after some games will in my opinion never be completely stopped but the police and authorities are largely on top of it now.

I got to know a Leeds fan quite well who I met in Prestwich. As I was writing a chapter about his team and supporters I thought it would balance it out having a say from a Leeds fans perspective.

Brian Searson Leeds United Season Ticket Holder from Falmouth, Cornwall.

I left Falmouth in 1982 and came to Prestwich with the dual intention of becoming a Psychiatric Nurse and to follow Leeds United both home and away. I first met Don near the old Victorian Kitchens at the hospital and people described him as a fanatical City fan and if you have read his other books you can understand why. I've not seen Don for many years now but contacted him to congratulate him on his books. Don told me he is writing his third and final one and as he mentioned Leeds United and would I like my penny's worth? Do bears shit in the woods? It was an opportunity not to be missed.

Don't Look Back In Anger

Don asked me loads of times how come I became a Leeds fan but either he or myself or both were pissed at the time so I will put it in writing, so he won't forget. I became a Leeds fan in 1968 when I was 10 years old. I liked two teams at the time Leeds and sorry to say your neighbours from Stretford. The first thing the City fans told me though was "We're the Only Football Team from Manchester". See how well trained I am as I never forgot? Well anyway the lot from Stretford won the European Cup and Leeds won the now defunct Inter City Fairs Cup as well as the League Cup. So thankfully I plumped for Leeds, probably because they played in White and I liked the kit (well I was only 10). I am glad I made that choice as I doubt I would have made mates with Don and the other Blues I got to know well such as Stany, Kev, Derbo (RIP), Mike Joyce, Ozzie and others whose names elude me at the moment. Well Don did say have a couple of drinks while you are typing, and stuff will flow. Thanks for the advice mate but the Cider down here is frigging strong!

The Hospital back then was huge and dominated the Prestwich/ Whitefield area and the majority of adults who lived locally either worked there, had a family member that did or at the very least knew someone who did. The football vibe was great and apart from the City and United fans there were some Bury, Bolton and Scouse fans with the odd smattering off Hereford and Shrewsbury fans as well as Rangers and Celtic plus there were a couple more Leeds fans as people in different professions came from far and wide to work and gain expertise at the hospital. For a country lad like me who was well into football coming to a city like Manchester with a great football vibe was just terrific. Unfortunately my team got relegated (not for the last time) five months after I made the move up North.

With others from the Hospital and some of the locals I got pally with, I occasionally went on a drinking tour starting with the Derby in Whitefield and finishing at the Red Lion in Prestwich. That was some session, especially if you were drinking Joey Holts as there must have been about a dozen pubs. Loads have sadly gone now including the Derby, Bulls Head, Church Inn, Wheatsheaf, Masons, Red King and the Junction in Whitefield plus the Grapes, and Wilton in Prestwich. I've probably missed a couple of others as well. I loved them pubs as there was a proper football buzz as we shared stories of who played who from the previous week and who was going where the week after, plus we had a laugh about the scrapes we got up to. In my early days in Prestwich most of the lads just called me Leeds and now and again something much worse but I took it in good humour. I am sure plenty will disagree or claim otherwise but I thought Prestwich and Whitefield were split pretty much fifty-fifty between Reds and Blues. Derby day was just mental round there and the piss taking, and the wind ups started a good week before. After most Derby games it seemed to kick off at one pub or another which was pretty crazy really, as most of the lads got on pretty well with one another except on Derby day, then anything could happen. I either stayed away or kept a low profile on Derby day in Manchester.

For me personally I have felt that Leeds and City have a lot in common as if something shit was going to happen it would happen to us, but both sets of fans had a siege mentality, and the ability to laugh in the face of adversity (as Leeds still do but City's luck has well and truly changed). Good luck I say.

I always liked City fans and I liked them even more after a couple of times on my travels when I came across them. I was going to Victoria station on my way to meet some mates as Leeds were playing Shrewsbury. Just my luck there were hundreds of City fans on their way to Bradford and this was the day and age when football hooliganism was rife. Well my arse fell out but to be fair not one of them gave me a crack or laid a finger on me, I got a bit of stick but I can take that all day long. On another occasion I was coming back from watching Leeds at Leicester when a sixty-handed mob of City fans got on the same train as us after watching the Blues play Sheffield United. I said to my mate "we've had it here" but thank goodness I knew some of them from Prestwich including Derbo and Kev, so we breathed a huge sigh of relief.

As a student nurse I couldn't always get to watch Leeds play, either because they played too far away or I was skint or studying or I was on shifts on a ward, but I still wanted my football fix. Sometimes I would go a few miles down the road to watch Bury, now and again I would go with Mario and stay with lads we knew in Scotland and watch Rangers play. I also followed England when I could but surprisingly, I rarely met City fans on those occasions.

I spent sixteen brilliant years in North Manchester and made friends with some great people despite being a Leeds fan. Although I am now *back in Cornwall, I still have my Leeds season ticket and get to as many matches home and away as I can. One day soon we will be playing you lot again and I can't wait for it.*

Cheers for that Brian I thought Leeds would have done it 2018-2019 but Derby thought differently and took your place at Wembley, don't think it will be too long though until you join us!

7: captains

OVER THE YEARS it has often been debated as to who was the best ever Manchester City captain. Fans' views will depend on their age and how good or bad City were at the time their choice of captain was playing. Also, what must be considered is the changing role of the captain in this day and age. Before football became a global brand and television companies, radio stations and Newspapers reported 24/7, the captain's main role was to watch the ref toss a coin in the air and shout heads or tails, then if he won the toss decide who would kick off first. He also acted as an extension of the manager and to be a leader out on the pitch. Nowadays the captain is representing the club in many different ways. Whether helping out with doing charity work or meeting with sponsors and fulfilling about a hundred other obligations, the captain has to be ready to give radio and television interviews in a very professional manner. It is hard to give an interview at any time especially if a microphone is stuck under your nose just after a game has finished and he is still dealing with the raw emotion of the match and if he's had a stinker and City were badly beaten it makes it even harder. It only takes him to say one wrong word or say something out of context and the so-called pundits are all over it like a rash and debating it until the cows come home. It's a bit like managers at press conferences, with some of the interviewers asking loaded questions just hoping for a negative response. I rarely listen to them now as you can more or less guess what the next question is going to be. Pep is a master as he has been there done that and got half a dozen of the shirts so there is nothing he can't take in his stride but at times you can tell he is getting pissed off with the ridiculous things he is getting asked.

When City favourite Peter Barnes won the Young Player

of the Year award in 1976 after we had beaten Newcastle in the League Cup final he was interviewed, and the poor lad just froze as the moment got to him. In contrast I watched an interview with young Phil Foden, and he handled it like a veteran. No doubt players in this day and age are given help, advice and training when conducting interviews. So it is not just the club captain who will get a microphone shoved under his nose and as every kid it seems has a mobile phone with a camera it is so important that the players behave ultra professional both on and off the pitch as any indiscretion can be beamed round cyber space straight away. As football is a multi-billion-pound industry and clubs are marketed as a brand, any bad publicity or indiscretion by players in general and in particular the club captain can lead to bad coverage in the press and a lot of negativity for the club. That is why over the last few years City have gone the extra mile to make sure whoever we sign is not only a brilliant footballer but can handle himself professionally off the pitch as well.

The beginning of this more professional approach can be traced back to a live BBC interview in March 2006, when 17 year-old Micah Richards described his dramatic injury time equaliser, which secured City a fifth-round replay against Aston Villa, as "f**king great" to a shocked national TV audience. A few days later former BBC Radio 5 Live presenter Susan Bookbinder, who still runs media training company Zamala International, got a call asking her to deliver some 'urgent media training' with City's young centre-half. Here, Susan gives us a fascinating insight into that session and of the state of the club at that time.

"As a life-long blue I was delighted to drive up from London with my camera crew. However, the session at the Carrington training ground was not what I had expected. Although I had spent much of my working life in London, I have City running through my veins. I was virtually brought-up at Maine Road, attending matches from the age of four with my father, who in turn had been going to the old Moss Side ground since he was seven with his father. I am also very proud that my brother John was a member of the iconic 1986 FA Youth Cup winning squad.

"At that time the club was hugely in debt to Chairman John Wardle and wanted their money's worth and threw into the session a few extra players and a couple of senior executives. As well as Micah, the players included the ambitious and intelligent Daniel Sturridge, a warm and enthusiastic Georgios Samaras... and Joey Barton. You maybe be surprised that I found Joey to be serious about the training and quite a charming young man. When I said I'd been a journalist for over 20 years and therefore well-placed to help the players get the most out of their media interviews, Joey commented that I must have started my career "whaa, like, from when you were four?" OK, I am easily flattered!

"The executive team at the time, excluding dyed-in-the-wool Blue John Wardle who I still see among in the crowd at matches, were not City diehards. I found it rather odd that they were pretty angry about City fans. They seemed particularly upset about the singing of the song "we never win at home and we never win away", which they described as 'disloyal' and 'depressing'. I tried to explain how the song is a battle cry. 'It shows how long we have been following City through the thin and thinner of being in the third tier and losing to Mansfield Town in the Auto Windscreens Shield', I told them to no avail. At this point of course, the FA Youth Cup in 1986 was the only trophy the club had won since 1976.

"The executives (one was openly a Liverpool supporter) just didn't get it, to the extent that it was difficult to deliver their part of the training. Nevertheless the players' media training was a success. Micah put the skills he had learned in the session into action in an interview with Ian Ladyman of the *Daily Mail* who wrote, 'Micah Richards approaches a difficult question like a hard tackle, with precision and skill...'. When I next saw Micah and Daniel at the 2008 Hall of Fame Awards, which I co-presented with John Stapleton at the Etihad, Micah wrote a tribute for my website, saying 'You taught me everything I know about the media'. It is somewhat ironic that after retiring from the game last summer, Micah is now a pundit on BBC's Final Score."

Thanks for that Susan. It just goes to show how far the club has changed over recent years and not just when it comes to the recruitment of players. As a fan you just want to read about the players on the back pages. Not read about some scandal or something stupid they have said or done on the front pages.

A discussion about the best club captain was recently debated on the Manchester City forum Blue Moon. The five favourites in no particular order were Roy Paul, Tony Book, Mike Doyle, Paul Power and Vincent Kompany followed swiftly by Richard Dunne, Mick McCarthy, Andy Morrison and Stuart Pearce. Obviously it is not a scientific survey and everyone has their favourites for different reasons, but what readily sticks out is that many of our fans would never have seen Roy Paul or Tony Book play as Roy was our captain in the 1950s and Tony hung up his boots in the early 1970s so those two must have left an excellent legacy passed down from generations of City fans and their families.

ROY PAUL

I never saw Roy play but by all accounts he was a great player, captain and gentleman. He was born in South Wales and was rescued from a life down the pits because of his skill as a footballer. The reason I never saw him play was that I was only a nipper when he led City out twice at Wembley in the 1950s. We were beaten by Newcastle in 1955 but he lifted the FA Cup for City a year later when we beat Birmingham City. As a youngster he couldn't even get into his school team but he went on to make over 150 first team appearances for Swansea Town. He had a reputation for being a hard-no-nonsense type of defender but wasn't out of place playing in a more forward role.

He ended up upsetting Swansea (and his wife) as along with a few other players from the United Kingdom he flew out to Bogota, the capital of Colombia, in search of a big pay day playing football on the other side of the world. Back then English footballers were only allowed to earn £12 a week. Colombian football had renounced its membership of FIFA the year before so teams could now acquire these players without a transfer fee and pay them huge wages in comparison. The likes of Stoke and England centre-half Neil Franklin and Manchester United winger Charlie Mitten were lured to South America by the fortunes on offer. As an example Roy Paul was given a £3.000 signing on fee and a weekly wage of £150 a week, so it was no wonder the Welshman jumped at the chance.

We have all heard the saying that "the grass is not always greener on the other side" well so it proved for Roy. Because of the different climate, tough regime, the state of the pitches and football grounds, he left Colombia after just eight days without even kicking a football in anger. Swansea were seething with anger as they thought he was being disloyal and straight away stuck him on the transfer list and City readily snapped him up and he was soon to write his name in our club's history. Swansea's loss was certainly our gain, as captain he was well respected as a leader both on the pitch and in the dressing room so quickly earned the respect of all his teammates. He wasn't shy in coming forward to tell people some home truths but was generally very well liked.

Roy was at Maine Road for seven years and played over 290 league and cup games. It was rumoured that he liked to mix socially with some of the other players and enjoyed a pint or two after a game. Well there was certainly nothing surprising about that back then. Roy's nephew Alan Curtis also played for both Swansea and Wales. Roy also was player manager at Worcester City before going back to live in South Wales where he worked as a lorry driver. He was well liked and adored in South Wales and his standing went up another notch when he toured parts of Wales with the FA Cup and visited schools and amateur football clubs with it. He is still remembered down there with great fondness.

TONY BOOK

While the term legend gets bandied about like confetti nowadays, if one person is worthy of that title it is the man affectionately known throughout the football world as "Skip". It took Tony a long time to reach the top level in English football as he plied his trade first with non league Bath City, then Plymouth Argyle before arriving in Manchester at the age of thirty-two. He quickly became captain of City and led us through the greatest spell in the club's history and it took thirty odd years for his achievements to be eclipsed. He was a very popular club captain who had time for everyone at the club including the staff behind the scenes and would stop and talk to the fans all day long. I don't think he has ever said a bad word in public about anyone and I certainly have never heard a bad word said about him. He is a true gentleman in every sense of the word. Even when the club dispensed with his services (twice) he kept his counsel and of course both times he returned to the club he loves. Besides winning a host of trophies as captain he also managed the League Cup winners of 1976 and he has held several roles with us and has been an assistant or advisor to a host of managers in his fifty-year association with City. Even now at home games he can be seen chatting with fans of all ages and signing autographs and having his photos taken with them.

I was fortunate to meet Tony on many occasions, when I was chairman of the Prestwich & Whitefield Supporters Club, he attended many of the events we organised, and he still makes himself available to attend supporters' clubs and charity events.

We organised a special event for Tony after he left the club when Frank Clark became manager. The decision to let him go did not go down well with the fans. It was standing room only as over 400 fans packed into Heaton Park Social Club to thank him properly for his services at the club. Such was his popularity, fourteen ex-players also attended and Paul Walsh, who then, as now, was working for Sky TV, came up from London to show his support as did Paul Lake and Andy Dibble along with many others. It was a fantastic evening organised spontaneously by the fans and as Tony himself said, it was a very touching and emotional evening. Although there have been many great captains in my time supporting City, probably because I have met and spoken to him on many occasions and of his long association with the club I would have to plump for Tony as my favourite all time captain just by a minute fraction ahead of Captain Fantastic.

Vincent Kompany

I am sure that many fans who weren't around during the Tony Book era would have Vinny head and shoulders ahead of any of our other captains. It is easy to see why. He is articulate in front of the camera and has loads of time for City fans and he even married a Manchester City fan. Of course he is a fantastic player who can motivate the people around him and spur them on to the next level, so he ticks all the right boxes both on and off the field. During his injury problems he has always remained positive and is always giving encouragement to the younger players who I am sure he inspires to be like him. He is a born leader and when he hangs up his boots for good I am sure he will make a success of any career he chooses to go into, Many fans hope there is a role for him at City in the future but whether he returns to the club in some capacity or works in the media or does something entirely different, he won't be short of opportunities as he also has a master's degree in business administration which he passed at Manchester University.

Vincent is a serial winner picking up the FA Cup, League Cup, Premier League and Community Shield trophies and medals. When Vinny was at his peak, with him in the team we didn't think we would ever be beaten as he is so inspirational and oozes so much confidence it rubs onto the other players. Granted in his final two or three years, because of his injuries he didn't play as much as he would have liked but there was always a buzz when he got onto the pitch. Vinny always gave his best and never let anyone down and whenever he gave interviews, he always had a captive audience, as he not only spoke common-sense, but he told it how it was without any of the bullshit that some players tend to spout. He seemed to enjoy every game and whilst never a prolific goal scorer he scored some vital ones and none more so then when he powered in that header against United in 2012. He must have jumped about ten foot in the air as the goal meant so much to him. The smile and celebration from 'Captain Fantastic' said it all. The best of the lot though must have been against Leicester on our way to win the league title in 2019, what a cracker that was and boy did we need something special.

It will be a long time until we get another captain of his calibre, but who ever is next will have big boots to fill and we wish him all the best and let's hope he wins as many medals and trophies as Vinny. Being a captain of any football club is an honour and it's a title that should be held with pride as you are a leader both on and off the pitch and that is something he did immensely well. Plus in his testimonial year he teamed up with the Mayor of Manchester to raise a substantial amount of money to help get the homeless off the streets. One lad from Bluemoon summed it up by saying both Vinny and Skip were his favourite captains but while he was sure Vinny had the capabilities to be captain of the team from Tony's era, he didn't think Tony would have been able to captain the teams Vinny did because of the demands of the modern captain and also the egos of some of the players. I am not so sure myself. While Tony was quiet and softly spoken, he was no push over and there were some people on proper ego trips in the teams that Tony captained. Having said that Vinny was our leader in 2019 when we went on to win all the domestic trophies including the Community Shield, an achievement that has never been done before so I should imagine he would top any future polls easily and all City fans wish him all the best in his new role at Anderlecht.

KIT SYMONS

While he was never the most popular captain we have ever had and endured some hard times on the pitch, it was his endeavours off the pitch and his work with charity events and supporters' clubs that endeared him to the fans. He was tireless in attending supporters' events up and down the country and his help with fundraising events was brilliant and he got many other first team players involved as well. When the Rochdale branch organised a charity ten pin bowling event at Pilsworth near Bury, Kit turned up with a few players and stayed for a few hours, bowling, eating, sitting and chatting to the fans and having photos taken and signing autographs for the fans.

That's the thing that fans miss now, or in some cases have never experienced, players just turning up to events without them being organised through the club. Those afternoons/nights/early mornings, have long gone. Any events involving players, management and staff at supporters' events are now sadly few and far between.

Looking back at some of the events we had and the state some of the players went home in, well in all honestly if you didn't attend any you would find some of the stories hard to believe. I am sure though like me, if you had the choice of players attending supporters' events on a regular basis or winning trophies, I'm sure most of you would opt for the latter. Maybe if Kit was at the club in a time when chaos didn't ensue, and we were more stable with better players around him he would figure higher in supporters' opinion. I am giving him a good mention as he is a really nice bloke and he did so much for so many supporters clubs and nothing was too much trouble for him. I must admit I am a bit biased as I got to know him quite well and as a family we have been up to his house for tea and we attended his wedding in Portsmouth. Since he left City, we have not been in touch that frequently but we did meet up with him in London when City were playing Crystal Palace and when the Last Royal Tournament was at Earls Court Cath and I met up with his wife Lucy and went to their house. Kit was away on International duty, so I just drank his beer instead. Each year we still send Christmas cards to each other. Maybe one day our paths will cross again and we will have a chat over old times.

STUART 'PSYCHO' PEARCE

Unfortunately we got Stuart at the tail end of his career. His progress up the football ladder was reasonably slow as he was a full-time electrician while playing part-time for Wealdstone FC which was the start of an illustrious career in football and he went on to play for Coventry City, Nottingham Forest, Newcastle United and West Ham United and was capped many times for England before joining us towards the end of his career in 2002. He was a very passionate player and always wore his heart on his sleeve, was extremely patriotic and very proud of playing for his country. He captained every team he played for and was a born winner and leader of men. As such, he was awarded the MBE for his services to football. Arguably his best times were at Nottingham Forest where they treat him like a legend and welcome him with open arms whenever he returns to the City ground. He was a no-nonsense player who never gave less than one hundred percent and even though his better days were behind him, that's what the City fans loved about him. I met him on a couple of occasions and what struck me instantly was how quiet and softly spoken he was as out on the pitch he seemed to roar like a lion. Stuart went on to manage City for a couple of seasons but his style of play during that time was uninspiring to say the least and that's me being polite. However, he had better luck when he was manager of the England U21's team and The Great Britain Olympic football team in 2012. Just watching him with those teams you could see how proud he was to have been given that honour.

One game Stuart played in must have been strange for him. It was Forest away at Brighton in the League Cup during the 1986 and 1987 season. Well it probably was just as strange for one of the linesmen as it was his brother Ray. Is that not strange or what? I don't think that would be allowed these days. That will be one for the pub quiz so remember where you heard it first. And here is another one for you at no extra charge. His other brother Dennis was the referee for his testimonial game: Nottingham Forest v Newcastle United. How good am I? If I ever need to set questions for a pub quiz those two are going in for sure. Here is another, again at no extra cost. Which two teams took part in the first ever FA Cup replay at Wembley?

KEITH CURLE

Now Keith was a wonderful player but didn't figure in the top ten of my very unscientific survey about City's captains, in fact he hardly got a mention so I am not even sure why I am mentioning him either. I must have lost the plot and now I'm waiting for the nurse to come round and give me my medication, but as someone must have thought he was okay I decided to give him a quick mention. I think one reason he wasn't highly regarded as a captain was because even though he was a decent defender and led the players well on the pitch, he never quite captured the hearts and minds of the majority of the City faithful, as other captains have. Now I know it isn't the 'be all and end all' of turning up to supporters' club meetings and attending fan charity events and I have no doubt he went to one or two, but he never ever seemed to have a rapport with the fans. Since he left, I doubt he's ever been back to any of the events or celebrations that the club has put on. I will never forget the time I saw him at the Platt Lane training complex. After finishing a training session the players were about to go upstairs to get something to eat and were signing autographs and having photos with the fans. Keith, who had not been training, got out of his car and before he went upstairs, a gentleman politely asked him if he would sign an autograph and have a photo taken with his son. Keith said not now but I will be back in five minutes. Of course, he never came back down for the next hour at least while I was there. All the other players were great, and nothing was too much trouble for them. Captains are supposed to lead by example, so I'm glad that the players that day didn't follow his example, and in my humble opinion that sums his attitude to the fans and why he is not highly rated as a captain.

PAUL POWER

Paul was not only a brilliant captain for the Blues, but he served City well in various roles at the youth academy until he was relieved of his duties in 2014 as part of an all round shake up following a review. I believe Paul was vastly underrated in some quarters while playing and captaining City, one reason being we never won any silverware during his tenure but who can ever forget that goal he scored against Ipswich at Villa Park in 1981 which sent us into the Centenary Cup Final against Spurs and the subsequent replay. Yes, if you took part in my mini quiz – City and Spurs was the answer, so if you got it right you have my permission to have a can of lager cheers, okay if you didn't get it right you can have one anyway, good eh?

Paul was a local lad and a City fan as were many other players at that time. While Paul was at the Academy, a host of young players went on to play for the first team, and like us he is chuffed that Phil Foden has not only broken into the first team but has won a load of medals already. Other young players are knocking on the door, but I won't put the mockers on them by naming them, as that would surely be the kiss of death, and we don't want that do we? The Academy complex is light years ahead of the Platt Lane training complex where there were never enough pitches for everyone to train or to play on and many Academy matches were played at Whalley Range High School for Girls on a Sunday when the facilities were not being used by the school. You can't even begin to compare that set up to what we have now, as instead of borrowed pitches at a girl's school there are seventeen pitches, a hotel, a restaurant, a state of the art mini stadium and a fitness centre which would rival that of any club in the world.

Paul's route into football was a bit unusual as he earned a Law Degree at Leeds Polytechnic before becoming a professional footballer in the mid 1970s. Paul also worked with the Professional Football Association and was held in great respect with his fellow professionals. His only other club was Everton, and would you believe it, he only went and won the league with them. I have had the privilege of meeting Paul on a few occasions and he is proper old school. He will talk football all day long and he talks fondly of his time at City especially when our teams were packed with Manchester lads. He still keeps a fond interest in City and visits supporters' events and helps with various charities. One thing he said about the Academy is that because the first team is so good it is very hard for players to break into it and he cited Kieran Trippier as an example who eventually went on to play for Spurs and England. In fact, at Euro 2016 there were nine graduates who had been released from City's Academy who went on to make careers at other clubs who were there representing various countries. So well done the Academy, even though the young players didn't figure in our long term plans, those players went on to fulfil their ambitions as a professional elsewhere and we also got to put some money back into the coffers in terms of the transfer fees.

Myself, Derbo, Kev and our wives (okay I'd better name them so I don't get into trouble, Cath, Sue and Julie) were having a meal in the Bem Brazil in Manchester and Paul was in there and he came over and had a natter and we had to touch on his goal at Villa Park as all three of us were in the end where the ball flew into the net. I still have tremendous respect for him. Thanks for the memories Paul.

THE LATE GREAT MIKE DOYLE

What a captain and leader of men he was; absolutely fearless and inspirational as well. A Blue stalwart who was as hard as they come, he was loved by all City fans and his reputation was enhanced by his hatred of United and he baited them at every opportunity. He also scored forty-one goals for us altogether and went on to play for England five times. There is one iconic moment I will never forget and that is when those "lovely" fans from over at the swamp invaded the pitch after Denis Law scored when they were relegated in 1974. Mike calmly walked through the lot of them and they just parted to make room for him and not one of them had the bottle to confront him. Among his many achievements was when he captained City to the League Cup final against a very good Newcastle team in 1976. A year later Mike was injured and was substituted when we played West Ham at Upton Park. As I was making my way to the tube, I saw the City coach parked up by the players' entrance and Mike was sat in it on his own. Being the shy restrained person that I am I got on the bus and had a chat with Mike for a few minutes and I was buzzing all the way home after that. Mike has left a legacy at City in the form of his grandson Tommy (who is also grandson of Doyle's City team mate Glyn Pardoe) who is getting rave reviews, so all City fans are hoping he one day graduates to the first team. Now what a story that would make!

ANDY MORRISON

Now if anyone was a contender to be as hard if not harder than Mike, Andy's name would be top of the list. If you have read his book "The Good, the Mad and the Ugly" you will recall the sort of shit he got himself into on a regular basis. I thought I had gone off the rails once or twice whilst in the Royal Navy getting myself into some mither, but Andy was in a league of his own. Whilst Andy only played around fifty games for us, we can't underestimate the desire, commitment and will to win he brought to the club. We were in a right old mess when he joined us, but he dragged us kicking and screaming out of the old Third Division. He was a no-nonsense type of player who didn't suffer fools gladly but had tons of time for the supporters from which ever club he was at. He came to many of our supporters' meetings and events. It was only after I read his book, I realised what a serious drink problem he had, but at all the events he attended he was very professional and only had soft drinks. The first meeting he attended was a fundraiser for Henshaw's School for the Blind, A group of partly sighted youngsters were in attendance and it brought a tear to my eyes seeing how well Andy interacted with them. At one charity event he came to we gave a special twelve-year-old bottle of whisky to all the guests. None of us knew at the time that he was a recovering alcoholic, and he could have taken offence, but he was as good as gold and didn't get the hump. I am sure he knew someone to pass it on to who would appreciate it.

He was another player who would do whatever he could for the fans and would attend supporters' club meeting and charity events whenever he could. The last time I met Andy was at an evening dinner to celebrate twenty years of the Prestwich and Whitefield branch of the City supporters' club. I hadn't been involved for several years so was chuffed to bits when I was invited to attend. I had a good long chat with Andy, and he was very proud that he was a Manchester City FC Club Ambassador. I asked him what that entailed, and he just explained that anything the club wanted him to do, he would do it, whether it was meeting club sponsors or going to supporters' events or meeting fans on match days in the lounges. That is why the fans loved him so much, nothing seemed to be too much trouble for him and he had a great rapport with the fans unlike another ex-captain I have already mentioned. Andy gave me his number and told me to keep in touch. Cath in her wisdom binned it as she knows what I am like and had visions of me phoning Andy at stupid o'clock in the morning after a few beers and talking nonsense as I have previous for doing that. So, if you read this Andy it is Cath's fault I have not been in touch!

RICHARD EDGHILL

Edgy was another local lad and City supporter who came up through the youth ranks to captain the club, what a great achievement. It was a pity then that some City fans turned on him and he was yet another victim of the boo boys who slagged him off for any minor mistake, but over the years City fans have had a tendency to find a scapegoat and give them grief. I remember Alan Kernaghan used to get booed when his name was announced before the game even started. Most players cop for a bit of stick now and again but towards the end of his career it was relentless. Astonishingly Richard played for nine different managers during his time at City and when Frank Clark took over it was five managers in five months. You would think that that must be a the record, however Ian Brightwell played under ten managers and three caretakers, four if you count Tony Books two different stints in charge. Those were the days eh, but we can laugh about it now, although it was not funny at the time. In his book "Once a Blue always a Blue" Edgy reckons Alan Ball's time at City was a disaster but thought Joe Royle was the best manager he worked under. He was disappointed though with how he was treated by Kevin Keegan and he left under a bit of a cloud. I only met Richard a handful of times but what a smashing lad he is. Richard is another one who has plenty of time for the fans and nothing is too much trouble for him. During Paul Lake's testimonial year Richard gave Paul loads of support and attended some supporters' events with him.

For the years of dedication he gave to City it would have come as a massive disappointment that the fans were getting on his back, plus he didn't think Kevin Keegan rated him highly and was gutted to have been only offered a one-year contract so eventually he left. He felt unwanted and thought he was shown a total lack of respect by the manager after the service he had put in. That to me is such a shame for someone who has given so much to the club. To be treated in such a manner must have been hard to take, as always though there are two sides to the story, and I remember at the time many City fans were not disappointed at him leaving. Well if I have counted correctly that's ten club/team captains I have written about. No doubt some of you will disagree with what I have written and question my choice of ten captains and wonder why others weren't included. The ten I wrote about apart from Curley Wurley were the ones most mentioned by the fans on Bluemoon. Others that I could easily have written about were Richard Dunne, Paul Lake, Carlos Tevez, Johnny Crossan, Mick McCarthy, Steve Redmond. Jamie Pollock (only joking) and David Silva to name just a few more. To be honest, we have been blessed with some great captains. Some did not wear the armband for long and some had bigger impacts than others. I hope that by writing about some of our captains it has triggered some good memories for you, it certainly brought back some belting memories for me writing about them.

8: a call to arms

EARLIER I MENTIONED how bad hooliganism was back in the day and even though there is still some trouble at grounds up and down the country and in Europe (A City fan in Germany and a United fan in France suffered serious injuries watching their teams abroad in 2019) the trouble is nothing like on the scale it was back in the day. There is one exception though and even though it was well organised and well planned in advance, the police and authorities took no decisive action to stop it. We are of cause talking about when thousands of Liverpool fans were "allowed" to attack our team coach with bricks, bottles, and other assorted missiles when City played at Anfield in the Champions League quarter final. The coach was so badly damaged it couldn't be driven back to Manchester and a replacement had to come to collect the team. Just after the draw was made leaflets were being passed round Liverpool encouraging thousands of fans to meet up two hours before the game and to bring flares, sand, pyro cans and bangers with the intent "To scare the Mancs back to Manchester with their tails between their legs." The internet and Facebook sites down the East Lancs were in overdrive and for weeks the Scousers were getting all giddy for their big night out. It soon became very clear to anyone who read any of the stuff on the internet that a recipe for disaster was on the cards. Liverpool have history with the "Welcome to Liverpool" "Call to Arms" events and other team's coaches have also been bombarded with missiles. The shocking scenes of parents swigging cans of lager with children on their shoulders while other fans were standing on the police surveillance vans as others were bombarding the team coach with missiles were beamed around the world. What made it even worse was not one fan was arrested. A police investigation was later launched but no one could be identified, and no one was brought to court.

Don't Look Back In Anger

Unbelievable, but we weren't surprised.

Liverpool's manager Jurgen Klopp in his press conference said all the stuff you would expect him to but then made a dick of himself by saying it was just a small number of idiots. No, it wasn't Mr Klippity Klopp, which part of the video did you not watch? Andy Burnham, the Mayor of Manchester, said precisely nothing about the incident and some ex-Liverpool players tried to make light of the situation. Prior to the attack the *Manchester Evening News* wrote an article highlighting the potential problems and the real concerns we had. Manchester City FC also made representations but it was still allowed to go ahead. The police even announced that they were changing the route and then gave details of the new route, no doubt so the fans could be better prepared. Now I am not sure how it affected the players, but I know if I was on a coach being driven through a baying mob of thousands of fans with missiles bouncing off the coach but I would have shit myself. Liverpool later issued an apology which was about as much use as a one-legged man in an arse-kicking competition. David Walker, a City fan who runs the City Facebook page 'Read But Never Red', commented "It is little wonder by their actions why many ordinary fans now despise Liverpool".

Liverpool police and council have years and years of experience of policing football matches, strikes, demonstrations, riots and all sorts of public order offences but despite the warnings they were either unwilling, unable, or incapable of preventing an attack of such magnitude on a football team coach at a massive sporting event. A few months after the event Liverpool police announced to the BBC that they had "exhausted" all lines of inquiry after sorting through CCTV, and phone footage provided by members of the public with body worn cameras. They admitted they had been unable to make any arrests despite viewing 130 hours of footage. It surely must be a massive embarrassment to Liverpool, UEFA, the police and the council that the most violent attack ever to a football team coach in England was not only allowed to happen when it could have been easily prevented but despite the violent scenes being beamed all round the world not a single arrest was

Don't Look Back In Anger

made.

The actions were in stark contrast to the actions of City's medical staff after the game. On the way back to Manchester in the replacement coach, they stopped at exactly the same place they had been attacked to treat an injured female Liverpool fan who had been involved in a collision with a van on Arkles Lane. They treated and stayed with the lady until an ambulance arrived.

City fans were not in the least surprised that not only was the attack allowed to happen but that no arrests were made and many went on social media to complain about the attack and also to explain that what happened to the team coach was nothing new and especially in the 70s and 80s fans' coaches were regularly attacked and away fans were regularly ambushed and assaulted by Liverpool fans. This is what some of them had to say about their experience in the 1981 League Cup semi final at Anfield ;

Tony from Blackley said it was an amazing atmosphere at Anfield that evening. Thousands of City fans were in the pubs having a great time drinking and singing. Before the game Tony didn't witness any trouble but after the game, he said going back to the train station was very scary with fights and running battles breaking out all over the roads and pavements. He hasn't seen trouble as bad as that since.

Tony from Clayton was on a coach which was ambushed near Stanley Park. Bricks and rocks were thrown at the bus and most of the windows were smashed. Whilst everyone on the coach were very scared and shaken up no one was seriously injured. Tony said it was a disgrace then and it was a disgrace what happened to the team coach as it was just allowed to happen.

Barry from Sale remembers families coming out from their terraced houses just to hurl abuse at the City fans.

Clive from Duckinfield ended up in the Main Stand with Liverpool fans who were great lads. There was no trouble where he sat and the lads he spoke to reckon the City support was the biggest following ever at Anfield. He kept his head down after the game and got back to the car without any problems.

Andy and his mate Steven from Cheetham Hill had a great time as they arrived at the ground just before kick-off. After the game they ended up in a back-street pub which had a lock in until the early hours.

Alan from Bury said it was the worst trouble he had seen at a football ground in over thirty years of following City. Two lads on his coach were stabbed and ended up in hospital. The coach was wrecked but instead of waiting for a replacement he and a few mates decided to get the train and ended up in running battles on the way to Lime Street station. Apart from the European night he never again saw any violence of that scale at Anfield.

Len lost his mates coming out of the ground and jumped on a coach to the train station. As he got off there was a pitch battle outside the station, and he saw some badly injured fans being taken away by ambulance.

Mike was with a group of lads who were being harassed by Police on the way to the ground. Police dogs were used to "encourage" the City fans not to hang about and to get to the ground as quickly as possible. Although he was not involved in any trouble, he witnessed a large fight further up the road. He was convinced that City should have won the game and as he has been back to Anfield on a few more occasions he reckons the place is still a shit hole.

Dave from Hulme was on a coach which was not attacked on the way to the game but on the way home it came under siege from bricks and bottles whilst it was stuck at traffic lights. Everyone was badly shaken, and whilst a couple had minor cuts from the smashed windows, no one was seriously injured.

I was in the Hare and Hounds in Manchester discussing Liverpool and Anfield with a group of City fans and they all had similar experiences. Nick said he was in a police escort from the train station to the ground and there was a lot of Liverpool fans hanging about looking for any stragglers they could attack. Mark said whilst the semi-final in 1981 was utter madness, the last few times he has been to Anfield he has seen no trouble at all and has had a good laugh and a drink with the Liverpool fans in the pubs near the ground. All the lads were pretty much in agreement that apart from the European game, Anfield is as safe as any other ground in the country and there is no problem having a drink with the Liverpool fans.

That's as it should be, going to an away game should be a pleasant experience and win, lose or draw you should be able to have something to eat or drink without being afraid of getting your head kicked in.

9: city 'til i die

This chapter is dedicated to Linda Sparrow
1/8/1963-24/2/2019

'CITY TILL I DIE' has become a club anthem down the years, even to the extent that other clubs seem to have copied it. It is a fact that once you are a fan of a particular football club you will carry on supporting that club until you sadly pass away. It's not like anything else in life, as if you got fed up with a particular pub or got pissed off at your local supermarket or you thought the service at a restaurant was crap, you take your business elsewhere. No, if you are a football fan you are in it for the long haul whether you like it or not. It might be the case for whatever reason, whether it's financial, ill health, pressures of work, family life or even logistical reasons that you might not go as much as you once did but you will carry on supporting your club in your own way forever. There is no divorce, no switching sides, and for City fans the saying "Once a Blue Always a Blue" really means that. Once City has got its claws in you there is no letting go. The fans that have been on the roller coaster ride that is Manchester City are now reaping the rewards that during our dark periods we would never have thought possible.

Many City fans, especially season ticket holders, are known to many other Blues whether it is because they sit near each other or have a pint together at the games or know one another from travelling to away games and on their European travels. Also, with the emergence of social media, fans are in regular contact via websites, Facebook, Twitter, and other stuff I haven't a clue about. They have debates, send each other messages and even if they don't see each other very often there is an unbreakable bond between them. Fans even get to know and meet each other through the various social media sites and tickets and travel requests are a way that fans get to know each other.

Once a City fan sadly passes away, obviously it is devastating and heart breaking for the family and close friends of the loved one, but it also leaves a void for the many friends made while supporting the Blues and it is also a very sad time for fellow supporters.

To this end the club must be applauded for their effort and initiative. Manchester City Football Club have installed a memorial garden at the Etihad Stadium near the Colin Bell Stand. Fans can come at any time to pay their respects, say a prayer, leave remembrance cards, messages, scarves, and football shirts in memory of their loved ones. Through arrangements with the club the loved one's family can scatter their loved ones ashes and the Chaplain will also come and perform a service and there is a Book of Remembrance for friends and family to sign. From time to time fans also arrange a minute's applause at a certain time during a home game and the whole ground as one stand and applaud the fan that has passed away and that act alone is a tremendous comfort to the family of their loved one. Whilst the club doesn't broadcast their efforts from the rooftops what City do is welcomed by all fans and top marks for their sterling efforts in such sad and sensitive times.

Eddie Sparrow is a lifelong City fan and an unsung hero who runs the excellent face book page *Let's Not Forget Past Blues* Eddie does a tremendous job making sure loved ones are not forgotten and produces memorial badges and wrist bands for fellow fans and he has also organised two very successful Memorial Evening Dinners and many ex-players came to support the events which were a complete sell out and a very successful evening with money raised going to various charities. The poem on his memorial flag reads

Our dreams our hopes our passion
Our love for you lives on
Although we are not together
Your memories live on
Each game we are the twelfth man

Don't Look Back In Anger

Still standing there with you
And when you feel that warm glow
I've put my arm around you
For City is our true love
And that will never end
Each game we are still here with you
Fighting to the end
City till I die they say
But that's not really true
We will be here for ever
Once a Blue Always a Blue

Wow just writing that put a tear in my eye and Cath has just brought me a hanky with my brew. Once she reads this, I think she will need one as well as it is very emotional. Eddie has the following message on his face book page.

"Blues if you have lost a Blue loved one and would like them remembered please visit the Facebook page called MCFC Memorial Let's not forget past Blues. Whether they sadly passed away years ago or recently, the group is here to support all City fans. The group has over eight thousand members. Just request to join the page and join us in remembering our past Blue loved ones.

Well I think both the football club and Eddie are performing an excellent and worthwhile role which benefits many people who are grateful for all their efforts.

I was having an argument with myself (good job I won!) about whether to put this chapter in the book. If I had been a lot younger I don't think I would have even considered it but the older you get the more you realise you can never forget those who have gone before you, plus when players and fans younger than yourselves pass away it brings the fact home. I also asked family and friends if they thought it was appropriate to include such a chapter in the book. Everyone I asked thought it was an excellent idea with many being surprised that something similar has not already been done. Once people found out I was writing such a chapter they asked if they could mention their loved ones in it, and it is an honour and a privilege to do so. So here goes.

In Loving Memory of **George Atkinson**, lived a Blue died a Blue. Gone but never forgotten

Joe and Molly Dempsey would be enjoying the success. God Bless x

Ian Mclelland 8/6/43 to 14/5/13 – an original Prestwich & Whitefield Blue.

Sam and Margaret Fisher.

Dave Woods Senior from Salford 26.4.1933 to 4.4.2018. The whole family went to all the games together and loved the Prestwich & Whitefield supporters' club meetings. Thinking of you always xxx your loving family.

Debbie Moore – she would party with you, fight with you, laugh with you, cry with you, but would always be there for you. Love you to the Blue Moon and back Deb. Love from Kim.

Me and my husband are lifelong Manchester City supporters and we were expecting our first child in 2012. We didn't have a name for her as we were unsure of her gender. We nicknamed her "Baby Blue" from day one. On the 5th of January we lost her as she was born sleeping. We named her **Blue Bell**. At the end of the season we clinched our first ever Premier League title. My husband and I and close friends still believe that this was her magical way of letting us know she will always be there. Love you forever Mum and Dad.

Joe Riley Prestwich.

Pauline and Graeme Thornley.

Tipping Tim, a Whitfield Blue

Alan "Milky" Brown from Prestwich.

Steve Davis from Prestwich.

Jaqueline Thomas from Brooklands who passed away 4.12.16

Elliot was one of City's longest serving ball boys serving from the age of nine until he was sixteen years old and it was Elliot who placed the ball in the corner for Dzeko's equaliser back in 2012 .He was diagnosed in Feb 2016 with a very rare muscle cell cancer rhabdomyosarcomo and was tragically taken from us in just 11 months. He suffered immeasurably spending nine weeks on life support, brain surgery and dialysis. He fought his way back to attend the first game of 2016-2017 in a wheelchair but for the Everton game he was back walking even though we were told he would never walk again and was taken onto the pitch and honoured by the club at half time. At the club's request Elliot spent the day with Aguero and Pep and it was a most magical moment for him, it is a day we will never forget and we can't thank City enough. Although we thought he was winning his battle, just six weeks after being given the all clear our angel gained his wings on January 22nd 2017. Our wonderful captain Vinny laid a wreath the first game after his passing and was given a standing ovation. He lived. breathed and bled Blue, I have been a Blue for 55 years and his grandpa has supported City for over 75 years, and we have formed a charity in his name, Elliot's Trust. Manchester City have been marvellous and they've been behind us every step of the way. Elliot wanted so much to help other children and young adults suffering from rare cancers and this is now our mission, working closely with the Young Oncology Unit at The Christie where Elliot was treated and Ward 84 at the RMCH and every penny we raise goes directly to helping these children and their families. Elliot will always be our 12th man

EXTRA TIER

There is an extra tier at the Etihad, we mortals cannot see
It seats all our loved ones, who get to watch for free
Though God will never influence the outcome of a game
He builds the extra seating, in the stand without a name
When City ran out on the pitch, the final match to play
My mate said how he wished his dad was here to see today

Don't Look Back In Anger

I told him not to worry, as his Dad was seated here
And although we couldn't see him, he was in the extra tier
He's sat up with my Dad, they've got a brilliant view
And every game that City play
They are there to watch them too
When Sergio Aguero, smashed the winner in the net
Their cheers were just as loud and proud as ours, I bet
It's not just us who has the stand I know the others do
Though knowing those in Trafford, they probably have two!
Long lost players, managers, groundsmen, saints and sinners
They roared the Blues on to the end, the Premiership winners
By Peter Harris written the day after Agueroooo day.

Eric Griffiths, Whitefield Blue and landlord of the Beehive for many years RIP mate.

David Leigh 1963-2019 – our amazing dad was a true Blue who fought to the very end just like City. He was a man with the most infectious sense of humour that will live on for many years. He inspired us to follow City even when we were shit. From freezing cold days in the Kippax with a cup of Bovril to the padded seats in the Colin Bell Stand, Dad was always there; passionate, shouting, singing, and jumping for joy and going mental and nearly ripping our heads off in excitement when City scored! We have always been avid Blues but now when we wear our City shirts we always think of our dad. Gone but never forgotten. Love from Kate and Jessica xxx

My dad **Alex Welch** died in his seat before the Etihad derby on April 17th 2010, If you've got to go I suppose it is the best place to go surrounded by fellow Blues.

On a personal note I'd like to pay my respects to a few club legends who passed away: **Joe Mercer**, **Malcolm Allison**, **Mike Doyle**, **Neil Young**. **Bernard Halford** and finally **George Smith** an ex player who lived in Prestwich for many years, Rest In Peace. Also to **Stan Gibson**, the best groundsman in the country back in the day who was a legend back at Maine Road.

Also I'd like to remember my Uncle Bob, **Robert Peters**, who was killed in action in Burma aged 21 in 1941 all the ex-servicemen and women who we lost in wars and conflicts.

FOR THE FALLEN

> *They shall not grow old as we that are left grow old*
> *Age shall not weary them, nor the years condemn*
> *At the going down of the sun and in the morning*
> *We shall remember them*

Alan Hardy 11-12-52 to 23/4/13. Alan, my brother, is the main reason I am a City fan. He took me to my first away game at Leeds when I was 14 years old. We went in their end as he said it would be quicker than going in the City end – it was character building to say the least! He was a true Blue and even managed to go to Vienna for the Cup Winners' Cup Final. I'm just glad he was about to see the good times come back to the club. We know he is up there loving what is happening and having a laugh at what is happening at Trafford. Always in my heart regards Dave Mitch.

I think it is amazing the tributes you are doing about all the loved ones from the Manchester City Family that have passed away. My father-in-law, **David Senior,** sadly passed away just before his 85th birthday. His ashes are in the memorial garden at the Etihad along with my brother Mike who died aged just 49. All the family meet up at the garden before every home game and we lay fresh flowers. You would not believe the comfort that gives us. The club do such a wonderful job and I know of no other club that does anything like it. The club chaplain performed the laying of the ashes ceremony and we all signed the book of remembrance which was a lovely touch. We are blessed to have such a wonderful place to remember our loved ones. Kind Regards Julie and David Woods.

Mrs Yvonne Salt 26.05.1947 to 03.12.2017. Mum's stepdad, a policeman at Maine Road, would let her and her friend Maureen sneak in by climbing over a fence back in the 50's. They were hooked. Mum saw league and cup wins in the 60's and 70's and her favourite player was Neil Young. As a family we have been to Wembley together in 1999, 2011, 2013 and watched the League wins of 2012 and 2014 together. She loved Vinny, David and Sergio, and after winning the FA Cup she pulled out a can of Mojito that I had stashed in her bag so we could celebrate in style. She is the reason we are all Blues and she is very sadly missed. Love from Dad, Anthony, Michelle, Joanna and all the grandkids and great grandkids.

Paul Buckley was a True Blue taken from this life far too young. As a young boy Paul played for his favourite club as a Junior Blue. As a teenager he saved up for a season ticket as he was so passionate about City and this became a yearly 'must have' item. He watched City in all his young life in the bad times as well as the good. In 2011 Paul sadly contracted an infection around his heart and not too long afterwards developed Hodgkins Lymphomas. He fought it with all his might. His family were always his main priority with City being a close second. On 27th April 2013 this True Blue who was a beautiful soul, a real gent and the best Dad, Son, and Brother sadly lost his fight, but his dream to see his club back at the top was fulfilled. He was buried in his 2013 shirt which was signed by Aguero and his passion for the club lives on through his children. He is loved and missed every single day. Paul Buckley, A True-Blue Forever.

On February 13th, 2016 we lost our son **Craig Tarry** in a tragic road accident in Sweden along with four other band members of Viola Beach from Warrington. Craig and I were both City season ticket holders who travelled to home and away games together. The day after the accident we played Spurs and the club paid tribute with a picture of Craig on the big screen in the 5th minute of the game. The club also sent a beautiful bunch of flowers, that's one of the reasons I love this club so much. I am so glad that I saw us win the FA Cup and our first Premier League Trophy with Craig. Miss You Son.

After beating Watford in the FA Cup Final my brother informed

Don't Look Back In Anger

me that 50 years ago in 1969, he went on a coach to watch City v Leicester in the Cup Final. Three lads who were on the coach with him **Pasty**, **Eric** and **Milky** are sadly no longer with us RIP Blues.

This is a tribute to all our loved ones who are no longer with us

Our love for you will never go away
You will be walking beside us every day
Unseen, unheard, but always here
Still loved and missed and very dear
Your life was a pleasure, your memory a treasure
You are loved beyond words and missed beyond measure.

Jon Grant, originally from Eccles and a fanatical Blue, born in 1996 but sadly passed away in March 2019, Regards Howard.

Stanley Beesley 09-10-1932 to 18-10 2014. None of our family would have been Blues if it wasn't for him. He is always in our thoughts. Many thanks, Vicky, Darren and Scott.

Remembering **Mike Burke**, a lifelong Blue and one of the original members of the Prestwich and Whitefield Branch who passed away on 12th October 2007. When Vincent Kompany announced he was retiring I realised Mike had never seen him or any of the rest of this history making squad. When people ask what he would have thought of our success, I tell them he made it happen from the Kippax in the sky. RIP my crazy Blue man xxx Love from Joyce.

Could you please mention my dad **Rick McCracken** born 18/08/1967 passed away 25/09/2012 xxxx many thanks regards Karen

DAD

Although we can't see you here with us today Dad
We feel you are with us still in every waking moment
You leave a space no one can fill
You never wanted to go Dad and that is what is hard to take
Because we all miss you so because like you our only wish

Don't Look Back In Anger
Is to be together still
Your loving smile, your gentle laugh still sounds proudly in our memory
Nowhere is the sound louder than here outside your spiritual home
And final resting place
For we can all remember the great times Dad both here and at Maine Road
And of all those away days when you would finally wander home singing with true friends in toe
For you not only watched out for us Dad but your mates too
That's why you still live in the hearts of every Blue, For you never really left us
Because you are besides us still, every second of every match you watch with us and every past Blue .
In the stand without a name

Poem written by Karen Houghton

I feel so honoured and humbled that so many have shared their stories, poems, and memories of their loved ones with us. We can all be inspired by what has been written and our loved ones will never be forgotten, we cherish the time we had with them and as the title of the book says 'Don't Look Back in Anger', just remember the great times you had.

God Bless You All

10: a norwegian blue

I WAS BORN IN a small suburb of Oslo on 26th September 1961, my story tells why and how I became so heavily involved in English football and Manchester City in particular. My parents are from a working class background, my mother came from a fisherman's family from northern Norway. My father's parents were postmen and housekeepers at the local council with little income, so my father's aim was simply to create a better life for himself. He started to work as an accountant for Hoover and as washing machines took off it was an expanding business for him to be at. My mother worked as a nurse and later on in life, when I was at school, at an old people's home. My mum like most young people after the war moved to Oslo to grab a chance for an education and a brighter future rather than milking cows and herding sheep or become a fisherman's housewife as was the norm if you settled in northern Norway back then.

England and Norway have always been close. Our nations share the same sense of humour and outlook on life in general; well at least they did in the time I grew up. One of the main factors was the closeness between the royal families in each country, and you can hardly be more closely bonded then circumstances from 1940–1945 when both nations were fighting for their existence against the same enemy led by Adolf Hitler and his Nazi comrades. Looking back to that period our country stood by the English and the Allied countries. Before the Second World War Norway had one of the world's biggest shipping industries and one of the world's largest fleet of ships which played a big part in winning the Second World War as we helped out in the dangerous convoys carrying goods from the USA to England. Many of our sailors lost their lives as their contribution to the Allies, whilst the English fought for our freedom in the air (RAF) and via the English army onshore.

Norway did not have the same strength as we have been poor in battle since the Vikings era died out at the Battle of Stamford Bridge (not the football ground) around the 11th century. As some of you may know, the people of Oslo send London a huge Xmas tree as thanks for the help during the Second World War. Every December it is lit up at Trafalgar Square in memory and thanks for all your help between 1940–1945, so there you go! Norwegian freedom fighters also blew up a huge industry that produced "heavy water" for the purpose of creating the atomic bomb. The film Heroes of Telemark was based on what the freedom fighters achieved. The Norwegian Royal Navy sank an important German battleship "The Blucher" on its way to Oslo with the use of an old cannon, a bit like Ian Brightwell's thunderbolt at the swamp in the 1-1 draw many years back. Nobody expected it, just like Vinny's goal against Leicester, but you should never underestimate your opponents I suppose.

So, to finally get to the point – what has this got to do with football? It was not a coincidence that our betting system over here after the war involved English football teams when Norwegian football had its winter break.

From October to April, during the Norwegian close season, English clubs would form the games on our weekly state-run pools coupon, (the thing same happens in Denmark and Sweden by the way). It became a fashion to follow an English team – the pools themselves were based on a bit of skill as well as luck; you needed to be able to pick 12 games with a correct score of either a home win, a draw or an away win. The pools became a really big thing in Scandinavia and when TV was introduced in the 60 s every Saturday a section of the news would involve a reporter reading out the English football scores. It became a big industry. In 1969 the television companies began live coverage of one of the English First Division games with live scores coming in along the way as well, so every Norwegian and his dog sat in front of the TV every Saturday afternoon with their pools coupons. It was the age with only one channel to watch; there were no apps or Internet streaming, so no wonder it caught on with the masses. Funnily enough, nearly all games at the start were from either the Midlands or London area, so a lot of Norwegians picked Stoke, Derby, Leicester and Wolves as well as London teams as their favourite club. After a while TV also introduced former Wolves and England star Billy Wright to us as the expert – he was phoned up every Sunday to predict the next week's results in the 12 games on the Norwegian pools coupon. I would not call his predictions successful, he always seemed to get things completely wrong, hence after a while he became known as " Billy Wrong".

I became a City fan for a number of reasons – I liked the Beatles, but never took to Georgie Best. I learned that City's home crowd were big and noisy and they always had huge gates. I wanted to follow such a team and the name City was also an important issue to me. Their blue and white colours were also important, plus I wanted a team that scored goals and attacked. So when I watched us play "live" on TV in my grandmother's flat (she had a TV with access to Swedish channels as we lived south in Norway very close to the Swedish border), I fondly remember that I finally picked City due to the Final against Gornik and it cemented that time because we also had the League Cup against West Brom which we won 2-1 with just weeks in between. It was also largely down to Francis Lee, as for me he was a great inspiration. *Shoot* and *Goal* magazines were also on sale over here, so whatever I could digest all City related stuff, as well as everything on English football. Naturally my bedroom was decorated with City players from said magazines. With one Norwegian and one Swedish TV channel and darkness from October to April and snow, bitter cold and no pubs, live football became a drug for most Norwegian on a Saturday afternoon. I would guess half the nation would watch the live games back then, it was that popular. British humour did not fail to deliver either with John Cleese, and some fantastic iconic British films plus the music from the Beatles, Stones, and the love affair with these essentials became just the drug I needed. As City were seldom on live from Maine Road I had do make do with Bryon Butler's commentary via BBC World service. For one reason or another it had to be dark to get proper radio signals, so I remember we could not really follow the games early Autumn and Spring time. Different times indeed compared with today!

The first Supporters Club for an English team in Scandinavia was formed in Norway in 1974 by Nils Martinsen, it happened to be Man City, and it also became an official Supporters Club the same year. In the beginning we were treated like heroes when we went to watch City and the club spoiled us. The first City supporters I met could not believe the distance we travelled to watch their team. The cost of flying back then was a lot more expensive than today. The norm was around £150 return Oslo-Manchester, a lot of money in the early 70s. Sometimes we would also go by boat from Gothenburg or Bergen to Harwich or Newcastle, and make our way to Manchester by coach as it was cheaper, but it took two days to get from Oslo to Manchester that way and a massive bar bill to go with it! I did not go to the League Cup Final in 1976, but those who did from our branch got an invite to celebrate with the players and staff after the Final, what a night they had!

I played a bit of football myself and I paid to go on a training camp in Germany in 1977 where Alan Hudson and George Cavanagh were our trainers. I did the same the next summer in Southport where we were based at Pontins Holidays on Ainsdale beach. We watched Everton's pre-season training there as well. We also had some great trainers like Emlyn Hughes, Bob Latchford, George Harrison, Steve Coppell and Brian Greenhoff coming to train us. I was only 16 years old back then but I had already found out that going in a pub was even more exciting than playing football. I only did 8 out of 40 training sessions that summer in Southport as I would prefer the beer and rock & roll on offer. It was also a great time with so much music so I would prefer that to playing football.

In a night club at Pontin's I also met a real City and England football fan for the first time, David Charnley, a welder and great snooker player from Blackburn. He had a 3-wheeler "Robin Reliant" so he invited me to stay at his house in Blackburn as he went to all City games home and away in his yellow Robin. So

Don't Look Back In Anger

I went to my first live match at Easter 79 with him to see City win 3-1 at home to Wolves, with Palmer, Channon and Silkman the goal scorers. I also went to the 0-0 draw at home to Everton played a few days later. I went in the Kippax; a dream had come true. In order to afford this I was working part time as a sports writer, writing articles for my local side Vestby, so I watched a lot of teams from various age groups and wrote in our local press getting paid £3 for each story which was great back then. I would save every penny to afford to go back to watch City, plus beer was a lot cheaper in England. I also liked the English humour and I was introduced to the typical British lifestyle, visiting chippies after the pub was shut. I also drank regularly in a proper working man's club with no women allowed and I found this amusing and strange. They were allowed upstairs when they had bingo and dances every Saturday and Sunday night. I also learned what "Grab a Granny night" was all about as we went out in a place called the Mecca in Blackburn. I got to know a few women and had a relationship for a while with a Polish Jewish women called Valda who was a lot older than me. I listened to her and her family's story and how lucky she was to have escaped Hitler's terror, it made a great impression on me to listen to her explaining how grateful she was when her family got away to the UK just before they were about to be captured and sent to hell. I also met a lot of crazy people in the Vulcan pub in Blackburn, a pub well-known pub for its juke box and mad clientele.

With the huge unemployment situation and the strikes back then most of them would spend the whole day smoking funny substances! When the pubs had a break we would simply carry on outside until the place opened up again. I did also visit Placemate 7 in Manchester as a great place to hang out. I liked a big variety of music from Punk to Ska to classic rock bands, it was great fun. Dave and I always went in his 3-wheeler from Blackburn and he had a key to Moss Side County club where he would play snooker before City's games. It was crazy; we used to meet in the Orchard Club at 9am to drink with the other lads who supported Everton, Blackburn, Burnley and Bolton, there were even some sad rags and

Don't Look Back In Anger

a couple of decent ones as well as you will find in any crowd, and they actually had a sense of humour too. And there were a lot of Celtic fans about as well as Rangers.

Dave and I also went in City's Social Club after every game and in the ground we always stood near the tunnel in the Kippax, closest to "windy corner" and the North stand. Only once did I not go there. I went to stand as close to the away fans segregation as possible on the Kippax when we met Spurs in September '81, this being after we lost the FA Cup Final a few months before. It was my 20th birthday that day, and I was mad keen on revenge. Revenge? City lost 1-0 in typical torrential Manchester rain and Gerry Gow never properly returned to City after that game. He was then my favourite player and got a really bad injury that day, I can't remember by whom but Gary Mabbutt scored from near the half way line. I went back to Norway to join the Navy but I only lasted three months. I got kicked out for doing all sorts of things apart from abiding by the rules. The Norwegian services were compulsory and the equipment was incredibly old. This was also the start of the 80s, a period of time in which our branch would arrange and set up quite a number of pre-season games for City. Can you believe members of our branch managed to sign contracts for local sides around Oslo - and even in remote areas of Norway and Sweden, City would go to play for next to nothing just to be able to stage a pre-season abroad. There were always some City fans around like Jocky, Mitch, big Alan Potter and a few others who would go to every City game wherever they played. This was truly the days of *The Boys in Blue* and we had the record to match. I myself signed a pre-season game contract worth £2,500 for City in order for them to afford to go on tour in which they played FC Grei of Oslo in 1989. They were a local Third Division side, and City nearly lost as they were 3-1 down with 10 minutes to go, but Dave Oldfield and Wayne Biggins saved us to make it 3-3. After the match we went with the players of both teams for drinks and food, this being under Mel Machin. We also invited some of the Manchester based fans along for free. I still have the copy of the contract at home. As our supporters club set up many games in the 80s and 90s, it always was and still is a very close relationship with the club. We had and still have great friendship with the Barnes family, the late Ken and his son Peter have both been our Presidents, Peter still is. Other great friends along the way have also been Tony Book, Tommy Booth, Joe Corrigan, Alex Williams, Asa Hartford, Ian Brightwell and Paul Lake. We still try and see them whenever we are over, they still take time out for a drink with me and our branch members which I think is fucking great and it also shows we have history as hardly anyone else can attend.

Our branch now has 2,450 members, and has gone up since we were around 600 in 1976. It was down to 189 when I took charge of the branch in 1989. In the late 80s and early 90s a member called Egil Svarstad went to nearly all City games, and for a period of the 90s he was staying for two whole seasons in The Lansdowne hotel on Wilmslow Road. Egil also went to all City's pre-season games including those in China under Alan Ball when the games were cancelled because City did not know they were going in the rainy season! Stupid management. I think the blue half of Manchester and the Parkside all knew Egil, as he became famous for his support for City. He even had his own key to Maine Road given to him by Stan Gibson, the groundsman, not a lot of people had that. When Joe Royle was manager, he often came out on the Main Stand to have a can of beer with Egil after the match. Can you believe Pep doing that now with a supporter? Crazy days indeed, but good days. My friend from Blackburn, Dave, stopped going when they introduced membership cards, his last game was when Imre Varadi scored at home. David was stopped and barred from getting in, and he never set foot inside Maine Road again apart from coming with me to the famous 5-1 in 1989.

A few memories from the City team's pre-season games; Gary Megson was a lot more skilful at sinking pints than trapping the ball, Brian Clough was correct saying that Megson could probably hardly trap a brick, not your David Silva of today but Gary worked hard and was a nice enough man, a real grafter. The pre-season when Uwe Rösler met his now wife Cecilia was a great trip for me as we met all the players in the little village called Horton (I kid you not) where City were based, this being strange as our manager was Mr. Brian Horton. It was very funny, they now have two kids named Tony and Colin after Tony Book and Colin Bell. As most of you know Uwe had a battle with cancer, and the support given to him back then from the City fans was something he will never forget. Tony Book was also very much involved on this trip and Tony always treated us in a great manner and always took time to speak to us fans. I will always rate him highly. He was also the first person I met when I visited Maine Road in the summer of 1978. I just stood on the doorstep of the main entrance at Maine Road and Tony asked me who I was, when I told him my story he invited me in for a coffee in his office. He made my summer. I also quickly understood how friendly this club was.

Back to the pre-season trip. City flew out to Trondheim and beat them big time as well as Rosenborg 1-0 after a Michel Vonk header. Rosenborg were big in Europe back then, so this was a great result by City. The day after City flew even further north to play against Bodø Glimt, and were thrashed 5-1. Quite a number of Mancunians made the trip all the way up north, including Jocky and Kevin and a guy called Tommy Boyle who would later return to Norway to arrange his wedding there, a great man Tommy. Kevin Cummins also made his way around this whole pre-season trip as was his norm back then. Niall Quinn and Keith Curle did not play in this 1-5 game, Niall was a very nice person, unfortunately Keith Curle ended up nearly fighting some of the City fans which I think was out of order, he must have had a bad day. Just a few days earlier Keith Curle, the then captain, was speaking to us in a very friendly way so I suppose he did have something on his mind that night, perhaps he did not like that the fans got some of the Norwegians birds and he ended up with nothing? Another player who behaved like a spoilt brat on this trip was ex Liverpool star Steve McMahon. He said to his City teammates that they should concentrate more about drinking with each other rather than socialising with the fans. I suppose in a way he was correct as he had been at Liverpool who were a great team in those days. I think City lacked a winning mentality back then.

On another occasion City played our local team Lervik and won 10-1, Nils Martinsen our branch founder went in nets for the last 10 minutes, he would dive the wrong way and helped Clive Allen to score no less than 6 goals in that game!

Another funny episode was when George Weah, and Paulo Wanchope were driving to their first match at Maine Road, this being a night match, Norwegian Alfie Haaland the captain was also with them. They got lost and had to pick up a City fan who happened to drink in the same boozer as us, The Beehive and he laughed as George and Paulo dropped him off outside the Beehive and they said thanks for guiding them to Maine Road. It is a true story, we even won 4-2 and Paulo got a hat trick that night! Alfie was popular in the beginning at City when he bought some City fans their petrol after City had played so badly, he felt he owed the fans an apology

Today we have a number of season tickets in our supporters club that we share between our members who are over for games. We also have a member who has bought a flat in New Islington and he seldom misses a home match and flies over for every home game. We also get some tickets for away games but not a lot as those tickets are hard to come by as we all know. We have also done our own Fanzine, *The Scandinavian True Blue* that we produce five times a season and have been running since 1976. We have a base of 2.500 members that we post out our magazine to, even in these days of e-mail. We also have our homepage www.manchestercity.no - it is a full time job these days to manage all the things we do as a branch and I have been doing it since 1989. The amount of time spent has increased with our success. This season, 2018-2019, I think I must have spent something like a full working day every day arranging tickets, travel and answering e-mails, so you can picture yourself how good I felt when we won the treble and Community Shield. What a team, what a story that we have behind us!

But it is a dream come true. We had great fun and amazing comebacks in 99 and the Aguero moment. In the old days City were shit, and the City fans were great together, now it is suddenly the other way around, now some of the fans are shit, and now the players are great. I am also aware that us Scandinavians used to be liked as fans who have followed City for decades and regularly travelled a massive distance, but I feel more and more that a section of City's fan base don't like us foreigners anymore. This is sad but I understand why. I think it is because a lot of City's fans find themselves priced out at the Etihad. However, I have some great relationships with the older City fans from back to the 70 s and 80s, at least some of them are still alive and we have our history together. I am happy to carry that with me, the same with the players at City. I went from having their respect, to a melt down with a pre-season in Karlstad (Sweden) under Sven Gøran Eriksson. He was friendly but some of the players, Danny Mills for instance, just hated us but I guess that's part of being more professional as well, you can't have it both ways! The same happened with City moving from Platt Lane, first to Carrington where it was difficult to watch training, but we did get in sometimes if we asked beforehand. Keegan was great, and special mention to Chappie the kitman who was always great to us when we were there and always made sure we were welcome. Even today Chappie is an absolute star to us and looks after us whenever he can, such a great man and a character!

It was back in 2001 when one of our members, nicknamed Blue Danube, died after we had been to Manchester. Going home he flew to Milan to meet his girlfriend and going back to Norway from Milan their SAS flight was hit by another jet at take off and Espen and his girlfriend were killed. He was a great lad and very well behaved, and also a tee total so that's why he travelled on this morning flight. Sometimes life takes freaky turns, he was only 30 years old when he died. We rallied round his family, and as we had a good rapport with some of the press in Norway, I like to think that our supporters club helped out his parents and sister and brother who went through a tough time. With 9-11 and later all the terror and bombs that we have all seen, I am afraid this has somehow drowned in all the misery caused by these other events. The world and society is indeed changing and we've just got to try and look after each other as best as we can.

On a lighter note, arguably the biggest moment for our branch and myself happened in October 2012. We learned there was a possibility that the PL trophy could come to Norway on a weekend visit. In fact, in Manchester City's confirmation letter to me it stated, "Manchester City will, as a gratitude to your branch commitment during the years, pay for the trophy to be flown from Abu Dhabi via London to Oslo". All we had to pay for, as a branch, was the return flight for two security guards and the trophy to be flown from Oslo back to Manchester. Plus we needed to commit to the trophy not being used for commercial purposes. The PL Trophy needs its own seat on the flight between the guards so at no time do they leave the trophy alone, so SAS took it upon them to sort it and we had a huge branch function the same day as we played West Brom away that autumn. We also invited Paul Lake, Tommy Booth, and Joe Corrigan to our function, as well as one of our main men in Manchester to help us, Alan Potter, I think you can imagine what it was like for us all to see the trophy on display in Oslo, with more than 150 members gathered. We had an absolutely fantastic weekend and a Saturday night in front of the trophy, so that moment will go down as the biggest moment in my life. We all knew that this was the icing on the cake, the absolute proof that we were back on top, and now it looks as if it is here to stay, but it can hardly get much better. The PL is by far the best trophy on earth, the ultimate thing to win, the marathon, not the sprint.

I said on a TV station that was present that this was the ultimate and I think the message got through that City were back, as even people I've never seen before, recognized that our branch had something of a history to be able to make this kind of event happen.

I also followed England in the 80s; I went to the games in Spain 1982 staying in Benidorm and Madrid, and did Mexico in 1986, where I met another great City fan Mick, also from Blackburn. We were based in Monterrey and Acapulco. Again, so many great memories, and I am happy to say that the friends we make along the way gives you unique opportunities. I can even walk into a Millwall pub next to Bermondsey station where their main nutters used to be camped, as even some of the Millwall lads are okay. I gave up following England after Germany 1988, as by then I had found a girlfriend, plus I had my own Carpet cleaning company called Kippax Cleaning to look after. I needed "The Kippax" to be able to afford to travel, it was just an extra job, I was also working full time as a financial advisor in a bank.

With the banning of English clubs after Heysel I, and some of the leaders from various Norwegian based fan clubs, got together and formed a Norwegian Association of Supporters Clubs called "Supporters Union for British football" in order to combat all the negative criticism that were thrown at us for simply being supporters. I can honestly say that I have met so many great friends and characters from a lot of clubs, not only City, when I have travelled around the world. I am happy to say it has been a fantastic ride but as society changes so do the fans, and I can see it is a bit different today. Even though City were mostly shit, we were always well respected and the club always treated us with utmost respect. I would also like to say that after forming the Supporters Union in 1989, it now has 120,000 members in Norway. I was also a very central person in setting up the first Sky pub in Oslo when the PL came in 1992. It changed everything. TV wise we could now watch every game live. I know some of you reading this might hate me for it but it really opened up a new dimension with the possibility to watch City live which we rarely had before. Nowadays all the games are shown, and I will only miss one or two games per season now, whereas in 1970 I would only be able to watch one or two games per season.

I retired three years ago at 57, I was one of many older workers who were told to leave from the bank I worked for, as many were told that when you pass a certain age you are no longer 'worth your salt'. After spending all my working life with them I managed to agree a leaving package which made sure I would receive wages for some time after my retirement. So I am really happy these days with only the supporters club to look after. However, it is not an easy task, as it is a ridiculous amount of time spent distributing and buying tickets for City home games. I also work as a Warden and Leader of the Board in the Building Society where I live now, so that is enough to keep me occupied on a day by day basis, and I also made some good investments along the way so I am happy now with life as it is. So as long as my health is good I shall be returning to Manchester as often as I can.

As great being a City fan was, it's even better now with trophies as well onboard, but as with everything please enjoy it while it lasts. Before home games we meet in Mother Macs, so please feel free to pop in and say hello. Hope you enjoyed this chapter and hopefully it gave you an insight into why so many Scandinavians follow City with a passion.

11: away day blues

THE ONE THING I treasured about going to away games, especially in the 1970s and 1980s, was that even if you went on your own you would meet up with someone you knew, or just get chatting and have a drink with a fellow City fan, and many a lasting friendship was made on away trips.

I was based down south for most of the 1970s mainly at Portsmouth, Plymouth and Weymouth. I went to many away games on my own and usually bumped into someone I knew or I would arrange to meet some mates from Prestwich or Whitefield in a pub near the train station or the ground. It wasn't always that easy to make arrangements as many people in the 1970s didn't even have a land line telephone. It makes me smile at how dependent people are on their phones nowadays, a group of people could all be sat together but instead of talking to each other they are either texting or speaking on their phones. I am still amazed how quickly technology has moved on and I'm baffled with all the things you can do with a mobile considering their size. It's a computer, video camera, sat nav and phone all rolled into one!

Anyway back to the 70s; if it was a game in London and I had not arranged to meet anyone I would just go to Euston Station to see if I recognised anyone getting off the train but if the pubs had already opened I would just go in the Royal George which was near the station as most City fans arriving by train would pop in there for a couple of beers before heading off to the ground. Sometimes, depending where City were playing, I might stop over in London on the Friday night for an early start on the Saturday as I wanted to be in a pub for opening time. Back then, the Salvation Hostel or YMCA in London were okay to stay for a night and cheap. So I would just have a few beers get my head down and get the early train to wherever City were playing. On occasions after the game, if it was the start of my two weeks leave, I would head on to Manchester or anywhere en-route that took my fancy. 'Have train pass will travel' was my motto, or if I didn't have a travel pass and was skint it would be have to be 'have thumb and travel' as I didn't mind hitch hiking to the games either. Obviously it was much more comfortable sat on a train with a couple of beers than hitching when it was raining but needs must at times. On one such trip I stopped in London overnight and in the morning got the early train to Norwich. There were only a handful of City fans on the train as they must have got the Manchester to London train at daft o'clock to have been in time for the one I was on. I didn't know any of them to speak to but I recognised one of them as he was a well-known lad from the Kippax. As I was sitting in the buffet carriage on my own having a drink, he called me over to sit with him and his mates. After that day I met George McGuire on many occasions on my travels including on a train trip in Ireland when we were on a pre-season friendly and if I was on my own I would join him for a drink. People often asked me if I was ever lonely or got bored travelling on my own all-round the country watching City. The truthful answer was that I was never on my own for long and would always get chatting to someone and I'm sure many City fans had similar experiences. I used to see a City fan and his young son who were from Oxford on occasions and once when I went to Stoke from London there were a lot of London based Blues and I joined them for a beer or two to make the journey more enjoyable, well it would have been rude not to wouldn't it?

I once went in a pub with George and his mates called the Compleat Angler which is a cracking pub and not long after we arrived it soon started filling up with City fans. I must have a bit of a knack as I can remember names of pubs all-round the country but when it comes to Cath's birthday oops, well anyone can make a mistake can't they? Another time at Norwich I met my mate Paul Holt who was from Hillock Estate in Whitefield which was and still is a huge Blue area, ex-City player Trevor Sinclair was brought up on the estate. Paul went to the game with his mates in a big removal van from Salford Van Hire and it was crammed with City fans. It was a cheap but uncomfortable way of getting to games but City fans at that time did the journey to many away games in Salford Van Hire vehicles, I wouldn't have fancied being the driver as they would want a piss stop every few miles and it must have stunk like fuck. I was going to get a lift back to Manchester with them until I remembered I had my suitcase in left luggage at Euston as I was going home on leave after the game so they dropped me off at the train station and they went on their merry way. It was at Ipswich and at Norwich (both away in the same week) in 1976 that I first heard the Vikings theme tune sung at a football match. Well I say sung but there were no words just a load of noise, but it sounded great. Then later on the words "City, City, The Best Team In All The World" was added. Apparently, the film the Vikings had been shown again on telly just before the games so after a few beers why not give it a go?

When the ship was in Rosyth in Scotland for a few days after some exercises with the RAF it was my turn for weekend leave, many of the crew decided to go to Newcastle for the night so, in for a penny in for a pound, I went with them. In the morning sporting a big hangover as it was a great night out and after a hearty breakfast we were going to get the train back to re-join the ship. However, City were playing West Ham United in Manchester, and as I still had some money left, instead of joining the lads on the train back to Scotland, I waved them goodbye and on another one of my spur of the moment decisions jumped on the train to Manchester. After the game instead of going straight back to Scotland which was my intention, I ended up drinking in Manchester, missed my last train and fell asleep on Victoria Station. On the Sunday morning, feeling a bit worse for wear and a bit scruffy, I boarded the train back to Scotland. We changed stations at Preston and as I had a while to wait for the next train and seeing it was nearly opening time, I popped in the local pub to wile away the time as it seemed the sensible thing to do – there's never a dull moment following City.

Sometimes I enjoyed the social aspects of following City even more than watching the game itself, especially when we were crap and playing shit football. Unlike these days, it was so much easier to go to away games and watch City back then, but for one or two exceptions you could just turn up at the gate and pay to get in. Getting to most away games was easy as well, even if you didn't know anyone driving a Salford Van, some supporters clubs organised coaches and there was always the "football special." Anyone travelling in one of those back in the 70s would probably come out in a nervous rash, just thinking about it. The good points were they were cheap and on time. Honest! Some trains once upon a time did stick to the schedule. That's it for the good points. Where do I start for the bad? The compartments were old stock, not very clean and not very comfortable, it was hit and miss if the bogs were still working by the time you got back to Manchester and until supporters clubs got involved, there were usually no refreshments either, especially at night games, and the heating never seemed to be switched on. I once saw a documentary about Everton fans and the special they had was run by the supporters club, it looked clean and smart and they had a disco on it, that's the way to do it. Many of the trains ended up getting wrecked though, either by the travelling fans themselves or by rival fans who attacked it with various missiles. Even though the standard of service was poor no one was really arsed as it was a cheap way of moving round the country to watch your team. Many people think the "specials" coincided with the mass out break of football hooliganism which was sweeping the country, as prior to that there wasn't the means for fans to travel in vast numbers up and down Britain. Some towns and cities were just not prepared for the influx of thousands of predominantly young men suddenly turning up on their door step and in the early days the police and football clubs couldn't cope. A big downside of going on the "special" was that the home fans knew what time you would arrive and have a "welcoming committee" prepared. Once the police got their act together they would be on the station to greet the away fans and usually were accompanied with some huge Alsatian police dogs, and believe me they put the fear of god into the hardest of football fans as if you got a bite from one of them you would certainly know about it. Unfortunately, many policemen viewed the majority of away fans

IMAGES OF MAINE ROAD
The Kippax Stand; a Kippax Turnstile; Helen the Bell in the North Stand and the City Store.

Don enjoying a reunion with the Prestwich & Whitefield City Supporters club (top). Don served on the HMS Devonshire, a Guided Missile Destroyer which went to Romania in 1976 on a goodwill trip (below) and Don as a teenage sailor (inset).

Phill Gatenby (above) with his grandchildren Phoebe and Lucas at their first City game. Sean Riley (five from the left) and the lads he's followed City with over the past 45 years; a birthday message sent via his wife Jane that appeared on the big screen at Villa Park.

Sean Riley Happy 48th Birthday for the 7th March – Sean hasn't missed a City game home, away or Europe for 24 years with love from your wife Jane, family and friends

King of the Kippax editor Dave Wallace and his wife Sue outside the Etihad.

The Ginger Wig (Anthony Rawson) in New York City.

Norwegian Blue Tor Soensteby with his wife and the Premier League trophy.

Manchester City's Memorial Garden at the Etihad Stadium has become a focal point for supporters wishing to pay tribute to lost relatives, and friends.

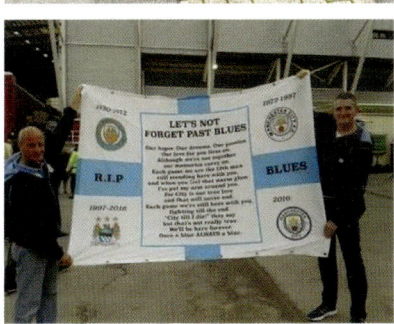

Eddie Sparrow began his popular Facebook page 'Let's Not Forget Past Blues' a few years ago and it has become the online equivalent of the Memorial Garden at the stadium, acting as a focal point for remembering former Blues.

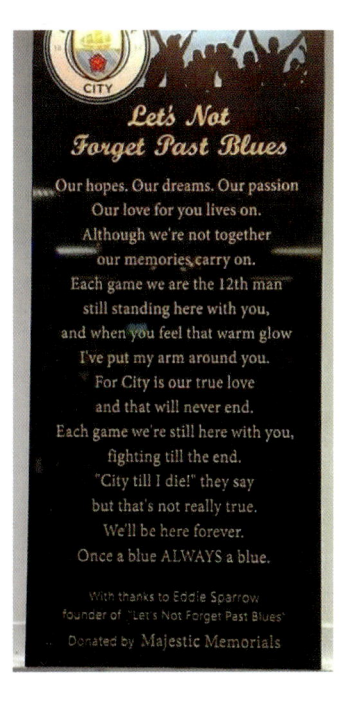

Let's Not Forget Past Blues

Our hopes. Our dreams. Our passion
Our love for you lives on.
Although we're not together
our memories carry on.
Each game we are the 12th man
still standing here with you,
and when you feel that warm glow
I've put my arm around you.
For City is our true love
and that will never end.
Each game we're still here with you,
fighting till the end.
"City till I die!" they say
but that's not really true.
We'll be here forever.
Once a blue ALWAYS a blue.

With thanks to Eddie Sparrow
founder of "Let's Not Forget Past Blues"
Donated by Majestic Memorials

IN MEMORIAM

Elliott with one of his heroes.
11/08/1997-22/01/2017

BRIAN ROSS

STUART KENYON
sadly he lost his fight
18.11.18.
RIP over the Blue Moon

DAVID LEIGH
We never win at home we never win away .. our angel love Kate and Jessica

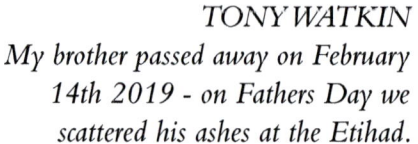

TONY WATKIN
My brother passed away on February 14th 2019 - on Fathers Day we scattered his ashes at the Etihad.

IN MEMORIAM

My Mum, Margaret Wall was an avid supporter for over forty-five years and following her death in September 1999 we were allowed to scatter some of her ashes on the pitch directly in front of her seat in the Main Stand.

My late Mum Alma (left) with the late Neil Young at a P&W meeting back in the 1990s with Sheila and Kath. I can't work out if my mum was giving Neil the Scotch or he had given it to her!

I met Debbie at the P&W meetings and we became the best of friends. Here we are with Shaun Goater. God bless you Debbie until we meet again!

Susan Bookbinder with media trainees Micah Richards and Daniel Sturridge in 2008.

Don's granddaughter Ayla who Don is convinced has a future career in City's Ladies team.

as hooligans and treated them as such.

Sadly, some still do, and in the 2018-2019 season at a game between Preston and Stoke City at half time the police pepper sprayed the Stoke fans including women and children. After footage was shown on YouTube, the police, as usual, tried to justify their actions but after many more complaints promised a full inquiry and debrief. Anyone who viewed the video will have been both mystified and shocked to see the police with batons drawn facing the Stoke fans on the concourse and then indiscriminately start spraying them, and a ten-year-old lad was in great discomfort after being sprayed.

The inquiry de-brief was soon over, and it will come as no surprise to many football fans that they concluded that spraying football fans, including a ten-year-old lad, was justified but that 'lessons would be learned'. No shit Sherlock what lessons can be learned? Lancashire police have been policing football games since year dot, if by now they haven't learnt how to do it properly they ought to pack their bags and go home.

Angela Smith, the chairwoman of Stoke City's supporters' council, thought it was disappointing that the police thought there was a need to pepper spray the fans at all, especially in such a confined area. A Stoke City spokesman said he was bitterly disappointed that they had issued a statement so quickly as it suggests they had concluded their inquiry already. "Based on our current knowledge, which appears to be zilch, we are unable to agree or accept their findings and conclusions they appear to have reached and would welcome further dialogue and investigation into the matter." So in a nutshell, for reasons that have not been made public the police decided to spray a group of football fans, including women and children, with pepper spray. Only after a huge outcry after fans had seen the video did the police hold an inquiry. There were no Stoke fans at the inquiry and there was no one from Stoke City football club there either. So, who exactly was there? Bet you have guessed already haven't you? If not, I will put you out of your misery. The police who were in charge on the day were present and so were the police doing the spraying, so the outcome of the inquiry wasn't a huge surprise. Just a pity the inquiry into the Liverpool hooligans' attack on the Manchester City players coach wasn't as quick.

Now loads of you were probably having a great deal of sympathy for the Stoke fans, but later in the season they proved that hooliganism can still take place in football grounds despite all the measures put in place by the clubs, the police, and the authorities. Away from home against their local rivals Port Vale in the Checkatrade Trophy, Stoke took around 4.000 fans and fought battles inside and outside the ground with the police, stewards, and rival fans. Coins, bottles and other missiles were thrown, flares were let off and chairs were smashed up. Fans also wrecked the toilet facilities on the concourse. Eleven fans were arrested on the night and more are expected to get the dreaded early morning knock as police study CCTV footage plus YouTube film taken by their own fans. To give them their due, many Stoke fans quickly got on social media to condemn their fans' actions. Typical isn't it? Just when you think violence on that scale at a football ground in the UK was a thing of the past, someone goes and proves you wrong.

The great thing about going to away games is that you visit towns and cities you wouldn't normally dream of visiting, even if it's just for a few hours. If you wanted to have a few drinks before and after the game, it was best not to go on the "football special" as the police wanted to take you straight to the ground and straight back to the train station after the game. I ask you where is the fun in that? Especially if you have been on the train for a few hours without any refreshments and an overflowing toilet. If you made your own way to the ground or sneaked away from the police escort you would be able to have a couple of drinks and have a chat with the locals. Sometimes if we weren't on the special we would be in the pubs early having a drink and a sing song when the fans from the special and the police escort came past. That was when the police had their work cut out as we would open back and side doors and windows to give fellow Blues a chance to join us for a pint, and the ones who managed to get in were grateful for our efforts.

There have been many classic away games over the years and

Don't Look Back In Anger

fans of different generations will have their favourite for many reasons. As I was only fourteen years old at the time and deprived of enough pocket money to go, I missed out in 1968 when it seemed half of Manchester converged on Newcastle to see City crowned as First Division champions. Not to miss out on my football fix though I went to watch Bury play Watford that day and Bury won the game to get promoted to Division Two. Although it wasn't my first choice of game to watch that Saturday, it was a lot cheaper as it was only about one shilling to get in the ground and a few pence return on the local train. The footage of the Newcastle game is in black and white and at the final whistle it seemed the majority of fans in the ground were City fans and they had a friendly pitch invasion to celebrate an excellent victory. Chelsea in the FA Cup third round was a belter, and we beat an excellent Chelsea team 3-0 at Stamford Bridge. Another classic played at Chelsea's ground was the beating of Norwich in a second replay of the League Cup, City won 6-1 and many fans in a small crowd of under six thousand fans were from Manchester. I'd fallen asleep on the train from Weymouth and didn't get to the ground until half time. It had been a busy weekend for me as I had hitched it to Manchester for a "Derby" game at Maine Road, then on the Sunday I got the 10 pm coach back to Weymouth from the coach station on Portland Street, then hitched it from Weymouth to the Naval Base on Portland arriving back at about 6-30 am. After a quick shit, shower and shampoo it was off to the galley to commence my duties then when I finished it was off to Stamford Bridge for the game, no rest for the wicked. I wouldn't even attempt that sort of schedule these days. I'm knackered just thinking about it now and fair play to the City fans who go to watch City all over Europe, especially the ones who go by plane and are there and back sometimes in under twenty-four hours. Beating a really good Ipswich team at Villa Park in the 1981 FA Cup semi-final is a stand out one for any City fan who was at the game, more so if you were in the Holte End as Paul Power's shot flew in the back of the net. Watching hundreds of City fans doing the tango at Ewood Park in 2000 was a sight to behold as we won the game to get promoted back to the

Premiership.

Another promotion-winning game was at Bradford in 1989 where thousands of City fans were in every part of the ground and the majority were waving their inflatable bananas about. Me and my mate Derbo were in the seats with the Bradford fans but they were all sound lads and they had smuggled a load of Vodka in the ground and were very generous with it. Now Vodka wasn't my tipple of choice, but it would have been rude to refuse, so I gratefully accepted their wonderful hospitality.

Then there are the ones we want to forget such as Halifax and Shrewsbury in the FA Cup and the likes of Bury, Lincoln, Southend, Stockport, Macclesfield, and York as all those games give us a stark reminder how shit we were not too long ago. One year when we were playing Notts County and our game coincided with the Nottingham Goose Fair, so instead of re-arranging the Goose Fair they moved our game instead, which shows how much respect they had at that time when a load of bleeding Geese have priority. James H Reeve did a brilliant take on that at a show at Bernard Manning's Embassy Club, it's on YouTube and I will be surprised if you are not in stitches watching it.

My earliest memory of watching City away was at Blackpool in the 1960s and joining in with hundreds of other City fans playing football on the beach. In the ground, the late greats Joe Mercer and Malcolm Allison applauded the thousands of City fans who had made the journey to the Fylde Coast. I recall not having a great view as we were all standing up, and as I was only thirteen years of age still a right short arse. City won 1-0 and Johnny Crossan scored for us, no I didn't remember the score or the scorer as it was over fifty years ago but I delved into the archives to bring the info to you as you would only have had a sleepless night wondering who scored and who the scorer was. As a young kid you, like me, will probably agree, it is a brilliant feeling going to watch a live game and it's extra special to watch an away game as well. Also in the 60s another away game for me was at Huddersfield, now I can't blame this on the drink but all I remember is getting off a packed train which was full of City fans, marching into the city centre chanting

City songs then that's it! Nowt else, a full stop. I can't remember going to the ground, the score, or getting back to Manchester, at least I don't think I had a drink, oh well another little mystery for me to dwell on. There have been far too many times I forgot the score or the scorer or even getting home from a game but at least I had some thing to blame, as we always said that City drove us to drink, not that we ever needed much persuading.

The first time I went to Nottingham to watch City it was eventful to say the least. I was home on leave and was only just turned seventeen, so it would have been 1971. I'd only got home late on the Friday night so hadn't been in touch with anyone about going to the game so I just went to Piccadilly to get on the "special" and as luck would have it I soon recognised a few lads that I knew. One thing that went on for years getting the train to away games were the amount of youngsters, some as young as ten or eleven, asking for money so they could get to the game. At first I used to give them a couple of bob until I realised most of the cheeky buggers didn't even buy a ticket but sneaked on the train and played dodge the conductor and police when they came checking for tickets. When we arrived at Nottingham we were all herded together and escorted to the ground. The locals were all out in force to give us a "welcome" but it was all huffing and puffing and the only thing that was thrown was lots of abuse, I'd take abuse any day instead of a bottle or a brick. After the game it was a different kettle of fish as the police were nowhere to be seen and it was every man for himself. I am not being sexist ladies but I'm convinced back then there wouldn't have been many if any women bonkers enough to set foot on the football special and I can't remember seeing any but please give me a shout if I am wrong. As there were so many City fans, I wasn't unduly worried, but we had all heard stories of away fans being thrown into the River Trent. In future years I went to the City ground many times and not once did I see any City fans taking an unwelcome dip so whether those stories were make believe and just an urban myth, I don't know but on my first trip to Nottingham I certainly didn't want to find out the hard way. As we were walking back there were scuffles and fights breaking out all down the road. I was with a group of around fifteen City fans and we were surrounded by a load of Forest fans, quite quickly we were hemmed into a huge glass shop front and as they forced us back I honestly thought the window would cave in and yours truly would end up inside the shop covered in broken glass. Fortunately, it held and after a bit of pushing and shoving we got out of our predicament and arrived at the train station in one piece.

Then that's where my trouble really started as I realised I had lost my train ticket. Now a few months earlier my mum had lost her purse while shopping in Manchester (probably stolen) she was very upset and went to the police who were very helpful and gave her money to get home which she repaid the next day. Now with that memory being fresh I went to the Manchester police who were travelling back to Manchester with us and explained my situation. I also explained I was on leave from the Navy and showed them my ID card hoping for a sympathetic solution so I could get on the train with no hassle. No chance, now the simple solution would either to be to let me on without paying, for me to pay again or hang around the station and get the next service train back. I would have been willing to do either, but silly me I should have realised that a simple solution and a bit of common-sense was lost on some police back then. Instead they put me in the "cage" on the train that the guard usually put the mail and other precious cargo in and said I would be interviewed and dealt with back in Manchester, but what could I tell them that I hadn't already? I hadn't realised losing a train ticket and offering to buy another one was a crime? Did it not occur to them that as I wanted to go back on the special, I must have arrived on the frigging thing? As it happens about another ten fans joined me in our make shift cell on the journey back to Manchester but I can't remember what they were supposed to have done. It couldn't have been serious otherwise they would have been banged up in a Nottingham police station. Back in Manchester once the rest of the City fans got off the train, we were let out of the "cage" and the police escorted us to wherever we were being taken. Now I didn't know if we were going to be arrested, get a slap, or both, and to be honest, I didn't want to hang about to find out. We were only being escorted by two policemen so I thought I would take my chance and do a runner to where the other City fans were and mingle in with them as I didn't think I had anything to lose and just hoped the police wouldn't come after me as that meant the other lads would do one as well. When I saw my chance, I just went for it and was on my toes. I wasn't the fastest of runners but thankfully no-one gave chase. One of the policemen did shout at me to stop but that was never going to happen, and I ended up getting away. But what a barmy situation to be in - if common sense had prevailed, I wouldn't have been knackered legging it through Piccadilly station. I never found out what happened to the other lads and it was ages before I chanced going to a game again on the train in case I was recognised and was also a bit nervous getting the train back to Portsmouth but all's well that's ends well. It wasn't the only time I have lost a train or coach ticket but, on those occasions, as it was not football related the problem was sorted out without any fuss. The next away game I went to on the football special was at West Brom, so I will get the song out of the way first

Oh, I do like to be beside the seaside
Oh, I do like to beside the sea
Oh, I do like to walk along the prom, prom, prom
Where the brass band plays fu*k off West Brom

The old ones are the best and before any youngster asks. No, West Brom is nowhere near the sea or a prom, it is near Birmingham in the Midlands but at least it rhymes and that's the main point even if it doesn't make sense. Anyway, going to the station I was a bit wary about being recognised by the police but my hair was a bit longer and I stuck a City hat on my head, it wasn't much of a disguise and James Bond wouldn't have been impressed, but there wasn't much else I could do and I would have stood out like a sore thumb if I had put a pair of sunglasses on. Once my ticket was checked I stuffed it down my sock as I didn't want to go through all that mither again if I lost it. Once we arrived it was the same scenario as at Nottingham with the local knob heads out in force to greet us and the local police also on hand to give us an escort to the ground. The West Brom fans did loads of gesturing and hand signals from a safe distance but apart from the usual abuse and football chants nothing untoward happened. I wish I could say the same after the game. Like after the Forest game there were no police to walk us back to the station, although there were some knocking about and pointing us in the right direction. I was talking to a City fan I had seen on the train and although there were plenty of other blues walking back it wasn't as though we were all in a group singing and chanting, most were trying to keep a low profile as we made our way back. As we were passing some waste land, we were suddenly attacked by a large group of West Brom fans, most of them weren't getting too close, but started to throw bricks and bottles at us instead. I don't know about you but I think I would rather take a punch than have a bleeding big brick hit me on my head. There wasn't much else we could do but try and defend ourselves as best we could as no-one else was there to help us and so we returned the compliment by launching the bricks back in the direction they had come from. There were also scuffles breaking out and eventually some police dog vans turned up. Instead of confronting the West Brom fans who were clearly the aggressors, they turned their attention and their dogs on us. Fuck me, I only wanted to go to a game of bleeding football and now, through no fault of my own, I was in a serious confrontation with both the home fans and the police. I had just picked a brick up to launch when a policeman, with what seemed to me the biggest dog in the world snarling like mad and looked like it would have enjoyed ripping my arm off, when the copper ordered me to put the brick down. I did so in a nanosecond as I didn't fancy being that monster's supper. I don't give a shit how hyped up you are or if you think you can take the world on but seeing one of those dogs up close and personal will soon make you see the errors of your ways and I guarantee you will be shitting bricks, I know I was. The talking point on the train back home was why didn't we get a police escort and why were the West Brom fans allowed to attack us? Over to you Sherlock as I still don't have a clue.

A few seasons after that little set to I was home on leave and my mate Paul asked me if I fancied going to West Brom with him. There was no way on earth I was going to go on the train again but as he had organised a mini bus I jumped at the chance. The trip going was great, the driver was sound and we stopped at a couple of pubs on the way and were with some great lads and there were loads of City fans in the ground. After the game we all got on the mini bus without incident and started making our way back. We hadn't gone far when, fuck me, our mini bus came under attack from a load of brick throwing West Brom yobs. Other City fans in cars and coaches also came under attack and surprise, surprise there wasn't a policeman in sight. This lot of brick throwers, probably because they had years of experience, were better shots than the last lot I had come across and apart from some hitting the roof they had a bullseye and one went through the back window and landed on the back seat next to my mate Kev Beesley. Luckily it never hit him on the head as he would have had a nasty injury. A couple of the lads on the coach, to their credit, wanted to get off to confront the thugs who targeted our mini bus and while I admire their sentiments I would willingly have joined them if we had anything to gain, but the most obvious outcome was that the minibus would have been wrecked and we would have got battered. To top it all, the police would have probably turned up late as usual and arrested us. I think it was Napoleon who once said, "choose your battles" and we all know what happened to him, and if it wasn't him who said it, he should have taken note anyway as some of his quotes are legendary "I would kiss a man's ass if I needed him" is a classic. Oh well, swiftly moving on. Since those bitterly disappointing times I have been to West Brom's ground a few times and I'm glad to report all the occasions were trouble free, for me at least. I have no idea if the brick throwing yobs were still allowed to attack visiting fans, it's just that I never witnessed it again. I have even been in West Brom's fans' social club and had a great time with their fans and one time outside the ground I spotted Steve Daley who once played for us and managed to blag some tickets off him.

Without wishing to sound like a nutty professor and stating the bleeding obvious, chucking a brick at someone could have a life changing affect on both the person it hit and the person who chucked it. People certainly don't think about the consequences as I am sure none of the lads who threw bricks at us wanted to seriously hurt us or even kill us but that is the reality that could have happened, and so is a spell in prison if they were caught. I was a split second away from launching a brick to defend myself and would have been horrified if I had done, and it caused someone some serious damage. Unfortunately, it still happens now and again in this day and age but thankfully not as frequently.

Going to watch City at Ipswich is always a great experience as I have never seen the police being heavy handed or witnessed any trouble with their fans. After the games you could go in any of the pubs and mix with the locals without fear of being set upon. That could be one of the reasons City always took a lot of fans down there as it is quite a distance and a bit of a pain to get to. I had been to Ipswich a couple of times when I was in the Navy but the best time I had was on my mate Dave Mitchell's stag do. We set off from the Ostrich public house in Prestwich in great spirits after first having a few beers and getting a carry out. The only downside was there was no toilet, so we improvised with a couple of buckets, just as well no one wanted a khazi plus we had a few pee stops. When we were over half way to Ipswich, we stopped at a little country pub as our beer supplies had run dry and we needed to empty the buckets. The landlord of the pub couldn't cope with a sudden surge of thirsty football fans so two of the lads on the coach who were also pub landlords went behind the bar to give him a hand. He must have thought it was Christmas as not only did we drink a lot, we also bought a large carry out each. The game was not until the following day, so we were in no hurry to get to the hotel. When we eventually arrived most of the lads went into town after a quick shower while light weights like me had a couple of beers then got our heads down. Before the game we all met up at a big pub near the train station and soon it was packed with City fans. Some of the lads had done a whip round for a stripper gram, and after she finished a local girl in the pub thought she could do better so jumped on the pool table and proceeded to get her kit off. The landlord was having a panic attack and quickly threw her out. All I remember about the game was everyone near me was steaming and that our midfielder, Ali Benarbia, was absolutely brilliant. After the game it was back to the pub for more beers. After an hour or so most of the other City fans had gone on their way and there was only us lot left. Now I have been in other pubs when the police want you to leave for whatever reason, they will just come in mob handed being very aggressive and turf you out. Ipswich police were much more civilised. The police advised us they wanted us to leave as they had intelligence some local yobs were on their way to cause a spot of bother, so not to spoil the rest of our evening they had contacted the hotel where we had stayed the night before and he was willing to have us back, I bet he was considering the money we had spent! What a great lot of police down there, no wonder there is hardly any trouble with football fans in Ipswich. Just a pity other police forces don't adopt their tactics. So, from all of us it was a big ten out of ten for the police, pub and hotel landlords of Suffolk.

On many away trips we visited the same pubs each year and they loved it when we came, as we were very good for business. Some put free sandwiches on and some opened early for us. One year we stopped at a regular watering hotel outside Nottingham. A policeman had seen us enter and came in the pub and advised the landlord not to serve us as there was potential for trouble. The landlord explained in no uncertain terms that we had been coming for years, were very welcome and we hadn't even smashed a single glass. The landlord would have been gutted if we had left as we always spent a fortune.

Another firm favourite ground of mine is Villa Park, they've had some great teams in the past who played very attractive flowing football and their fans were a credit as well but deserve better than the dross they have been served for many years. Although there are signs of improvement massive investment is needed until they can seriously compete at the top level and compete for any silverware again, although they've just got back in the top flight. You could have a drink in the pubs with them near the ground with no hint of hassle, the only downside of having a chat with them was that bleeding accent, I always needed an interpreter, after saying that they probably said the same about me.

Although Birmingham City's ground wasn't too far from Villa Park their fans were like chalk and cheese by comparison.. Although I have never personally witnessed any trouble there, you always had to be on your toes as tension was always in the air and it seemed to me it would only take a little spark for it to kick right off and that is probably why our away support was always so much larger at Villa than at Birmingham. One game though at Birmingham that will always bring back memories. It was 0-0 until the 89th minute when City scored. The Birmingham City fans were not amused and I thought "oh shit it will kick off outside now" but I needn't have worried as the City fans were still cheering when Birmingham equalised. We were still recovering from that shock when Birmingham went on to score the winner. We have, unfortunately, had bigger shocks than that though with the likes of Halifax and Shrewsbury knocking us out of the FA Cup and York and Bury beating us in the league. We still occasionally suffer the odd shock in one of the Cup competitions but that is usually because we have put out a weakened team, which is something I could never get my head round and it always did my head in. Teams like Liverpool, Everton, Newcastle United, Spurs, Burnley and West Ham haven't won the FA Cup or League Cup in donkey's years if at all but come the Cup games they will usually send out a team of fringe players and then wonder why they get knocked out. All the teams mentioned except for Liverpool at the moment have little or no chance of being serious contenders to win the Premiership but continue to put out under-strength teams in the Cup competitions is a mystery. While fans will accept one or two changes it annoys fans from all clubs when managers put out a second string team that is virtually unrecognisable from the one that plays week in week out in the league. Yet fans are expected to travel the length and breadth of the country and fork our good money to watch what is basically a mix of reserve and junior players. One season at Chelsea we were easily beaten as we had many youngsters playing for us who had never previously been in the first team, while Chelsea had most of their first team in action.

One of the biggest shocks in the FA Cup recently had nothing to do with a weakened team but just that the underdogs were better on the day. That's how it was when City were beaten by Wigan Athletic in the FA Cup final the same season that Wigan were relegated. Although Wigan fans were bitterly disappointed that they were out of the Premiership it softened the blow that they had beaten us in the Final. All fans want to see their team play at Wembley and it is so disappointing when they get easily beaten by not playing a full-strength team in the early rounds of a tournament. I know a few Everton fans and they feel let down that most seasons they make little progress in the cup competitions as realistically they have no chance of winning the Premier League. Talking of Everton, until the take over at the Etihad they seemed to have a lot in common with City. Both teams for a long time lived in the shadows of their neighbours but the fans remained loyal and carried on supporting their teams through thick and thin. Goodison Park like Maine Road was a proper football fans ground as the fans were close to the pitch and the atmosphere in the 1970s and 1980s was always good , but the old place could still do with a bit of an upgrade. It was a ground I always enjoyed going to but you had to keep your wits about you as there were always some scallies lurking about ready to turn you over given half the chance.

A few months after I left the Navy in 1977 City were playing at Goodison a few months later and I arranged to see my mate Dinger who was home on leave. I had arranged to meet him in the bar at the station (where else?) but before he arrived the police escorted all the City fans away from the station and on to buses as loads of Everton fans had turned up to give us "a welcome" and the police obviously didn't want a mass brawl in and around the station so we were moved on. Mobile phones were something we'd only seen on Star Trek, so there was no way I could contact him and was bitterly disappointed that we couldn't meet up before the game. Dinger though had a brain wave and after the game went around to where the away fans were congregated, and he spotted me on the way out, so we had a few beers together before I got the late train back to Manchester. I'm still in touch with him and had a drink with him and a few other lads from the Navy in a pub in Liverpool. I told them though next time we meet up it will have to be in Manchester as at least I can understand people's accents.

One evening game in the 1990s I was there with my mate Ken from Whitefield. At half time after going to the toilets we were making our way up the stairs when he took a tumble as the stairs were very wet. A policeman came over and like an idiot I thought he was going to assist him. Doh! I should have known better and the tosser arrested him for being drunk. I kid you not he did absolutely nothing wrong and although like the majority, of fans in the ground we had been in a pub before the game we were not even close to being drunk, more's the pity. If the police seriously want to arrest people that have had a few drinks, all they have to do is go in the corporate hospitality lounges or the private boxes that have sprung up in all the football stadia then they would have literally hundreds of people to choose from. It was really annoying but what made matters worse was that the police with their sick sense of humour waited until the last train left Manchester until they let him out. Another time we booked a minibus from Prestwich to take us to Everton for a midweek game. I wondered when I booked it why it was cheaper than usual. The driver only thought we were going to Atherton. Why the hell would anyone who didn't have to, want to go to Atherton? We used to call the driver "Blind Dave" after that it was "Deaf Dave". He got some stick for that for a long time. Bloody halfwit, only joking, Dave was a top bloke, he had to be to put up with us lot on away trips.

Now I don't want to portray all police at football grounds in a bad light as some can be really helpful at times, and while some are quick to arrest people for trivial matters, others will use their common sense. Many police have risked injury to help fans, many have been injured at games protecting innocent fans from gangs of hooligans, sometimes police are the first at the scene of

Don't Look Back In Anger

an injured fan and will give emergency first aid while waiting for paramedics to turn up. With some police you can have a laugh and a bit of banter, while some suffer from a serious sense of humour failure. Some will go out of their way to help, just like the two I encountered on the first time I drove to Hillsborough, home of Sheffield Wednesday. It was in the 1990s and when I woke up in the morning, I had no intention of going to the game as I was working on the late shift at Prestwich Hospital. Before I was due to start work I gave Derbo and Kev a lift to the train station as they were going to the game. On the way back from dropping them off I got a severe attack of jealousy as I was now really gutted, they were off to the game and I was off to work. I was getting myself wound up on the drive home and it was a minor miracle I didn't crash or get involved in a road rage incident. Once I got home, I phoned work up and sweet talked them into giving me the day off, fortunately I still had loads of holidays to use up, so it wasn't a problem getting the time off. Back in those days for a game like Sheffield Wednesday away in the league tickets weren't required and you could just turn up and pay to get in. I hadn't long passed my driving test and had little experience of motorway driving and I had absolutely no idea how to get there but that little obstacle wasn't going to deter me in my quest to watch City play that day. I set off in my trusty little Fiat which I had bought for £200 just after I passed my test. Sat navs weren't around then so in my wisdom I just got on the motorway and thought if I keep driving, I will come across a sign for Sheffield. Oops another clanger dropped by yours truly so eventually I stopped in a service station and got proper directions. So, after a quick chat with the guy in the petrol station shop, I set off with renewed confidence to get to the ground. I made it with minutes to spare and straight away came across Derbo and Kev who were surprised to see me as they thought I would be in work. After the game I came very close to leaving my car in Sheffield to go for a few drinks as loads of City fans were staying for a few bevvies. My intention was to come back the next day by train to collect it. What the bleeding hell was I thinking of? Fortunately, common-sense kicked in and I shelved that idea very quickly. I hadn't got far in my car when I discovered I had a puncture. Not having the faintest idea what to do to fix it I phoned the AA who said they would be out in under an hour. A passing police patrol car stopped, and the police had a chat with me about what I was up to. Once I explained my predicament, they told me to cancel the AA as they would change my wheel. Result. They went on to say how they would rather help me than get involved with splitting up rival fans. I wasn't bothered what their motive was I was just glad that my new 'knights in shining armour' came to my assistance. It is not often a football fan will praise the Sheffield police, but they got ten out of ten from me on that occasion.

Another favourite away trip was to Derby and City always took a huge following, but the state of the pitch was always a bit iffy and one season Derby were awarded a penalty but a member of the ground staff was called to measure out and repaint the penalty spot as the pitch was a mud bath and no-one was clear where to take the penalty from and big Joe Corrigan was booked for his protests. Another year I was on another of Paul Holt's mini bus trips. As it was a glorious day, we stopped off in Buxton for a couple of ice-cold beers. We ended up in a nice pub and it seemed pretty quiet. Unbeknown to us there was a huge lounge bar packed with United fans. They soon realised we were there and as they outnumbered us by about ten to one they just came in the room we were in and launched an unprovoked attack. Luckily none of us were seriously hurt (wasn't for the want of trying) and we eventually got back to the minibus relatively unscathed except for some lumps and bruises but more importantly the mini bus was not damaged. United fans still have a reputation these days for attacking small groups of opposing fans when they have superior numbers. They did just that when we thrashed them 6-1 at Old Trafford and hung about to attack City fans as they made their way back to their cars and coaches. I used to love going to Old Trafford and there were some classic games, but we were without a victory there from 1974 to 2008 but it is a different story now a days. City fans were ecstatic when Keith Curle scored from the penalty spot and Ian Brightwell's goal is my all-time favourite there and City fans celebrated in most parts of the ground as we had so many fans all over the swamp that day.

Another ground I liked was Fratton Park, it's just a proper football ground with very passionate fans and another one of those clubs that has been mis-managed over the years and seen some dark times. I was never fortunate to watch City play there but it was always a great atmosphere as I went there a few times whilst in the Navy. Whenever we played Oldham, as it is on our doorstep, we always had a huge following with City fans in every part of the ground. One year we were getting a police escort, and I recognised one of the policemen as he used to be a chef with me on HMS Devonshire, what a small world! A highlight for City fans is when we play Blackpool away as most City fans stay over and make a weekend of it. Many of the grounds I have mentioned have been modernised or rebuilt over the years, as they needed to for Health and Safety reasons and then the Taylor Report recommendations brought in after the Hillsborough disaster and most have lost their character and the atmosphere in general has declined as a result.

I am never sick of telling this story but I watched Pele play at Plymouth who were in the old Third Division at the time when the great Brazilian was on tour with his club Santos. Over 35,000 fans crammed into the ground to see arguably the greatest footballer on the planet, but the chairman and directors could only see money signs and were not too concerned for the health and safety or the comfort of fans. There was some atmosphere that night and something that people who were there will never forget.

One-year City had a massive travelling army of fans at Bramall Lane in the FA Cup against Sheffield United and before the game City fans let off hundreds of blue and white balloons which at that time was a bit of a tradition. Unfortunately, some were still on the pitch when Sheffield United launched an attack. One of our defenders, Michael Ball, got himself a bit confused as to which was the ball and which was the balloon. The Sheffield striker had no such problem as he rifled the ball home much to the amusement of the match day commentators as City went on to lose the game and take an early exit from the FA Cup.

City have often taken a massive number of supporters up and down the country and abroad and their loyalty cannot be questioned, so it came as no surprise when we played in Germany for a pre-season friendly against Hamburg. About eight thousand City fans made the journey and about three thousand went to Thailand for another pre-season tour. Thousands made the trip to Cardiff when we played TNS in a qualifying round of the UEFA Cup even though we were winning the first leg 5-0. My mate's son, Mark Ellis, who was over from Australia came to the game with us as did local radio presenter James H Reeve. Swindon and Bournemouth are both nice and friendly clubs and so are their fans and we always get a warm welcome whenever we visit but City's Kevin Horlock got sent off as the referee at Bournemouth accused him of "aggressive walking" which is the only time I have heard of a player committing that offence. The promotion win at Blackburn was something special and half the ground was filled with Blues with hundreds watching from up a hill.

I'm quite sure many of you have your own favourite grounds and favourite away games for various reasons but in this day and age it is getting increasingly difficult to get tickets for away games as most clubs either use a loyalty points system like City do at the moment, or other clubs put names of fans who want a ticket into a ballot or random draw so it is a bit hit and miss whether you get a ticket or not. Fans of all clubs though if they really want a ticket for a particular game, will find one way or another of getting one. Whilst I could probably write a book just on away games I hope this chapter stirred some memories for you.

12: the fall and rise of city

THE LAST FEW YEARS have seen City reach heights previously not even dreamed about. Many of our supporters have followed the club through the bleak times and at long last are being rewarded with not only watching brilliant football but picking up trophies as well. The following are comments from lifelong City fans, I am sure you will all have similar thoughts and opinions so grab a brew and please read on.

Loud and proud football and great to see City fans, families and grandchildren filled with pride at the 2019 celebration parade. Great for being alive and witnessing the 1969 Cup Final and the roller coaster years that followed. The icing on the cake was the incredible 2018-2019 season when we broke all records to win the treble (plus 1) I'm blessed to be a Blue. **Alistair Hay Prestwich & Whitefield branch organiser.**

I'll never forget getting back on the coach after we beat Gillingham in the play-off final. My two daughters said "Dad now I know why you cry about City" back then I could only dream of what is happening now. **Tommy Muir Chairman of Cheadle branch City Supporters Club.**

I was born into a big Blue family in 1977. My dad was from Chorlton-on-Medlock and I went to Maine Road with him before I could walk. I've got great memories of Maine Road and made friends for life. While we are now enjoying great times, we have been served with some rubbish and the Stuart Pearce era was very challenging. Like many others I was tempted to give my season ticket up, but I kept the faith and got a bit of a taste of what was to come when Sven was in charge but was brought back down to earth when we were thrashed 8-1 at Middlesbrough. In the summer Sheikh Mansour took over but I couldn't understand all the hype over Robinho. For me it was Kompany and Zabba that got the ball rolling, things really changed under Bobby Manc and with players like David Silva, Yaya, Sergio and Dzeko the mindset of the whole team changed and turned us into the winning machine we are today.

Now Pep is making everything click and the football is just amazing. It's just a pleasure to watch City and it makes the 31 years of being a season ticket holder worth it. The football I have witnessed in the last three years is the best I have seen in my life and playing against York, Wrexham, Macclesfield etc is just a distant memory. The 2018-2019 season topped it off for me though, as to win 14 games on the bounce to pip Liverpool to the title by winning at Brighton on the last game of the season was just incredible. Older fans will have had similar emotions, winning at Newcastle in 1968 on the last game of that season to also win the title. To sum it up, we have had some special goals, especially from Sergio and Vinny the last few seasons have been incredible, and I have watched the games and had a drink with some top City fans. Being a Blue isn't a choice, it is a privilege, it's in the blood, it is an extended family. IT IS LIFE. The 2018-2019 season was a dream come true. **Strongy, Bury Blue.**

I've been a supporter 60 years and never ever seen such great football from any football team. **Roy from Prestwich.**

After living painfully in the shadows of the red team from Stretford for many years it is great that we are now the dominant force, not only in Manchester but in the whole of England **Aide" from Crumpsall.**

In the future people will be talking about this team like those that know football talk of the great Brazil team circa 1970. **Howard from Prestwich**

I am exiled in Holland at the moment, so imagine my joy when we drew with Ajax a few years ago and then recently with Feyenoord. When organising a trip to the Etihad I couldn't think of doing it without my two City mad sons who were born in 2008 and 2010. We get good coverage on Dutch satellite networks but get cheesed off when they choose to air Formula 1 instead of the EPL. Under Pep we are something special and the style of football we play is something all football fans appreciate. **David John Lyons, exiled Blue in the Netherlands.**

Growing up with a small group of lads who were City fans was brilliant; Steven and Sean Price, Kevin and Lee Holt, Rob Mitchell, we all experienced City at their lowest ebb with our dads on the Kippax or sat in the North Stand or Family Stand. Those memories will never be repeated nowadays. Nowadays we have a glamorous stadium, mind blowing football, superstar players, and trophies galore. The first part makes the second part sweeter, for fans of my age. It completes the story of what it is like to be a Blue. **Darren originally from Prestwich now exiled in Middleton.**

City will be with me until the day they put me in the ground. Where we are today is fantastic and every City fan deserves it as over the years we have had to endure our fair share of rubbish, enough to last us a lifetime to be honest. Onwards and upwards and the last few years have made up for the lean times. Remember those words "Not in my Lifetime" yeah dream on. **Marc Hayes ex Audenshaw now living in Poole.**

The last couple of years being a Blue and long-time City fan have been majestic, days that even the most optimistic of our Blue hearts would have dreamt of seeing. We have been down but never out and right now we are riding the crest of a blue wave. We were there in the bad times and we will be there again if ever the bad times come back. But now it is our time CTWD. **Ger Browne Wexford, Ireland.**

As City fans who have seen us at our lowest it is hard to believe and take in what we are actually seeing. It is only when you take a step back and have a minute to think about it that you realise just how much we owe to Sheikh Mansour. The scary thing though is there is a lot more to come from this team. **Scott Beesley original Prestwich lad.**

I had a dream, as Martin Luther King once said, that my team Manchester City would play the most perfect football imaginable. I've lived through that dream the last couple of years and have to ask myself; is it really happening? I had the joy of commentating on the Aguero goal and interviewing the players on the top deck of the open top bus as they paraded through Manchester and wondered if I was imagining the whole thing, then along came Pep Guardiola. I'd salivated at the football Barcelona played under Pep's stewardship, but I was watching from afar on TV. Move forward a few years and here I am watching the dream team playing the football I could only imagine right in front of me at every game home and away. I've marvelled at Bernardo Silva, David Silva, Kevin De Bruyne, Fernandinho, Raheem Sterling and Leroy Sane led by our captain Vincent Kompany and just sat/stood in awe. I don't communicate out loud anymore, but I have found myself in the last couple of seasons going "Wow" and wondered if those around me had noticed me shouting out. I grew up watching Bell, Lee & Summerbee and Jairzinho and Rivelino - but this is even better. I love seeing City lift trophies but that is not the most important thing to me. It's seeing my Boys in Blue playing with a smile, like it is just a practise game among best mates and making my dreams become a reality. **Ian Cheeseman City through and through.**

City is in my DNA and I can trace a family line of City fans all the way to the side lines at St Marks and watching Ardwick F C play. With Don and his brother Bob Price our heyday team was the golden age of Colin Bell, Franny Lee and Mike Summerbee, however the last few years have even eclipsed the achievements of those greats. Now my son Mark is carrying on our family's proud tradition and he is the "Only City fan in the Village" living in Kitzbuhel, Austria and It makes me so proud that he is a big Blue and enjoying the success that eluded us for many years. The best game we ever attended together was the beginning of the new era with our one-nil win over Stoke in the FA Cup Final. Both of us cried with joy and relief, then it was cigars and brandies all round, a day never to be forgotten. I still have two Cuban Cigars left for us both when we finally win the Champions League, but you know what? Having supported City for 68 years all I want from each season is to beat the rags! Nah nah nah nana nah nah nana nah nah CITY! **John Ellis Prestwich born and bred.**

WHAT THE EX-PLAYERS SAID

My first season as a season ticket holder led to glorious success at Wembley. It would be an incredible 35 years until the Blues would be there again to compete in a major final. More than any one goal or any one game it was the fans' ability to turn up ready to party through mainly thin times that kept the club afloat. They are fully deserving of the great success story the club has become and long may they continue to enjoy it. **David White.**

Manchester City fans in my opinion are the most loyal in the country, after years of living in the shadows of their neighbours they still turned out in their droves to support the Blues, especially the away support. One of my favourite memories was the New Year away game at Stoke City where thousands turned up in fancy dress with their inflatable bananas and all sorts of other inflatables. Not sure if the team I played in would have given the present team a game. I would be fearful of a Huddersfield result. We did have some great young players though including Paul Lake, Ian Brightwell, Steve Redmond and Paul Simpson to name but a few. There was a great crop of home-grown talent that should have stayed together for longer and I think may well have emulated "the class of 92" from over the road. I used to love playing at Maine Road, being a Wythenshawe lad hearing the Kippax sing my name after I scored, great memories. **Paul Stewart.**

Throughout the last 20 to 25 years the Prestwich & Whitefield supporters club was one of the best organised branches to go to. Don Price and the committee would always organise the meetings very well and at the end of the season there would always be about 4 or 5 ex-players at the meeting telling stories and answering questions to a packed house at Heaton Park Social Club. The fans at the meetings always made us very welcome and as ex-players we used to love going there as the fans were so passionate. I am now though proud to be the President of the Scandinavian Branch having taken over from my father Ken who sadly passed away a number of years ago. Ken knew two of the lads, Egil and Tor, from the Maine Road days where they would chat and have a brew and a smoke at the Oasis Suite over at Platt Lane and chat about the history of the club and what it was like back in the day. When my father passed away in 2010 it was such an honour for me to be asked to become their branch President. I am often asked to attend events in Norway and recently attended one in Oslo which is always a pleasure. I often meet up with their branch members as at most home games over 100 fans come over for each game and we have a 'catch up' and a couple of pints in Mother Macs.

I would like to wish Don well with this book and I am sure you will enjoy reading his stories. What a great few seasons we have had, and our fans truly deserve the beautiful football the team is playing and I'm sure dad would have loved to have a chat with Pep. I just wish dad was alive now to see the total football we are displaying every week as he was always an admirer of that style of football, as he always said the best form of defence is to attack and to create and score plenty of goals and that is how the City teams he played in during the 1950s and 1960s liked to play. And it was the type of football I used to enjoy when I got into the team in the mid-1970s and we were always challenging for the League and playing in Europe at that time. I would just like to pay tribute to the fans who have stuck with the club over the years and are now reaping the rewards.

Peter Barnes

"I'll never forget my home debut, in fact the first half a dozen times I played at Maine Road. I'd be overlapping down the flank by the Kippax to receive the ball from Colin (Bell) and the wall of noise was deafening. But I couldn't fathom out what was affecting my balance, I thought I had some sort of underlying medical condition, and I was worried. I asked Colin about it, and explained my 'symptoms' to him. He laughed and said 'yes, that's perfectly normal Kenny, it's the sound waves coming out of the shed (the Kippax terrace)!' To say I was relieved to hear him say that was an understatement, I genuinely thought I was ill - true story!

Kenny Clements

"From the moment I walked into Maine Road I knew I'd arrived at a special football club. Being part of the squad that took City back where it belonged with back to back promotions to the Premier League, along with leading the team out at Wembley in the Play Off Final, remains the highlight of my playing career. Through the dark days of Second Division Football the fans stayed loyal and followed the team wherever we went. After being named captain a group of fans explained to me in the car park outside the Kippax what was expected of me, they didn't hold back, I'd like to think I never let them down. Players and managers will come and go, the strength of a football club is and always will be its fans. From York away in the Second Division to winning the Premier League title; whether it was shit or champagne the fans of Manchester City have always been there, stood proud right behind their team. I'll never forget I was lucky enough to captain their club."

Andy Morrison

13: 25 years and were still here

IN MAY 1994 a group of 80 or so City fans met in the Welcome Inn on Bury Old Road in Prestwich to form what was to become one of the largest and proactive City supporters club. It wasn't an easy start though as the branch was formed on the backdrop of the 'Swales out, Franny in' campaign, which divided many supporters' clubs and also many members. Most of the people who attended our first meeting were not necessarily bothered about the politics of the club, but just wanted somewhere to go and meet fellow Blues, have a drink and a laugh and on occasions travel to away games together. During the third meeting, where Tommy Booth was our guest, one of the lads refused to give someone their pint back and ended up spread-eagled on the floor having knocked over a table or two on his trip to the deck. Needless to say, the landlord was not too happy at our version of extreme sports and from that day on we were no longer "Welcome at the Welcome". We decamped to the British Legion Club at Heaton Park where we lasted about a year until, we upped sticks again and for the next 10 years or so our base was the Heaton Park Social Club. We pulled off some great events and at one time or another all the great and the good from Manchester City attended our events. We held family fun days, Christmas parties for the kids, charity events, race nights, gentleman's mornings, sportsman's dinners as well as regular monthly meetings when special guests would turn up for a question and answer session and obviously a few drinks as well.

Sometimes we had as many as 400 people at the events which were usually held on a Tuesday evening. The late great Neil Young even took our younger members for football training in St. Mary's Park in Prestwich. The kids got nearly a bigger buzz out of those sessions than their parents did. We did manage to get many serving and ex managers to the meetings including Malcolm Allison, Tony

Book, Brian Horton, Alan Ball, John Bond, Kevin Keegan and Stuart Pearce. Phil Neal was going to attend during his spell in the hot seat but was sacked the day of the meeting, so he thought it inappropriate to attend. Steve Coppell wasn't there long enough but he still got an invite. We pestered Joe Royle and Frank Clark to attend but to no avail, though it wasn't for a lack of trying on our part. One of the highest profile guests we had was "Rogue Trader" Nick Leeson and probably the most controversial was the late Bernard Manning as his humour was not to every ones taste.

It was great for the parents as well as the kids to meet the players and managers up close and personal and get photos and autographs with them. It was not easy by any stretch of the imagination to get guests to the meetings but our enthusiasm and persistence knew no bounds and we were relentless in our pursuit to get guests to the meetings each month. We also, on a couple of occasions, took the members down to Platt Lane to watch the players train and then finish off a great day with a packed lunch in the City social club. We also managed to get an allocation of tickets for both home and away games which made it easier to plan trips and hire coaches. For many away games we stayed either overnight or for the weekend.

Southampton, Bournemouth, Norwich, Swindon, Blackpool and Newcastle were always popular away venues. At one stage, while not for any means being complacent or taking things for granted, we just expected players and club officials to attend and to be supportive of us and by and large they were. By the time I stood down as branch Chairman, ten years after the branch was formed, it was getting very difficult to secure guests on such a regular basis and it is so much harder nowadays, virtually a near impossibility which is such a shame. For most of the time I was Chairman City's team was pretty poor and the club needed to keep the supporters onside, so that is why I think in those days it was a lot easier than the present time to get people to the meetings.

One thing that the club did excel at back in the day, and they still do nowadays, is the work they do for the community and for charities and good causes. They go about their business quietly and without any fuss or publicity and the people they are supporting are extremely grateful we have a club which offers help and support when it is needed. For many years our branch sponsored Henshaw's School for the Blind's childrens Christmas party, a fact that to this day makes me proud as it is always great to help people less fortunate than ourselves. In the age of the internet and social media you would think there would be less need for supporters' clubs especially if guests from the club are not coming to meetings but thankfully that is not the case and more and more people are joining their local branch and new branches are being formed on a regularly basis.

As we are winning trophies most seasons the club has been great in getting the trophies out and about to supporters' clubs not only in the UK but abroad as well, which is something that goes down well with fans of all ages as it is a great experience having your photo taken with a bit of silverware as we went so many years just dreaming we could win something. The men and women who run supporters' branches have my utmost respect as it is largely a thankless task and as the saying goes "you can't please all of the people all of the time". Phil, Paul and Keith do a great job keeping the Prestwich and Whitefield branch ticking over, but after doing it for so long I don't envy them but wish them all the best. And the branch celebrated its 25th anniversary in style with a great event at Saint Bernadettes Social Club in Whitefield and as well as yours truly being there some ex players turned up and so did the trophies

We have had so many great meetings, I think it is hard to pick any out as being the best, but a couple of them stand out. To get Bert Trautmann to a meeting was a brilliant achievement considering the logistics involved. Kevin Keegan once turned up unannounced and uninvited which was pretty incredible, but we all thought it was a brilliant gesture. One event saw all the first team players come even they had been at the *Manchester Evening News* award ceremony in the city centre then they turned up at about 10pm at the social club which was just mind blowing and we spent the rest of the evening just having a craic and singing songs when all the players joined in. Ex City goalkeeper Eric Nixon also turned up with them and he sings a great version of

"Living Doll". Yes, we certainly had some brilliant times and the branch played a great part in keeping the players and club officials in touch with the fans who had supported the club in which can only be described as a shit period for Manchester City Football Club. Cheltenham & Gloucester, The Leicester branch, London and the Scandinavian branch are among the most active of the branches and it is testimony to the people who run them that they still organise travel to all of the games. Rather you than me lads and lasses, as I know what a headache it can be, but it can also be very rewarding as well. If you are not in a branch, look your local one up on Facebook as it might be worth your while joining and if you live near Prestwich & Whitefield, if you have not paid this year's subs yet give Phill a shout as he will be hunting you down.

If Pep ever gets around to reading this book (I'll send him a copy) Prestwich is only about four miles from your gaff mate and I'm sure Phill will sort you out a taxi if you fancy popping down when the trophies are next on display. Well it's time for my hot chocolate and an early night as I am on granddaughter sitting duties in the morning. I know it's only a small chapter as I wrote a lot about the branch in my first book The Royal Navy, Manchester City and Me, but I hope you got the flavour of what supporters' clubs are all about.

14: the ginger wig

ONE COMMON FEATURE at City games over the last 20 years, as the club has risen to the top, has been the sight of a supporter wearing a ginger wig and tartan bonnet. Many have asked why? Including that supporter on many occasions! Those on Twitter may follow @TheGingerWig and many will have seen me wearing the Ginger Wig to matches over the last 20 years. It's been worn at Maine Road, the Etihad and Wembley, as well as a few away grounds. I've yet to break my Champions League away debut but hopefully you'll see the Ginger Wig abroad soon!

But why The Ginger Wig? It's a question I've been asked many times! Some people ask me, is it because I'm Scottish? Well no, I was born in Greater Manchester. Even this month I spoke to someone for the first time having been friends on Facebook for years. He couldn't get over the fact that I didn't have a Scottish accent. Is it because my family are Scottish? No, they're all from Greater Manchester or Derbyshire. It was my Manchester born Grandad who got me into City. Having raised my mum and uncle in Levenshulme, whilst working at Woodford for British Aerospace with Nana working at McVities, he moved the family to just over the county border into Derbyshire. It's here that I grew up and spent time listening to Grandad's stories of supporting City from the 1930s onwards. As his eyesight deteriorated, he'd encourage me to improve my reading skills by getting me to read the match reports in the newspaper to him. He was from the generation of watching City one weekend and United the other, but City were always his team. He was at the game against Stoke along with 84,568 others that remains the record attendance at a home game – I'm not letting Spurs take the record as Wembley wasn't their ground! Such stories inspired me to support City, so it's him I have to blame/thank depending on the result!

I never got to go to a match with my Grandad as his health was poor when I started to want to go to the games. However my mum managed to arrange a tour of Maine Road with my Grandad. I still look at the pictures fondly of us sat together in the wood panelled rooms of the Main Stand, surrounded by various exotic trophies from matches played in far flung places. There was a fantastic wooden display which highlighted the first international games of City players. I do wonder if there's one at the Etihad, it'd be much fuller now with all the internationals we have.

As we were shown around the ground we met Tony Book outside the changing room. I don't think I'd ever seen my Grandad as giddy with excitement. The internal architecture of the Main Stand was very grand, and the concourse area felt very regal and it was always my favourite stand at Maine Road. It was where I first sat so I'm probably a bit biased! This was all a long time before the Ginger Wig though!

THE GINGER WIG'S 1ST GAME

On August 8th, 1998, City were about to enter a whole new world little did I know that 20 years later the Ginger Wig would still be going. Never before had the club been in the third tier of English football, a team that had won every cup in English football and a European trophy were playing in the same division as Macclesfield and Wycombe. Surely this team, with a ground holding more than triple that of many others in the division, would storm the league.

Joe Royle had come in as manager late the previous season but he had not been able to save City from the drop. He'd steadied the ship somewhat but a lot of the big earners had to go. Fan favourite Gio Kinkladze was seen as a luxury and perhaps wasn't the right fit for the struggling team. He left for Ajax for a pretty good fee at the time. The '98/99 season certainly started off well in a game that was to see the debut of the Ginger Wig. Goals came from Shaun Goater (24), the much-maligned Lee Bradbury (62) and Kakhaber Tskhadadze (80) sealed a 3-0 win at Maine Road against

Blackpool. Thanks to them I'm still wearing the same Ginger Wig 20 years on!

Having worn the Ginger Wig to that first game of the season and City winning (we didn't win often back then!), all the other season ticket holders around me said "You'll have to wear it again, it's good luck!". So, I have! It's had the odd wash since and it's not like Trigger's broom, it's the same hat and wig as when I first bought it (admittedly the hair is thinning – just like its owner!). It has lost its bobble along the way thanks to a vicious attack on it by someone who really doesn't like it (you know who you are!). Since then it's seen us promoted three times, won the FA Cup twice, League Cup (4 times) and Premier League (4 times). Admittedly there was one relegation in there as well and that Wigan FA Cup final loss (that was an awful experience all round – although I did get to meet Shaun Goater.) People often asked when I'd stop wearing the Ginger Wig.

In the early days, I did say I'd throw it on the pitch when we won a cup, but when we won the FA Cup in 2011, I'd been wearing it over a decade so chickened out. I then said I'd do it when we won the league but the very next season was that of Aguerooooooooooooooooooo and I chickened out again! Currently I'm saying when we win the Champions League – over to you Pep.

BUT WHY THE GINGER WIG?

It's a simple story of friendship and a mischievous sense of humour. Back in the summer of 1998, the family holiday was to Scotland and a lovely stay just outside Edinburgh. Towards the end of the holiday we went into Edinburgh to buy some gifts to remember the holiday. At the back of one of the souvenir shops was a large selection of wigs and hats. After some tomfoolery trying on various ones, I decided I'd buy the Ginger Wig. With a tartan tam o' shanter, blue bobble and ginger wig it was destined to join the other novelty hats in a box in the loft, alongside such gems as a Scouse wig I'd bought in Southport and an Austrian shepherd's hat (complete with cowbell).

On the eve of the first game of the 1998-99 season the ginger wig was still on my bedroom desk. My mischievous side kicked in and I decided to wear the wig to embarrass my fellow season ticket holding mates. Back then I sat in block BB lower in the Kippax with my two mates. We'd abandoned our Dads and younger brothers who were still sitting in the family stand in the corner of the Platt Lane Stand (or Umbro stand as it had then become). I never got to stand in the Kippax but enjoyed the freedom of the new stand, being able to grab a drink and programme from inside then sitting on the floor behind the stand. I'd love the turnstiles to be moved to the outer fence at the Etihad so we could have the same freedom.

So having got to the game ridiculously early due to my dad's fear of being late, we'd parked up as we always did in the Platt Lane training complex. I took my seat in the Kippax and donned the ginger wig for the first time awaiting my mate's arrival. I still remember the look on their faces as they walked down the steps to our seats and the shaking of their heads after spotting me!

After that first win I've worn it ever since, even trying to embarrass them further on the last games of the season at Maine Road by wearing a kilt and going full 'Brave Heart' with face painted blue and white. We never won the games when I dressed up, such as the last game at Maine Road so I abandoned that tradition when we moved to the Etihad but I kept the Ginger Wig obviously!

I was kind of late getting into social media and joined Twitter at the same time as City started winning trophies. After trying a few Twitter handles with my name and finding they'd been taken, it seemed that no one else was @TheGingerWig. Little did I know then that 10 years later I'd have close to 20 thousand followers! A few years after joining Twitter I started a blog/website focusing on Man City gifts. Having spent time trying to find unique City gifts for my friends and family, I felt there were lots of excellent gifts, but no one place to find them all.

Originally the blog looked just at this but grew to look at City kits as well as interviewing City authors and artists. This is how I first had contact with Don Price when I interviewed him after his first book – A football fans story! The site grew and now we sell City related gifts, working with artists to create City prints, t-shirts, mugs and coasters as well as designing hats, socks and badges based on past kits and iconic City moments. We sell online (thegingerwigscitygifts.com) as well as artisan markets around Manchester. At the markets I often get asked "where's the Ginger Wig" while the lack of a Scottish accent surprises a few who've seen me at games and on Twitter. Social media such as Twitter, Instagram and Facebook are great for finding and showcasing work that wouldn't normally make it into mainstream media. There are some fantastic football artists and authors out there.

But there is one thing I'd like to clear up. Many times, on Social media, people have tagged me into a video of the play off semi-final home leg against Wigan in 1999. Often on the anniversary my notifications will suddenly go mad as an account has posted the video. On that great day the Goat bundled the ball into the net, setting up the Gillingham Final allowing Dickov to score that goal at Wembley.

I was there at Maine Road against Wigan, sat in the same seat that I'd watched that first game against Blackpool. I was wearing the ginger wig as I had throughout that promotion winning season and would wear it to Wembley for the Gillingham game. However, I didn't go onto the pitch that night against Wigan. I was living away at University during that season. One of the reasons I'd chosen the university was that there was a direct train line back to Manchester that avoided the Pennines in case of snow! I'd caught the train to Manchester the day of the Wigan game and had to dash to the train station to get the last train back to my Uni digs. So, I didn't get to enjoy the celebrations on the pitch and the gentleman in the video who was wearing a tam o'shanter is *not* me. His ginger wig was a much redder tartan than mine. Plus, he was probably older then than I am now yet people still think it's me! I can categorically say that it isn't me running onto the pitch and kissing Gerard Weikens!

THE END OF THE GINGER WIG?

As I said the Ginger Wig is getting a bit thin and I tend to only wear it inside the ground now to protect it from the Manchester weather. Will I throw it on to the pitch when we win the Champions League? We'll have to wait and see, hopefully that's not too long off. Here's to the next 20 years of the Ginger Wig and winning trophies. I hope to see you at the games or at the markets – just don't expect me to have a Scottish accent!

Anthony Rawson

15: heed over heels with city

MY NAME IS Craig 'The Heed' Simpson, a proud Scotsman, born in March 1960, and I grew up on the huge Wester Hailes estate on the outskirts of Edinburgh. Life certainly wasn't easy surrounded by a concrete jungle of tower blocks. We all came from the hard school of knocks, but my mates were the salt of the earth, and whilst we might have got ourselves in bother from time to time, we were good kids. Of course, the majority of my pals were Hibs or Hearts, with Rangers and Celtic thrown in for good measure, my heart was with the green and white hoops of Celtic, spurred on by The Lisbon Lions, as the Bhoys became the first British side ever to lift the European Cup. In common with English fans living south of the border, most of us picked a second English club at school, in role reversal which in my case was Everton FC.

But a holiday to Benidorm in 1984 was to change all that forever, let me explain. A group of us did what most lads in their late teens did, a couple of weeks in of sea, sun, plenty of Sangria, and a future wife if you were lucky! We'd found a local bar that we liked and were in one evening when I noticed a group of English lads gathered close by us. Putting all the Scotland/England rivalries to one side, I got talking to them, and they seemed just like us, 'happy go lucky' lads who were immediately welcoming. Two lads in particular, John Wilkinson ('Wilky' as he is known to Blues far and wide, and another lad by the name of Sean Riley). We got on really well, both groups of lads, there was loads of banter, they couldn't understand what we were saying half the time, and we couldn't understand them either but one thing I knew even then, within an hour of meeting them, I knew I'd be friends for life with these guys. As for the football, well they were from the Manchester area, and even then, it didn't surprise me when I found out the vast majority of them were City fans, with a couple of reds amongst their ranks. Even the slight sense of disappointment when I found out their second club (England lads tended to pick a Scottish team of course) was Glasgow Rangers, soon paled into insignificance. They showed me nothing but respect, the banter was brilliant, and we had the holiday of a lifetime. Of course, there were no mobile phones back then, and I pleaded with my pals to cut short a Medieval Night we were attending so we could say 'see you' to our English pals. We did, and saw them off, but nobody thought to exchange telephone numbers!

Back home I remembered the lads drank in their local pub called the Boat and Horses, so I went to the BT Centre in Edinburgh and searched the Yellow Pages for pubs with that name, and eventually I found one listed in Greater Manchester. I made a note of the number and rang from the telephone box soon after. I asked the nice lady who answered if she could help, and she said she would try, I asked if she knew a lad by the name of Sean Riley (Sean's name was easier to remember!) and to my surprise and delight she did! I duly left my contact details with her, and Sean got in touch, and a trip down to Manchester was arranged in November of that year. I'd arrived on the Friday night, and stayed at Sean's house, his mam kept asking me why do I keep asking for 'Ken' whenever she heard me say 'ye ken' (Scottish for 'know). I felt so welcome and part of my extend family of Sassenachs!

Saturday at 3pm back then was the match day ritual, wherever you lived in Britain, and this was no different. My English pals were off to Maine Road to watch City play Birmingham City, and despite City being in the second division, a healthy crowd of over 25,000 still turned up, City were managed by former Celtic player and manager, the legendary Billy McNeill, which gave me an added interest, although at this point, I have to stress I had no inkling of what was going to happen next. I entered the large gloomy covered terrace, affectionately known as the Kippax. It was huge, and it stretched the complete length of the pitch. I followed Sean, Wilky and their mates to the spot where they stood religiously every other Saturday, they explained they all had their own little bit of concrete step which is where they stood, others could join them but would need to shove up; their spot, was their spot! The thing that grabbed me, more than the fact City won the game 1-0 (David Phillips), was the atmosphere and camaraderie of the thousands of die-hard fans gathered around me. I was introduced by Sean and Wilky to other City fans and they were all genuinely delighted I'd come to the game to lend some support. The fans I spoke to were at pains to say that whilst the football was incidental at best, their support for the Blue side of Manchester was unconditional, a love of hopeless causes perhaps, but nonetheless it was *their* cause, and I quickly realised that after one game, watching a Club who played their home games 250 miles away from where I lived, in another country, it just felt so right, so natural, to want to became part of the very same cause… I felt an attachment and connection to Manchester City Football Club, forget the fact I'd just seen a second division match between two big clubs who had fallen on hard times, I'd traded in my green and white hoops for the sky blue of City and that afternoon spent in Moss Side had changed my life, as well as my football allegiance.

We kept in touch by landline and writing letters to each other, and Sean and Wilky came up to Edinburgh, once even by complete surprise, they just turned up the at the Longstone pub on our estate one Friday night but as is normal in life we didn't keep up contact, as most of us moved on with our lives got married and had children, It's just how it goes, and of course, a couple of years, became 5 years, then a decade, a house move or two included no doubt, and we'd lost contact for good, or so I thought. The advent of social media and Facebook in particular soon changed all that. A few years ago I was on Facebook one night – and something just clicked, I wonder if my long-lost mates in England were on Facebook too? Surely, they would be, and to my delight, I found Sean Riley –messaged him and he got back in touch!

So me and my Hibs/Man City pal Derek made the pilgrimage back down to Manchester, although watching City now playing at the Etihad, and being successful, was something I'd never expected or anticipated. By now I had no fewer than 5 City tattoos, to only

1 of Celtic. And then of course it happened, I saw the Champions League draw live on TV, and City were only drawn against my first love Celtic in the group stages! They would of course play each other twice, and I immediately thought 'what the hell do I do here…?' So, I phoned up Mr. Riley and asked him, he would have some sound advice! He said 'Craig, Celtic is your first love, and City is like a love affair' which didn't help me at all! Tickets were scarce for both matches, so I watched both in the privacy of my own home. I was shouting "c'mon the 'Tic", and then the other half of me was saying 'C'mon City!' It would be fair to say my thoughts were torn right down the middle. I had a split personality for 180 minutes, and I now think I know what it's like to be schizophrenic! But in the end I realised I could not win and I could not lose. Both games of course ended in honourable draws, and for me personally, that was the best outcome. I was neither sad nor happy about the results, but I was relieved I hadn't been forced to choose.

The final part of my City story relates to the Manchester Derby played at the Etihad towards the end of the 2017/18 season. We thought we had absolutely no chance of tickets for the game, and when it became clear City could win the league by beating them on the day, the already inflated prices for tickets went through the roof! Unbeknown to me Sean's better half Jane (I call her the Princess of Manchester, and I mean it!) had purchased a couple of additional tickets months in advance, and when she rang me to say 'you're going to the game!' I couldn't actually take in what she was telling me. Not only were me 'n ma son Jordan (Hearts/Man City) and my pal Derek attending our first ever Manchester Derby but we could actually win the Premiership by beating them! We flew down to Manchester the night before, well we drove, but you get ma drift. Mr. Riley said to me, 'just think Craig, if we win the league against them, you can take it to your grave…!' (nothing is ever guaranteed in football, or life, for that matter, as I was about to find out, on both counts!).

In the pre-match build up, we were interviewed by the Match of the Day TV team, they tried to trick us into saying today was a nailed-on win for City but all of us are far too old in the tooth for falling for that one! I'd actually not felt well all day and getting up to the third tier to take up my prized seat took a major effort, I was sweating profusely, and out of breath far more than I'd normally have been. Any concern about my well-being was easily forgotten as City stormed into a 2-0 first half lead, and if truth be known, we should have been at least 4 up and home and dry. That second 45 minutes saw the arch enemy somehow find a way to come back from the dead, to deny us, no one dared say it, but everyone was thinking it – 'Typical City' snatching defeat from the jaws of victory. It was a bitter pill to swallow, and the sight of seeing their fans celebrating pissing on our parade just added to it, but the reality was we were still going to win the league.

We said our goodbyes and travelled back up North, and the illness I had felt earlier had come back with a vengeance, as I went through the front door of our house, I collapsed, and the next thing I knew I was waking up lying in a bed in an Edinburgh hospital. I'd suffered a major heart attack and required stents fitting. Now how many times have we all said jokingly watching City will give me a heart attack? It was a shocker though when it happened. When the doctors spoke to me when I was well enough, they asked if stress had contributed. I told them too bloody right and that I'd been to the Manchester Derby (they soon worked out I was a City fan!) and I can vividly remember cursing Raheem Sterling for missing two sitters! (no offence Raheem, I know you've got to be there in the first place to miss em...!). Thankfully I'm now back at work, and I still get down to see my best English pals and take in City games whenever I can – 'fresh air, not armchair' – that's our motto!

Craig Simpson

16: typical city

WE FIRST CAME ACROSS Don in the 1990's when he attended City games with his sons, and sometimes wife Cath, in the Umbro/Platt Lane family stand at Maine Road., sitting next to Sue and Alex, our youngest, who was about seven at the time. He appeared at games with a beer bottle in each top pocket which made a big impression on Alex and Don confided to Sue that he was unimpressed with the official City supporters club in Prestwich, and was thinking of starting one up himself. "Just a few mates round, game of darts and dominoes, and chat about City." Wow, credit to Don he and 'his mates' developed it into a tremendous club with great meetings, and guests, which helped to keep Blues' spirits up during the dark times.

Don has now produced this, his third book, in conjunction with Sean, and he asked me to do some proof reading, plus 'requesting' me to contribute an article.

I left off in Don's last book, *'We Never Win At Home, We Never Win Away'*, at virtually the time of the takeover, saying that "the rest is history". That is true of course, and the last ten years or so are quite fresh in the memories of most Blues. However, I cast my mind back to September 2008, and a group of us, including ex City full back Bill Leivers and his son Glyn, were doing a TV interview about the takeover, outside the City store.

"Even City can't cock this one up" I said.

"Bring on the trophies" Glyn said.

But I have to admit, after years of 'Typical City', I wasn't totally convinced. This was compounded by Paul Wilson reporting in *The Observer* saying something like "it's in City's DNA, and that mentality will have to change if they're to be successful". He had a point. Of course all the crap came out from various quarters, "Sunderland spent money but went down" spouted Alex Ferguson,

(Sunderland went down in 1958, 50 years ago and not too relevant in 2008!) and "the trouble is when you've got money you can spend it willy, nilly". And all that 'noisy neighbours' stuff. Amongst other jibes, were of course "you can't buy success", "you're just a team of mercenaries, players have only signed because of the money". "You're a bunch of individuals, not a team", and from Ian Holloway "City have no history". Plus this absolute classic from Michael Calvin – "It's a pantomime at City, they signed David Silva instead of David Villa" (We actually signed Villa later but for New York City) and of course, the woman in the pub. You know the type, she's the one who's been banned from other pubs for fighting. Gets up on karaoke wearing a Man United baseball cap and changes the words of songs to glorify her love of United, even though she's probably never been to the Swamp. "They'll still win nothin'" she tells everyone within earshot. "Gob on a stick" Tony the Blue, confides to me. But you wondered and hoped. By the way, the 'lady' in question, has now moved with her long suffering hubby to Scarborough, and the pub is now an Indian restaurant. Damn. But was it all bad?

Since our formation in 1880, sorry 1894, as Manchester City, we've had our moments; good and bad, the good is generally glossed over. Into Division 2 in 1892 as Ardwick, promoted in 1899, relegated in 1902, promoted in 1903.

Typical!

In 1904 we were the first team in Manchester to win the FA Cup and were runners up in the league, we were then made scapegoats for paying players Illegally, as most clubs did, and half our team were snapped up by the rags who then won a few trophies. Of course they don't count as that was with a joint City/United team. Well my theory anyway.

Typical!

We recovered from that setback but were relegated in 1909, quickly bouncing back in 1910.

Typical!

A few seasons later, in 1915, United and Liverpool fixed a match so that a draw would keep United in Division 1, but after investigation, the verdict was 'no punishment'. That set the trend for the two clubs over the years, so no more on them.

Typical!

After the war years of 1914 to 1918, we were runners up to Burnley in 1921. In 1923 we moved from Hyde Road to Maine Road, a 90,000 capacity venue, the biggest and best in the country outside Wembley.

Typical!

Then in 1926, we reached the FA Cup final beating Palace 11-4 in the 5th round, United 3-0 in the semi-final, but lost 1-0 to Bolton and were relegated, despite registering our first 6-1 win at the Swamp - the only team to reach the Final and be relegated until... 1969.

Typical!

In 1933 we reached the Final again wearing numbered shirts, 12 to 22, losing to a Dixie Dean led Everton, but returned the following year, as predicted by captain Sam Barkas, to lift the trophy against Portsmouth. On the way, to the Final, after 30 years without a trophy, City attracted a crowd of 84,569 to Maine Road, sure there were a few Stokies there but it remains the highest attendance at any ground outside Wembley.

Typical!

Further success followed as City lifted the title in 1937, despite only winning 3 of the first 14 games, and losing 5-3 at Grimsby at Christmas. We were then unbeaten until the end of the season as United were relegated and we weren't very gracious about it. However City were relegated the following season, the only Champions ever to do so, despite scoring more goals than Champions Arsenal and having a positive goal difference/average.

Meanwhile United were promoted.

Typical!

After the war, during which Old Trafford was bombed, City were in Division 2 and United were in Division 1 (who had a better team), and despite United not allowing City to use O/T in 1922 when the Hyde Road Main Stand was burned down, City allowed United to ground share at Maine Road. The theory is that United took advantage and fans defected from blue to red, and their gates increased. The fact that we pissed off our greatest player, Peter Doherty, who was transferred to Derby County, may have also had something to do with it!

Typical!

We were soon promoted in 1947, went down a season later, signed an ex prisoner of war, Bert Trautmann, which didn't go down well initially with some of our support so soon after the war. However, Bert soon won the hearts of City and football fans nationwide, with heroic performances and helped to improve Anglo-German relations to became a legend. We regained our rightful place in Division 1 in 1951.

Typical!

In 1953 we erected floodlights, ahead of the game there, and in 1955 reached the FA Cup Final as hot favourites with the Revie Plan against Newcastle United, who'd scraped past 3rd division York City (the Minster Marvels) after a replay. We lost 3-1, their opener was the quickest Cup Final goal (45 seconds) for many years, and City were down to ten men for most of the game. We entered the field in snazzy tracksuits setting the trend for future style and class. 'The Don' was named Footballer of the Year.

Typical!

That was Newcastle's last domestic trophy, their 3rd cup win in the 50's, and they've won only the Inter Cities cup in 1969 since. City played that Final in the beautiful sky blue colours which inspired Coventry's future Chairman to adopt when he took over at Highfield Road, and check out how many teams have adopted the colours as their second strip. England even wearing it when they won the cricket World Cup in 2019.

Typical!

Naturally, we returned the following season, as Roy Paul predicted, to lift the trophy 3-1 against the hot favourites, 'The Iron Men of the Midlands, Birmingham City'. We did it playing an out of favour forward, Don Revie, an inside forward with his dicky knee strapped up, Bobby Johnstone, and a goalie who played the last 15 minutes with a broken neck! Bert was named Footballer of the Year.

Typical!

We then benevolently allowed United to play European games under our floodlights, as they hadn't yet cottoned on, so we probably lost a few more fans to them. When the Kippax was roofed we had covered accommodation for 50,000, which no other club could match. Then we went into decline, but we both scored and conceded a century of goals in 1957/58, the only club to do so.

Typical!

In March 1960 we paid a record fee of £53,000 for Denis Law and in 1961 beat Luton 6-2 away in the 4th round of the Cup, Denis scoring all six goals, but the referee abandoned the game with 20 minutes to go and we lost the replay 3-1!

Typical!

There was another City moment in 1962 when we beat high flying Tottenham Hotspur 6-2 at Maine Road in the snow, with people phoning the MEN offices to enquire if they'd printed the score the wrong way round.

Typical!

Relegation came as almost a relief in 1963, after 6-1 defeats home and away to West Ham following a home game with United when Denis Law (now with United) kicked Harry Dowd in the head and the ref gave them a penalty to allow them to draw the game and stay up. We had a centre forward Alex Harley who scored over 30 goals in that season, becoming the first 'King of the Kippax'.

Typical!

There was no quick return this time, with crowds down to around 8,000, and a Cup exit to Shrewsbury, though we reached the League Cup semi, losing to First Division Stoke over two legs, City, unlike others, taking the competition seriously.

Typical!

With the introduction of Joe and Malcolm we bounced back in 1966, and lifted the title in 1968 when half the team had been part of the relegated 1963 team. Malcolm announced that we'd "Terrify Europe", but, we went out in the first round of the European Cup to unfancied Fenerbahce.

Typical!

Nevertheless we lifted the FA Cup, then the League Cup and the European Cup Winners' Cup (first team to win a domestic and European trophy in the same season!) in the following few seasons, erasing the 'Typical City' tag, but taking on that of 'Cups for Cock Ups', strangely.

Typical!

In the 70's we were one of the first clubs to install under soil heating, Tony Book was named Footballer of the Year, jointly with Dave Mackay. We turned down first dibs on Ian Rush from Chester. We lost the League Cup final 2-1 against Wolves with a forward line including Bell, Lee, Summerbee, Marsh and Law, but returned in 1976 to lift the Cup in a 2-1 win against Newcastle, some revenge for 1955.

Typical!

After finishing 1977 as runners up to Liverpool, Peter Swales was persuaded to bring back Malcolm Allison by the love struck directors. Unfortunately Malc had, as Swales later put it "lived a little in the meantime" ('glamour model' Fiona Richmond especially coming to mind, lucky bugger!). The team was decimated, and fortunes were spent on players who weren't up to it. Despite an upturn under John Bond, losing the Cup final in a replay after Tommy Hutchison had scored for both teams in the first game, we lost the replay 3-2, and Ricky Villa's goal has been featured at virtually every Spurs home game v City since then.

Typical!

The 80's gave us relegation in 1983 when a draw at home to Luton would have saved us, promotion on the last day of 1985, 5-1 against Charlton, on the day of the Bradford fire, 5-4 loss in the Full Members' Cup Final v Chelsea, 10-1 win v Huddersfield losing the return 1-0. Relegation in 1987 at West Ham, then promotion in 1989 on the last day at Bradford, after a 3-0 half time lead the week before at home to Bournemouth was squandered to a 97th minute penalty. City fans embracing fancy dress and the banana inflatables during the season. We then registered the 5-1 win over 'Fergie's wallets'. Machin went and Kendall took over.

Typical!

The 90's were looking promising, but Kendall left and Peter Reid took over. We finished 5th, 5th and 9th, but lost to Spurs in the 6th round of the Cup at Maine Road, when City fans sadly invaded the pitch. Horton took over from Reid, Swales was eventually ousted, Franny Lee took over but we went from bad to worse, Horton was sacked, which he found out via the media, and we were finally relegated in 1996 under Alan Ball on the last day, at home to Liverpool when he thought a draw would do. We needed a win.

Typical!

After having five managers in one season, Frank Clark was replaced by Joe Royle, but we went down again in 1998 to the third tier. Not to worry though, as crowds maintained at around 28,000, and we came up in the play-offs against Gillingham, City fans were unfazed by the rags' treble singing "you can stick your f*cking treble up your arse" which made me feel proud. Unfortunately Maine Road's development wasn't forward thinking and capacity was reduced to 35,000 with a couple of temporary 'Gene Kelly, singin' in the rain' type stands having to be erected in the corners.

Typical!

We then went up again at Blackburn, but were relegated in 2001. Keegan came in and promotion was sealed. City took advantage of the Commonwealth Games and moved to the 48,000 capacity City Of Manchester Stadium in 2003 after 80 years at Maine Road. Pearce took over, then it was Shinawatra, and Sven. In 2008 we doubled the rags, winning 2-1 at the Swamp in the Munich memorial game, but lost 8-1 at 'Boro on the last day of the season, though we scraped into Europe on the back of the Fair Play League as we couldn't tackle. Sven was sacked and Mark Hughes came in.

Typical!

So there you go. What had we achieved before the Sheikh came in, during that fateful summer of 2008? Well we hadn't won the League for 40 years, the FA Cup for 39 years, a European trophy for 38 years, or the League Cup for 32 years We hadn't even managed a semi-final since 1981 (discounting the Full Members Cup) when we reached two.

So was 'Typical City' still in our DNA, succinctly put by a Stoke fan before the 2011 Cup Final as "underdogs, often beaten by underdogs"? We had a lot of catching up to do, as the big 4 had streaked away with the Premier League money, and Champions League benefits. But could we cast off our Typical City title?

We were making steady progress, tempted Carlos Tevez over from United, compounded with the famous 'Welcome to Manchester' poster (*wish we'd thought of that*) and went head to head with the rags, signing top players, had a set back when we couldn't beat Spurs in 2009 at home to play in the Champions League, having a film, 'Blue Moon Rising' made, commented on by rags "I see you've made a film about finishing 5th!"

The breakthrough finally happened in 2011, United were defeated in the Cup semi, and Stoke in the Final to take down the bitter, club supported rag banner at the Swamp. Saddos. United were then beaten 6-1 at the Swamp, and we dared to dream. We lost to them in the FA Cup 3rd round but had a 'Typical City' moment winning 3-2 over QPR when all looked lost with minutes to go. We were Champions and finally established as a top club again.

We went on to win the title another 3 times, the League Cup 4 times, and the FA Cup once again, plus 3 Community Shields. Raheem Sterling even winning Player of the Year, in 2019.

We've not been without '**Typical City**' moments though. Gary Cook's gaffes, sad Cup exits, the sacking of Mark Hughes on the day of the game against Sunderland which we won 4-3. The firing of Mancini on Cup final day when we lost to Wigan, who hadn't even scored a goal against us in seven previous defeats, and who became the first team to win the Cup and be relegated in the same season. We announced that Pep would be coming whilst Pellegrini was still in charge, losing to Wigan home and away in the Cup, and to the rags 3-2 at home after being 2-0 up but having to wait only a week longer to lift the title in 2018.

The Etihad was host to the UEFA Cup Final in 2008 between Zenit St Petersburg and Rangers, then expanded in 2015, to take the capacity up to 55,000, with future plans to extend the North stand to increase it to 63,000. We've acquired clubs in Australia, USA, China, France, Uruguay, Spain and Japan plus we're gaining fans from all over the globe. We also have a very successful women's team, and our owners, the best in the business, have invested in the Etihad Campus and in the infrastructure.

However there is a slight downside, Points of Blue has been replaced with City Matters, and I don't believe the club are engaging properly with fans. And now we've just won the domestic treble, showing tremendous resilience and have beaten Liverpool in the Community Shield on penalties after 1-1. So is this the new Typical City? Your shout!

As far as the fanzine goes, it's given us some great front covers. We've gone from joking about the 3rd tier trophy in 1999, to winning proper trophies, with surely the European Cup to come. UEFA have brought in the ludicrous Financial Fair Play farce to try and curtail City's progress but we are still progressing, and indeed are now financially self-sufficient.

Sadly the media has plumbed new depths, and have gone from "you can't buy success" to "City have bought success", even though recently United have outbid us for Berbatov, Van Persie, Sanchez, Fred and Maguire. Liverpool have also paid out record fees for Van Dijk and Alisson.

The amount of media coverage for Liverpool and United and the level of anti-City reporting has reached epic proportions, and personally I find it quite sad that a club who've been a laughing stock, and in the shadows of the most obnoxious neighbours in world football, (though Liverpool have now taken over) for years, are not being given the credit we deserve, as we fans enjoy our current place in the sun. The club, however, seem unperturbed.

Media wise, we are still in the frame, being interviewed recently for the French newspaper *L'Equipe* on the possible effects of Brexit on City and football. We've also had a German film crew round to view and video my Bert Trautmann collection and to sample the atmosphere of our Cup match at Swansea on TV at the local Astley and Tyldesley supporters club, to inform German fans of the passion of City's support as the film 'The Keeper' is released over there.

Onwards and upwards, in Pep we trust.

Dave Wallace

SEAN RILEY

prologue

MY NAME IS Sean Riley, not Sam Tyler and this isn't the unmissable TV drama 'Ashes to Ashes' but I want to take you back to 1981 - Saturday 7th March to be precise. It was a special day for any teenager, my sixteenth birthday but it was also an equally important day for my team Manchester City who had a tasty FA Cup quarter-final at Goodison Park.

At that time the FA Cup really meant something to all clubs, big or small, rich or poor, famous or unheard of. It was widely regarded as the most famous domestic cup competition in world football and that day was no exception. The game attracted an all-ticket 54,000 sell out crowd to Goodison with 13,000 City fans (Johnny Bond's Blue and White army!) making the short trip down the East Lancs. Despite the large allocation, tickets were at a premium. As a birthday treat my dad had organised for me to go to the match with his pals. I'd started going to some away games with mates, and I'd even travelled away on my own but I was well aware of the hatred that existed between Manchester and Merseyside; regardless of whether you were a fan of either the blue or red sides of either city, a trip to the other city was like running the gauntlet with feral youths ready to pick off stray fans upon hearing the wrong accent.

I knew the scouse Perry Boys would be ready and waiting; they were instantly recognisable with their flick hairstyles, brightly coloured V-neck jumpers, cords and Pod shoes. They also had a reputation for carrying Stanley knives and weren't afraid to use them on visiting fans either.

However any worries I may have had about my own personal safety were truly brushed aside (just like my hair) as I would be in very good company. The blokes who I affectionately knew as my Uncles Joe, Jimmy, Vinny, Louis and Brian were well-known men around Manchester and Liverpool. The real clue was in their surnames – The Monaghans (aka Swords), Schiavos and Grimshaws. Along with Jimmy Riley (my dad) and others, they were better known as part of the Quality Street Gang, or QSG for short. They were feared and revered in equal measure as a hard group of men. Most of them, my dad included, had been born and bred in the Ancoats district of the city. Like most inner-city districts it was a notoriously deprived area, where large families lived in squalid conditions. Most of these men had literally fought their way out of poverty. Ancoats Lads Boxing Club was where many had plied their trade and some were very good amateurs. By hook or by crook they had made their way in life, and in some cases, their fortunes. The tentacles of the gang spread beyond the streets of Ancoats as exemplified by high profile cases later in the decade that exposed the links between high-ranking people in authority and the Manchester 'underworld' that ended the careers of a few police officers and ended with jail time for a few of dad's mates.

I was blissfully unaware of this as I set off for the trip to Liverpool back in 1981. I was just going to a match with my adopted 'uncles'; my mam and dad's pals, the very same men who were friends with Rock legends Thin Lizzy. The band's lead singer Phil Lynott had penned arguably the band's best ever song 'The Boys are Back In Town' about these men and although I never went to Deano's Bar and Grill, or found out who their subsequent single 'Waiting for An Alibi' was about, the song title which included Jimmy the Weed's name was self-explanatory!

Making the trip to Merseyside were a mixture of Blues and Reds and tensions between the two arose before we even set off. There were two car loads of us ready to leave the New Cross motor vehicle pitch they all jointly owned; The Cheshire Cheese pub and the *Daily Express* Newspaper Printing Plant were directly facing on the opposite side of Oldham Road but we had a problem. Brian Grimshaw, or 'Tag' as he was known to everyone, was far from happy. Why? Because 'one of their own' who was in the same car as me (JT) wasn't of the sky blue persuasion. He was a United fan and his team had already been knocked out of that year's competition in the Fourth Round by European Champions Nottingham Forest. Now, it wasn't unusual for men of their age to watch both Manchester teams, my Uncle John being a case in point, he was a Red but had a season ticket to watch City as well.

Yet despite knowing each other more or less all their lives, Tag simply wasn't having any of it. "I'm not fuckin getting in the car with him", he ranted, "he's a Red!" The rest of the group looked embarrassed, as I watched in bewilderment before saying "Come on Tag there's no need to be like that" as the others tried to restore some order. This simply got Tag's goat up even more, "No! If he doesn't get out of the car, then I'm not getting in, he shouldn't even fucking be here!" And so, to ease the tension, JT got out, tutted, and travelled in the other car, so we could get on our way. The row wasn't mentioned again during the short journey down to Merseyside and it was all but forgotten during a pulsating cup-tie in which City twice clawed their way back from a goal down. Fans favourite Gerry Gow had got us back into the game just before half-time before we went behind again only for a late Paul Power equaliser to make it 2-2. It was a proper cup tie and the tension and atmosphere was unbelievable.

On our way out of the stadium the scenes resembled something out of a Wild West movie. There was absolute carnage on the surrounding streets, except this was for real. Gangs of hooligans from both clubs ran amok and with no club colours on show it was very difficult to work out exactly who was who! Some fans lay battered, bloodied and motionless in the streets as we walked by - it was a sickening sight worthy of a war zone, not a football match. Then something struck me (metaphorically speaking!) - nobody was hassling us nor were they asking us 'have you got the time?' which was a regular stunt pulled by scousers to establish you weren't one of them before they started wading in. Nor were they giving us the dubious advice, "stick by the bizzies Mancs". No, we just walked through this battlefield completely unhassled and unscathed.

Perhaps it was because my companions looked like kind of tough guys you'd see on The Sweeney; leather jackets, turtle neck jumpers, side burns which needed mowing, and boxers hands as big as shovels.

Years later my good pal Wilky told me of the horrors of having to hide in a telephone box while he and his mates pushed their feet up against the door to stop scousers dragging them out and cutting them up. Younger fans who grew up with all-seater stadia will think I'm exaggerating but every weekend was like this. Hooliganism wasn't just rampant, it almost seemed to be part and parcel of the game. God knows how the game survived but survive it did, principally because some people will literally fight for the right to watch their club week in and week out.

This is the story of how I became a City nut. Some people get into football and then wives, girlfriends, children, work commitments or mortgage repayments get in the way but I've been lucky enough to be able to follow the Blues almost every week for the past 45 years.

It's been a blast!

1: sweet suburbia

SO WHERE DID this obsessive, compulsive, lifelong addiction of all things Manchester City begin? Well, I arrived into this world as Sean James Riley, in the early hours of a March Sunday morning back in 1965, the first of three siblings.

My family roots are firmly embedded just to the North side of the City of Manchester. My dad James 'Jimmy' Riley, was an Ancoats lad, while my late mother Shelagh Magdalene nee Carroll (RIP mam), was brought up in neighbouring Collyhurst. After they'd tied the knot I soon came along but there was to be no poverty stricken, cramped, slum like up bringing for me to endure, as my parents had managed to scrimp enough together to escape the inner city so I was fortunate enough to spend my formative years in a small but pleasant semi-detached dwelling in Kew Road, Failsworth. Despite having an M35 postcode, the town comes under the jurisdiction of the neighbouring district of Oldham, hence the reason my mam was taken to Boundary Park Hospital and not St. Mary's for my birth. Nobody attached any significance to where you were born and who you 'should' support based on what it said on your birth certificate back then, besides which, in my case, it is an undisputed fact I was made by two Mancunians!

A few hours before I took those first gasps of fresh Lancashire air, it had been very much business as usual around the country with a full schedule of football fixtures with it being a spring weekend. Every game kicked off at 3pm back then of course. One of these games took place in Moss Side, a tough inner City suburb of South Manchester, attended by a sparse crowd of just over 14,000 hardy souls dotted around a vast stadium with a capacity of 63,000, the ground we all knew and loved as Maine Road. Manchester's first club by that name had fallen on hard times and City, then in the old Second Division, having just drawn 1-1 against Middlesbrough.

Don't Look Back In Anger

England would win the World Cup in 1966 of course, but football wasn't really on the agenda in our household, besides which, I was far too young to take in this momentous occasion. Similarly the great trophy winning City sides of the late 1960's didn't have any impact on our family; my dad was busy building his scrap metal empire with his brother John in Miles Platting, while mam was busy bring up all three of us; my sister Sharon and brother Martin had also arrived on the scene by 1968.

It wouldn't be until 1970, and two house moves later, that I can trace the beginning of my insatiable passion for 'the beautiful game'. That summer the World Cup was staged in Mexico and a series of World Cup Coins were released by Esso petrol stations nationwide to celebrate the competition and of course England's participation in it as defending champions. Just down the road from where we lived was a Citax garage and petrol station, now why on earth would a group of 5 year-old kids have such an interest in a place which sold fuel? I'll explain - any family fortunate enough to have owned a car (plenty didn't back then!) would go and fill up there. I remember the tank would take a fiver's worth filled up to the brim and that used to last us two weeks! Upon paying for the fuel, the attendant would hand the purchaser a coin or two if you were lucky and it was these coins we wanted to collect. Me and my oldest living pal, Bradley 'Brad' Powell (from the red side of the city) would, with the older kids, harangue the station's staff and beg for coins, sometimes off complete strangers who'd inadvertently qualified for one by filling up. Colin Bell was one of the coins everyone wanted, fellow City players Francis Lee and Alan Oakes (who subsequently didn't make it when England named their 22 man squad for Mexico) made up the trio of City stars, but there were a good mix of players from what seemed like every club in Division 1.

Like any addictive pastime, the passion had started and next up was primary school, where the main interests among us boys was Lego and Meccano sets and of course football cards. These were sold in packets (5 cards per pack) at the local shops, for a couple of pence a packet. The wrapper would gently peel off to reveal orange backed football cards and a stick of bubble gum. There were 219 to collect in total, and the set included cards for 11 City players, including two keepers Corrigan and Healey, which always baffled me as a child - we can't play two keepers in the same team, surely? They were given to me by our two baby sitters (the Pritchard family from Moston), all of whom were staunch Blues. Some of the pictures gave you a tantalising glimpse of the football ground, stands and floodlights behind them and so I was hooked and that's how, quite simply, I became a City fan!

All of us wanted the cards of the top teams; Leeds and Liverpool were highly collectable because they were the teams who were winning leagues and cups, while Jim Barron, the Notts Forest goalkeeper, was a hard one to get. I had managed to acquire him in my set, the card was creased to hell, but I didn't care, I had him, and that was all that mattered. There was even a card (only one of two) of a recently relegated Huddersfield player with the wonderful name of Dick Krizwicky, probably the first Polish sounding name I'd ever heard of wearing a black top. What kit was that I wondered? There was a Newcastle player with the unusual name of 'Ollie' Burton, the purple sky behind Derby County's Alan Durban always fascinated me, was it real? But when I found out there were not one but two Roger Morgans of Tottenham Hotspur I thought, how could this be? Two different pictures of the same player with the same catalogue number from the same set. I just had to own both of these cards! I did in the end, I'd have gladly swapped or traded in my somewhat underwhelming life savings of £3 (premium bonds in my name from birth) to get the ultra rare version of him but I got it and even now, as I type, I can still remember that feeling I had back then of wanting the full set of cards so badly it hurt.

My persistence paid off, I was proud as punch on the school playground, a carrot top kid I was the only one to have them all and I knew it was such a privilege. I lost count how many of the chewing gums inside each pack of card I'd gone through in the process but I do know my milk teeth weren't cut out for the constant intake of sugar, and every kid in our class who collected them had more gaps than teeth each time they smiled. Seeing the packed crowds on the TV during the early 70's drew me in even more. I was fascinated by all those heads in the swaying crowds showing masses of people. So much so that the inside cover of our Monopoly became my sketch pad, I'd gone into a Lowry mode of sorts and I started drawing loads of tiny circles with a blue biro. The circles denoted the heads of fans, City fans. Now to even things up a bit, I also acquired a red biro, to put some heads in of United fans but I made sure the vast majority of fans were blue, and tried to portray the image of this small pocket of United fans being surrounded by hordes of Blues – this was a Manchester Derby picture, probably worth a fortune now and it was on City territory!

2: *total football in troubled times*

MY FIRST MEMORY of watching sport of any description on the telly was the ill-fated Munich Olympic Games in 1972. It was supposed to be a huge spectacle of sporting excellence, watching the World's finest athletes compete in many different types of events, although sadly the sack race, something I excelled in at school, didn't feature. The names of Mark Spitz, the great American swimmer, and David Emery, the English long distance runner, are names which roll off the tongue. Unfortunately my abiding memory will always be that of murderous men clad in black with guns clambering around the chalets occupied by competitors and shooting to kill. It was absolutely shocking, the sombre voice of sports commentator David Coleman having to report the loss of life to watching millions followed by the news doing exactly the same. What with this, the Northern Ireland conflict, the miners strikes and the three day week which meant we had to live by candle light for periods because we had no electricity, well it wasn't a pleasant time!

The following year I turned 8 years old and I can vividly remember watching live televised games for the first time. The FA Cup Final was a traditional must watch event for households everywhere, even if your team wasn't competing in it. The mighty Leeds United were facing Second Division Sunderland in a clash billed as David versus Goliath but the highly unfancied Wearsiders had already taken the prize scalp of my very recently adopted Manchester City, after a replay, in the 5th round. Incidentally, both those games attracted in excess of 50,000 fans (the return game at Roker Park was subsequently voted the best ever seen at this famous former old ground by Sunderland supporters), but the Wearsiders had also gone on to beat cup kings Arsenal (winners in 1971 and finalists in 1972) in the semi final too.

Don't Look Back In Anger

The Leeds team was packed full of internationals, most of them household names. Don Revie's men were feared and grudgingly admired with I couldn't name a single player in Sunderland's team, in fact the first time I had heard of most of them was when the team line up was shown during the warm up in the days when type setting and image didn't really matter, it was as though someone had gone up to your telly and scribbled their names down! But if you ask me now, the names of a few, in fact nearly all of that victorious Sunderland team, immediately spring to mind, in particular. Of course there were future Blues Dennis Tueart (King of all Geordies!) Dave Watson (still the finest centre half I have ever seen play for City and England) and Micky Horswill who all moved to City from Sunderland within a season or so of the final.

The question is: why was this game so memorable, apart of course from the shock result? Well, I could scarcely believe my eyes as one of the most magical moments ever seen under those famous old twin towers. Sunderland had taken the lead in the first half but as the game went on Leeds hemmed the Wearsiders into their own half. It was at this point that Sunderland goalkeeper Jim Montgomery wrote himself into football folklore forever with a double save that defied the odds. If you haven't seen it, I implore you to stop reading and google it now but don't worry if you can't, I'll try to explain what happened next. A cross came in from Leeds full back Paul Reaney and he dived acrobatically to stop a diving header in the six yard box by Trevor Cherry but as the ball landed at the feet of Leeds hotshot Peter Lorimer (famous at the time for possessing the fastest shot in football) an equaliser looked certain when Montgomery, seemingly stricken on the floor, managed to leap and palm the ball up on to the crossbar, to the amazement of commentator Brian Moore, the Wembley crowd and the millions watching around the country. You just knew then that Sunderland's name was written on the trophy and it just wasn't going to be Leeds' day.

At the final whistle Sunderland manager Bob Stokoe, complete with bright red tracksuit bottoms, a cream coat and trilby hat, came galloping on to the pitch like a pantomime horse who had trained for this moment all his life, to hug the goal scorer and his goalkeeper. Stokoe was another exiled Geordie, now an honorary Mackem for life, with possibly the finest moment Wembley had seen in its 50 year history. I just loved everything about the day and the occasion. Even the classic kits worn by both sides added something, Umbro (the trade name of the Humphrey Brothers, who began their sportswear business in Wilmslow, near Manchester) had their branded diamond logo proudly stitched on their jerseys, with each clubs initials woven in to the shirt where the club badge would normally be. Former City player Don Revie's mighty Leeds had been humbled and everyone (apart from Leeds and Newcastle fans obviously) were genuinely pleased that Sunderland, the undoubted underdogs, had had their day.

With the long summer holidays to look forward to it was a combination of football, cricket and tennis which would keep us occupied until dusk, our parents simply never saw us from after breakfast until teatime, happy days indeed. The following season (1973-74) was to prove the real beginning of my 45 year football journey. Little did I know the impact this year of football would have, not only in Manchester but to English football as a whole.

It was a certain World Cup Qualifier which grabbed the attention of the nation. The game in question, England versus Poland played at Wembley, on the evening of 17th October 1973. Live football was a rarity when we were kids, and was normally restricted to the FA Cup Final, England v Scotland in the Home International Championships, and the odd England Qualifier where public interest was extremely high. Well the games didn't get much bigger than this one - England had to win to qualify for the World Cup Finals being held in West Germany a few months later, anything less than that meant the unthinkable, and I don't think anybody really thought England would fail to qualify. I was like any other football mad kid, and was desperate to watch the game, but it wasn't that straight forward, as the rest of my family were not really football orientated (okay my mam had been to Old Trafford when she was a teenager, but that was only because her and her friends fancied the players). The biggest problem was convincing everyone else to miss whatever was on the other side so I could get my fix of football. Fortunately, after much persuasion, I was allowed to watch and I perched on a chair close to the telly. ITV was showing the game, and while Hugh Johns wasn't the most well known commentator at the time, he certainly had a unique style which I was more than comfortable with. Brian Moore had been promoted to the match analysis team in the studio overlooking the Wembley pitch with the one and only Brian Clough and Wolves player Derek Dougan among the guests. The playing of the National Anthems, both teams lined up as though they were ready to meet their final fate at the hands of a firing squad, it all just added to the intensity of the occasion. Again, going back to the kits worn by the teams that night, it was the classic retro look. The England shirt; pure white with a round neck cotton shirt, a large shield sewn on the breast bearing the three lions, navy blue shorts and white socks with the number on each shirt emblazoned in red on the back. Simplicity and style personified, we looked the part. After all the build up, our national team had 90 minutes to deliver the victory to an expectant nation. A capacity 100,000 crowd packed into the famous old stadium, with millions more tuning in. What do I remember of the game then? Well, as you would expect, I can't recall every detail, but I do know that England bombarded the Polish goal for most of the game, and a certain Polish goalkeeper, by the name of Jan Tomaszewski (pronounced 'Tomashefski') almost single-handedly prevented what could and should have been a 10-0 scoreline in England's favour. The game was that one sided. But prevent us he did, much to the chagrin of the late, great Brian Clough who had called the big Polish stopper 'a clown' during the build up!

Against the run of play Poland took the lead following a mistake by Norman Hunter and poor attempt to save by Peter Shilton before Trevor Cherry equalised from the penalty spot. But despite wave after wave of England pressure the Poles somehow stood firm. The enormity of the fact England were not going to the 1974 World Cup Finals didn't really sink in but our failure to qualify for the Finals was a shock to the world of football. We'd won the tournament in 1966 of course and were widely considered the second best team in 1970. It was unthinkable but it had happened. Norman Hunter would shoulder the responsibility and blame for decades to come, and having seen the goal on numerous occasions since, I've often wondered what if Peter Shilton had made what looked like a routine save, of course, we will never know. Scotland were to be Britain's sole representative, and as football daft kids, with no reason to dislike the auld enemy (indeed City players such as Willie Donachie, Denis Law, and future Blue Asa Hartford were seasoned Scottish Internationals), my school pals and I were quite happy to cheer the Scots on, that's what you did when you were kids!

My opportunities to watch Match of the Day on a Saturday night were still extremely limited, but my memories of Leeds United marching on together are still clear. In our class at school it was mainly City or United, but also Leeds and Liverpool because they were of course the successful teams of that era, and an Oldham fan (his uncle played for Latics). My colour by now of course was the sky blue of Manchester City, courtesy of those football cards, and our baby sitters!

My best pal, Bradley 'Enoch' Powell, was a United fan and his dad used to work at Granada TV so we used to get special trips to the studios to watch either City or United play 'live' on the screens they had there, with commentary provided by our regional commentator Gerald Sinstadt. I always thought Gerald was foreign because of his surname, and his unusual accent seemed to confirm this for me, although he was actually born in Folkstone, Kent, well it wasn't that far from France after all. Even then I can remember Brad's dad saying to me that United were the team to support, but my allegiance was to City, they were *my* team. I just needed to go and do what kids then only did if they were very lucky, actually get to go to see a game with your dad.

Just before my 9th Birthday City played Wolverhampton Wanderers in the League Cup Final at Wembley. Brian Moore was doing the commentary and Wembley looked huge and intimidating, with a noise to match. The massed ranks of sky blue at the tunnel end of the ground, with the contrast of the black and gold colour of the Wolves fans at the opposite end. City were the bookies favourites to win. Both Clubs had a rich history, but City had been dominant in English football in the late 60's and into the early 70's, but even with a forward line of Bell, Lee, Law, Summerbee and Marsh, we somehow contrived to lose a game we should have won. I felt so disappointed, City weren't supposed to lose, especially a final!

A couple of weeks later, I was to get my first ever tantalising glimpse of Maine Road, albeit from the armchair next to our telly, as Granada showed highlights of the match played a day earlier. Just like the Final, I didn't know City had actually lost (again!), I thought I was watching it in 'real time' (even though it was of course just the highlights). City hosted Sheffield United in a league game. My memories are somewhat sketchy, but I know we lost 1-0 (why do we always lose when I tune in, I thought), and the manner of the goal kind of summed up City in so many ways, Geoff Salmon (another name I'll never forget) took their corner kick, and curled it straight in the net at the North Stand end, this kind of bad luck seemed to be a trait within the club.

I didn't know it then but my dad, who I had constantly pestered about going to a match, was also getting earache off my mam to take me, so he spoke to his pals and got tickets for him and me to attend our first ever City match, and let's face it, if you want to go in at the deep end, a Manchester Derby at Old Trafford is about tough as it gets, talk about a baptism of fire!

The date was Saturday 27th April 1974. It was the 92nd meeting of the two clubs but that day had an even greater significance as even a victory for United wouldn't guarantee their First Division status the following season. To be fair, City weren't in a much better position but the 6 point advantage we had (remember it was only 2 points for a win back then) over the Reds had seen us safe. None of this seemed relevant to me; as a young kid I was just excited to be going to a game. My dad bought me my first ever City scarf, it was sky blue and white with thin maroon lines. For those who haven't read what happened in 'We Never Win at Home…', I'll cut a long story short; a group of United hooligans were after nicking my scarf outside the ground, but my dad knew what they were up to and put them in their place with a few choice words of warning, Ancoats style.

As for the game itself, well both teams seemed almost reluctant to win it. Something else which sticks in my mind of that day was that our sub was Phil Henson, and United's was Paul Bielby, neither of these locally born players survived and had to move on, I wonder what their chances would have been of trying to making the grade at City or United today? It also turned out to be the end of an era for some of the players out on the pitch, it was Francis Lee's very last game in a City shirt, and Denis Law's last ever domestic league appearance in football.

When Mike Summerbee crossed the ball into the United penalty area directly in front of us, none of the near 57,000 crowd inside Old Trafford realised what was about to happen next. Denis Law, the King of the Stretford End but who had been given a free transfer by Tommy Docherty and joined City for a second time, did what Denis does best, and conjured up something out of nothing. I just remember the sight of him back-heeling the ball, instinctively, and the ball deceiving United keeper Alex Stepney, before nestling in the corner of the net. At that moment time stood still, the utter thrill, the exhilaration, the adrenalin rush I felt. It was the first City goal I'd ever seen in real life with my own eyes. I suppose it wasn't a bad way to star; possibly the most important goal ever scored in a Manchester derby. I felt on top of the world, I jumped up out of the seat I was in and quickly raised the scarf I had managed to keep from around my neck (thanks dad!), and hold it aloft in the air, arms spread as wide as I could, just like I'd seen the fans do on TV.

I had never done this before in my life, and now here I was, a kid mixing it with a huge crowd, the majority of whom were not sharing the same elation as I was, in fact far from it. They had just seen their team condemned to Second Division football, although their fate was already sealed by results in matches elsewhere. I saw brawls and punch ups all around me, my dad seemed unperturbed, but then again no one in their right mind was going to provoke him, so I needn't have worried. In the aftermath which ensued following the goal Denis almost wished he hadn't scored (the TV highlights the following day with the classic quote by Sindstadt of 'Denis has done it!' became the quote he will always be remembered by) there was a large pitch invasion by disgruntled home fans, in a half-hearted attempt to get the game abandoned and hope for a replay. Meanwhile, the fighting continued beneath us in the Scoreboard Paddock, I kept wondering is this normal, is this what happens at every game? I have since spoken to many Blues and Reds who are older than me and were there that day. Their recollections of the events which unfolded still make me shiver. Some Blues were kicked up and down Warwick Road like rugby balls, the City fans who wisely decided to cover their colours soon made their exit when it became apparent that anyone not wearing red was having aggro whether they liked it or not.

Those were the days when real football hooligans were allowed to flourish, equally I've heard stories of City 'fans' chasing and ambushing any Reds they could find, who in turn, ran for their lives. I hadn't the faintest idea of the simmering hostility between the sets of fans, it was clear the feelings of hatred clearly ran deep.

Despite pleas by the referee, United Manager Tommy Docherty and even Matt Busby for fans to leave the pitch to enable the game to continue, the home fans were having none of it. Reluctantly the ref was left with no choice but to call the abandonment of the match with 6 minutes left to play but the result stood. We escaped the pandemonium outside the Scoreboard End without further incident thankfully, I just couldn't wait to go to my next game!

3: the moss side academy of footballing excellence

THE SUMMER OF 1974 meant our very own kid's version of Holland's total football revolution. Inspired by Messrs Cruyff, Neeskens and Krol, we tried to recreate the Dutch dream team in the school playground and on the playing fields every night, and some of us had now swapped the Denis Law back heel for the Cruyff turn. The whole of the football world had fallen in love with the Dutch style of play, they were without doubt the best team in the tournament, they had taken football to a new level. They also had a great kit, it looked every bit as stylish and classy as they played. Soon the new football season started and we were back in school after the summer holidays. I came home from school one night in early September to find that my dad had only got us season tickets for City! I could not believe my luck! These were prized tickets too in Block C of the Main Stand. I couldn't wait to tell all my mates but at the same time I felt sorry that their dads weren't taking them, or that some of them couldn't come with us. The sense of anticipation that morning was palpable, we were going to meet my dad's pals down in Ancoats, then join the queue of football traffic that had formed on the Mancunian Way all the way to Maine Road. The tickets had come via Freddie Pye, a fellow scrap metal merchant just like my dad, Freddie had close connections to City, and when my dad had told him that I was desperate to go to games, Freddie said "leave it with me Jimmy, I'll sort it…" and sort it he did!

Now I would just like to add here there was a scurrilous rumour going around that my dad had also called Jack Trickett, a local business man with big connections to United, and that Jack upon his return from his holidays, had called him back to ask how he could help. When my dad replied 'don't worry, Freddy has already sorted it', Jack had replied 'sorted what?' My dad explained we now had season tickets for City, at which point Jack turned round and said 'Jimmy send them back, I'll get you and your lad the best seats for Old Trafford!' to which my dad replied 'it's too late Jack, my boy is City daft!' Now if my dad and Jack happen to be reading this, I would only add that the die was already cast, besides which, why on earth would I change allegiance to a club whose fans thought it funny to try and nick a young kid's City scarf? I rest my case.

So, getting back to the main story, we even had the luxury of a car park pass, the main car park adjoined the Platt Lane end of the ground, and this was sometimes used by the club for players to train on, when the pitch wasn't fit for use, bearing in mind it was concrete hard standing!

On that first Saturday we parked up, it was really busy, which would normally be the case when a team like Liverpool were the visiting team. I was actually on a full priced adult season ticket, and acutely aware of what a privileged young child I was, football was very much male-orientated, and families were not catered for as they are today, it was also relatively expensive back then for a child to be taken to a game, let alone have access to the exclusive use of a prized season ticket.

So, excited and ready to make my full home debut, I finally took my place among the throng, on Saturday 14th September 1974, and like every other game that day, it kicked off at precisely 3pm. We queued outside the Main Stand patiently, rows of fans waiting to go through each turnstile. You had to check the number above the entrance, and tear the corresponding number out of your season ticket book but they used to swap the numbers around from time to time, so it always paid to have your book with you, to avoid the embarrassment of tearing the next one out, assuming that would be the correct one. I had the job of tearing out all 3 and I soon became well versed in the practice. Once inside, we went up flights of steps, before I finally got my first view of the pitch, and the Kippax Stand which loomed large in the distance, I was blown away at the sheer size of the place! It looked and felt as if it was already full! The crowd were shouting 'CITY, CITY!' as I took my place in my seat for the first time inside this awesome looking football ground, and I just sat there and marvelled at the tightly packed Kippax terracing, which ran the full length of the pitch. I, along with my dad and my Uncle (who incidentally was a United season ticket holder, who watched both Manchester teams like many of his era) and 45,191 others against a Liverpool side who were current holders of the FA Cup and Charity Shield, and one of the hot favourites to wrestle the league title back from Leeds.

The noise when both teams came out from the players tunnel was electric, it felt so different to my only previous experience at the derby the season before. It was loud and buzzing, but in a good way, not an intimidating way, if that makes sense? The sun was blazing, the Match of the Day cameras were there, so I knew highlights from the game would be shown later that evening, and I knew that I would be given permission by my parents to come downstairs after my brother and sister had gone up to bed so I could watch them, I was thinking, does life get any better than this?

The City team that day had plenty of our own international stars on show. Perhaps the greatest of them all, Colin Bell (aka Nijinski and known affectionately as 'the King of the Kippax') alongside Rodney Marsh, one of the most flamboyant players to grace the league, and another who would become my idol, and still remains my all time favourite to this day, Dennis Tueart. Mike Summerbee, although in the twilight of his career, was still a winger good enough to play regularly for England, and we had two seasoned Scottish Internationals in our ranks with Willie Donachie at left back and recently signed midfield schemer Asa Hartford. Add to this skipper Mike Doyle and Alan Oakes at the heart of defence, and you could see why many had tipped City to be up there competing for the major honours. Although this was only my second live City game, Keith MacRae was in goal, in favour of local lad Joe Corrigan.

So, sat in what was to become my very own personal seat for the next 5 seasons, 3 in from the end of the row, with my Uncle sat on my right, and my dad next to my Uncle. I hadn't forgotten the importance of getting a match programme and with 10p in my hand (that was probably my weekly spends) I excitedly handed it over to the old man with flat cap and black rimmed glasses stood behind a white wooden stand. He would often shout 'Programme!' but I didn't need any encouragement to buy one. 45 years later and I still have it in my possession, the front cover showing Dennis Tueart in City's change kit of black and red stripes, firing a shot on goal away at Coventry City the previous Saturday. Naturally I got Dennis to sign it.

So what did you get for 10p back in 1974? A 24 page booklet, with the only colour being sky blue used as background and borders on the pages. The referee that day was John Yates, a former goalkeeper who played league football, and like every referee from that era, this wasn't his main job, he actually worked for British Leyland full time. City Manager Tony Book gave his insight in his thoughts for the season, while Peter Gardner of *the Manchester Evening News*, gave us a low down on our opponents, including a record of the games played against the opposition over the last 5 years at Maine Road. The fans letters page made for interesting reading, a certain Mr. RT Goble from Sussex, wrote in to recommend how the club could improve the programme with more detailed statistics about the players. Ray Goble, as I knew him, would go on to be author one of the first detailed books about the club called 'City, the Complete Record' which first appeared on the bookshelves in the 1980's. A revised edition would subsequently be released a few years later, with the original edition sold out and now collectable.

There were also plenty of adverts from local businesses, including Freddie Pye's collection of no fewer than nine scrap metal companies! We then learn in the news and views section that 3 year-old Nicholas Summerbee, son of City legend Mike, had taken to drinking a cup and a half of petrol, which was the fuel used for his dad's lawn mower! Nick would survive and go on to follow in his father's footsteps playing on the wing at Maine Road in the 90s. The 'Fan-tastic' page reflects on the considerable efforts and lengths some Blues would go to in order to see City. Exiled

Don't Look Back In Anger

Blue Norman Urmston would make the 400 mile round trip from his home in Broxbourne, Hertfordshire for all the home games and use a tenner's petrol in doing so - inflation doesn't sound that bad now when I consider it, it would cost me about £60 nowadays to do the same in my car. Then we have superfan Morten Andersen from Honefoss in Norway, who would spend £250 to come over and watch City, and he was only 15 years old, he must have had one helluva paper round to find that kind of money back then!

The main player focus of the centre pages was devoted to the career details of terrace idol Rodney Marsh, who had been given the captain's armband at the start of the season. We learned that Rodney had won the last of his 9 England caps nearly 2 years earlier suggesting that at 30 years of age his England career was as good as over. Another player profile focused on the wife of a current City star and the honour went to Janice Booth whose husband Tommy had already given years of sterling service to the club. Janice tells us how she had converted from Red to Blue when Tommy signed for City!

The advert for British Rail tells us that Soccerail/Footex special trains would be going to our forthcoming games away at Middlesbrough (cost £2.30 return and no half fares!) and to Carlisle (£1.80) on the Tuesday night, it should be noted the return time quoted here of 21.55 didn't give the fans much time to get from Brunton Park back to the station! A half page advert to eat at the Bell-Waldron Restaurant (co-owned by City's Colin Bell and Burnley's Colin Waldron) sounded too good to be true - Sunday lunch for £1 (+ Vat at the rate of 8%) and 65p for kids! All roads to Whitefield must have been jam packed in those days. Inside the back cover, 'In my view' by City vice chairman Simon Cussons, focussed on football violence and his thoughts on how to counteract it. It's a pity governments and parents didn't take the trouble to read it as he highlights perfectly what needed to be done back then and still needs to be done today.

I digress. It was a fine end of summer Saturday afternoon, as third placed City took on top of the table Liverpool and we won! There was a goal in each half and a couple of disallowed efforts to boot, but we beat the nation's favourites and beat them well. Rodney Marsh would have the honour of scoring the first home goal I ever saw with my own eyes and Dennis Tueart, already my favourite based on only 180 minutes of football, finished them off with a fine finish in the second half. In the days when it was two points for a win, we went joint top of the league. What a baptism for this boy blue. And it was to get better, as I was given permission to come down that evening and sit quietly in the seat closest to the telly to watch the highlights on Match of the Day, as this was one of the two games chosen for highlights (no round ups of the other games back then!). After two games in the flesh I was absolutely hooked, I didn't even have the hassle of knowing that Manchester United existed in my little world of City although of course I had mates who supported them, but none had been to a game yet and bearing in mind the trail of destruction left in the wake of the Red Army at Second Divisions grounds up and down the country, that is probably not surprising!

I now had a fortnight to wait until my second visit to Maine Road and despite our poor form away from home; a 3-0 defeat at 'Boro followed by goalless draw at Carlisle which simply reinforced Tony Book's views that we were a soft touch away from fortress Maine Road. Next up were Rodney Marsh's old team Queens Park Rangers who were a quality team, who would go on to finish runners up to Liverpool the following season. Their team was packed with internationals, including former Blue and local lad Stan Bowles.

I wouldn't get a chance to see the famous blue and white hooped shirt today, as the visitors turned out in their change kit of red shirts with black shorts. Despite our win against Liverpool, the one point return from two away games put a dent in our early season title challenge, and the crowd that day, just over 30,000, seemed to reflect that, this being a drop of almost 15,000 compared to the Liverpool gate. The game was all about patience, as City bombarded the visitors goal, and found a determined Rangers team, with big Phil Parkes between the posts, in inspired form. And so the scene was set for Rodney Marsh to cement his place in

City folklore with an outrageous piece of individual skill, creating a winning goal out of nothing. I sat transfixed as Marsh, with his back to goal as we attacked the North Stand and a penalty area full of defenders, flicked the ball up on to his knee, juggled it, before launching himself into an overhead kick. The ball flew over keeper Parkes, and the ball rolled on the inside of the net on the underside of the crossbar, for a quite brilliant goal. The Kippax roared its approval "Oh Rodney, Rodney, Rodney Rodney Rodney Rodney Rodney Marsh!". You didn't see goals of this quality in English football that often, it was the type of goal you would expect to see from the Dutch or Brazilians at a World Cup. It was probably the best goal I ever saw scored in all my years going to Maine Road, thank you Rodney!

The Kippax Stand, complete with adverts for 'Trumans for Steel', TV rental companies, John Player Special cigarettes and Greenhall Whitley, became part of the furniture in my frequent visits to Maine Road. I repeated what the Kippax choir sang just like any other kid would do. 'City City' was the obvious one, 'You're gonna get your fuckin heads kicked in' from the boot boys to any away fans, was a obviously a song for grown ups to sing, and one which I knew not to chant but when we played Wolves, and they broke out into a chorus of 'Kindon is a wanker!' I saw no harm whatsoever in joining in the chant myself! My lone high pitched voice seemed to carry to everyone in the vicinity of where we were sat! I could see my dad and uncle smirk briefly before having a quiet word to say it wasn't a song I should be singing but the damage was done as the well to do professional people around us had already heard it, and their look of shock and disapproval said it all – I was the son of a Miles Platting based scrap metal merchant, after all.

With the Reds consigned to Division 2, albeit for only a season, there were no league derby fixtures to fulfil, although as luck, or bad luck would have it, we drew them at Old Trafford in the League Cup. For this match we ended up in the United Road paddock, which was about as far away from our fans as we could get, unintentionally of course. I don't remember anything too violent happening for my second derby, apart from the fact the underdogs won thanks to a hotly disputed penalty which went their way to decide the tie. I was bitterly disappointed at tasting my first ever derby defeat, so much so that I defaced the cover of the programme, a copy of which I still have, my writing wasn't great, but I'd scribbled out United and wrote 'Rubbish' in what must have been an early attempt at 'real writing'! I also change the score to read Rubbish 0 City 45! Ironically that number has remained my favourite number ever since, if only we could have done that to them in 90 minutes.

The one home game I had to miss that season, due to my dad being otherwise engaged due to work commitments, was Stoke City at home, a game we won 1-0. I was absolutely inconsolable that day; the tears flowed as the realisation dawned that my dad wouldn't be back in time to take me. It was my worst nightmare and I was devastated – maybe this absolute fear of missing something I cherished so much even as a kid was a precursor to my compulsion to attend every game in later life, who knows?

Our FA Cup defeat at home to Newcastle (despite being drawn away – the tie had been switched due to crowd trouble – a recurring theme back then), saw our hunt for trophies effectively over for another season. I'd also gone with my dad to my first proper away match at Elland Road, home of reigning champions Leeds United. We came away with a creditable 2-2 draw, I remember large numbers of City fans being at the game, and without checking, I can tell you the official attendance that day was 47,489 but by now my parents had big plans in place for my education, I certainly didn't have a problem with numbers, being able to recite them decades later!

4: from the twin towers to hampden

IN THE CLOSE SEASON City manager Tony Book splashed out £275,000 to secure the services of another Sunderland FA Cup Final winner, man mountain Dave Watson. Centre forward Joe Royle was looking sharper after half a season with us, although my Uncle John wasn't a fan, if Joe made a mistake, he'd refer to him as a 'lemon' or a 'duck egg', harsh perhaps but I've heard worse! The return of our near neighbours meant league derby matches were back on, and the eagerly awaited Maine Road derby (my first), saw a hugely entertaining game, albeit we had to settle for a 2-2 draw.

A few weeks later and the teams would meet yet again as the League Cup Fourth Round saw the reds come over to Moss Side once again. The game was an all ticket sell out, mid week games under the lights at Maine Road were a sight to behold, there was a huge buzz of anticipation. We all met outside the Main Stand, when it transpired they didn't have enough tickets between them to get a couple of us young uns in! We needn't have worried though, as they had a cunning plan B. One of the older generation Schiavo's from the Italian quarter of Manchester used to drive from his home in a light blue three wheel car, the type of invalid carriage that was a familiar sight at the time. The car would pull up outside one of the vehicle entrances which went into the Main Stand, and drive on to the perimeter track around the pitch. As he pulled up, we were bundled into the back where there were already several young kids hidden in the dark! The car park ticket collector peered in while we were all trying to duck down and make ourselves invisible. To this day I'm sure he must have seen us but to our relief he seemed happy enough to let the car through without the need of a spot search, which would have revealed half a dozen ticketless kids!

Once in we were allowed out of the car, and watched excitedly from pitch level as the ground filled up and the players trained. With over 50,000 (well 50,182 from memory!) packed in, it was a tremendous atmosphere and City went at United like a steam train from the off. We scored the opener inside a minute and we danced with delight along the touchline and before we knew it City were three up and the game was won! But the major talking point was a tackle by Reds skipper Martin Buchan on the great Colin Bell. We could hear him screaming in agony and the St John's Ambulance brigade were soon in attendance, as they carried our legend off the pitch and down the players' tunnel for treatment, it didn't look good. As young kids we didn't realise that what we had seen was effectively the end of the playing career of one of the finest inside forwards the world has ever seen (as the chant goes). Showing our playground mentality, when the players from either side came over to the corner flag near where we stood, we'd play a game of tig and the unsuspecting players would shoo us away, they were trying to concentrate on winning an important local Derby, while we were dossing about! Imagine that happening today! City were to score a fourth in what became known in some quarters as the Demolition Derby and when we battered Middlesbrough 4-0 in the semi final second leg, the ground broke out into a full chorus of 'WEMBERLEE, WEMBERLEE, WE'RE THE FAMOUS MAN CITY AND WE'RE GOIN TO WEMBERLEE!!'

I hadn't even completed my second season and I now had the chance to go to London for the first time in my life and hopefully watch the Blues play and win the Final in front of 100,000 fans! Our season tickets guaranteed us one ticket per book but my dad had a friend looking desperately to find one, and I mentioned to my dad about the programme vouchers attached to each programme. Of course I'd been to every home game and had a programme from each game. We cut the vouchers out and the voucher sheet, and stuck them on with glue, I think we needed 18 to qualify for a ticket and we had enough! It also meant that I didn't lose my ticket to enable an older person asking to go instead, a couple of Blues I know had this happen to them, and to this day, they have

Don't Look Back In Anger

never forgiven their fathers for missing out on such a momentous occasion.

A week before the final I was privileged to watch the first team squad train on the pitch at Maine Road and collected all their autographs on a *Manchester Evening News* commemorative poster, although sadly this didn't survive. We went down in my Uncle's brand new recently purchased Ford Capri, it looked beautiful. It seemed to take ages to get there, and parking up around the ground was a nightmare, even more so given there were nothing but huge Geordies proudly wearing their black and white striped football shirts everywhere. The seats we had were directly opposite the Royal Box, the brass band played on the pitch, the famous old stadium was rocking, a mass of sky Blue and White at the tunnel end, contrasting with the black and white at the other, I couldn't actually believe I was there to see it. The noise was electrifying and when our young local born prodigy Peter Barnes smashed the ball home early in the game, half the stadium erupted to celebrate. Newcastle equalised of course, but just after the re-start in the second half, I saw something I never thought was possible, the most spectacular goal ever to grace and win a Cup Final. Willie Donachie launched a ball into their penalty area, where Tommy Booth rose majestically to head the ball back into the danger zone. Dennis Tueart, the Newcastle born winger who had been rejected by his local club and went on to play for and win honours with their great rivals Sunderland, got himself quickly into position and executed a perfect overhead kick. It seemed the whole stadium held its breath as Dennis was airborne and upside down, so he couldn't really have known much about the outcome but the ball, after one bounce, nestled neatly inside keeper Mike Mahoney's far post. It was a quite brilliant goal, of such quality that even the most die hard Geordies there that day would begrudgingly acknowledge it was a goal worthy to win any game. My hero, the 'King of all Geordies' had just given me the best moment of nearly 11 years on this planet, I remember crying with pure emotion, I literally couldn't believe what I had just witnessed and Mike Doyle went up to lift the Cup, the first, I thought and hoped, of many...

Don't Look Back In Anger

The next day there was a victory parade in Manchester City Centre and my dad was only too happy to take me down, huge crowds gathered around the town hall and Albert Square and the rest of the City, with an estimated 150,000 City fans in attendance. To be honest, it was all a bit overwhelming for me, my 11th Birthday was just around the corner, yet I felt I'd won the pools and gone to heaven. Life was good.

A few weeks later my Uncle John got me and my dad tickets for the FA Cup Semi Final at Hillsborough where his team (United) had been pitched against the current Champions of England, Derby County. Whilst realising I would have to go with flow, and be seen to be cheering on 'the enemy', make no mistake about it I badly wanted Derby to win the match! Unfortunately it wasn't to be as they surprisingly lost the game 2-0 and to cap it all, on the journey back home via the M1 my dad was stopped by the traffic police. His explanation as to why he was doing 110 miles per hour in a Pontiac Firebird was a good try, 'I thought it was in Kilometres per hour' (110km = 70mph) but even the comment that he was rushing to get his son home in time to watch Match of the Day (which of course I wasn't as Derby County had let me and the country down) didn't wash, and a speeding ticket was duly issued, that was the first brush with the law, and it wasn't to be the last.

My Uncle asked me if I wanted to go to the FA Cup Final but I just couldn't, it felt like it would be the ultimate betrayal, so I politely declined. Sod's Law would dictate that the team I'd have supported that day, Southampton, caused a major upset by beating the nation's favourites thanks to a Bobby Stokes goal, but I didn't care, we'd won a Cup, United hadn't and I was comfortable with that. After the final there was a derby fixture to fulfil, which had been postponed. The midweek game at Old Trafford attracted a crowd of nearly 60,000. We were sat in the top left hand corner of the Main Stand, at the back. To our left was the corner of the Stretford End Paddock adjoining the Stretford Groundside where fans clung to the railings, hurling abuse and spitting. They beckoned me to come to the fence, no doubt wanting to relieve me of my City scarf. I stayed close by my dad's side, knowing I'd be safe there,

Don't Look Back In Anger

but I can still see the image of them in my mind, it was like a scene straight out of the monkey cage at Chester Zoo! 3 star jumpers, scarves tied to their wrists, Doctor Marten boots; these were the young hooligans of the day, and our close proximity to them kept me on my toes. With nothing riding on the game and United anxious to restore pride after their defeat in the Final, they ran out comfortable 2-0 winners, in a game which saw father and son on opposite sides of the divide; United manager Tommy Docherty's son Michael was playing for City.

At the end of the season me and my pals had the British Home International Championships to look forward to, and with kit suppliers Admiral and Umbro scrapping it out to see who could make the best kit, all the football mad kids of our era craved them all! My first England admiral kit was something I treasured, it just looked the part, and the shiny blue and yellow admiral motif just looked brilliant, along with the England shield sporting 3 lions. I was the first kid on our road to have one, even in those days, when pennies were tight, the competition between kids for football strips (regardless of whether your preference was that of your own team, or someone else's, if they had a better kit!) was fierce.

I'll never forget the weekend of Saturday 15th May for as long as I live. My dad asked me on the Thursday night if I fancied going to Scotland to watch the England match, I looked at him in semi disbelief to confirm I had heard right! He wasn't joking, he was deadly serious, and straight from school on the Friday, we made our way down to Manchester Victoria railway station where we would met up with my dad's pals and families, all of them Blues; the Henson's and the Rooney's. I was dressed up in my Sunday best, with a fake sheepskin coat and an England rosette proudly pinned to my collar. When we got on this long sprawling train I got my first shock, it was absolutely jam packed, and the smell of alcohol and spirits was so strong I felt sick, especially when added to the thick layer of tobacco smoke which hung like a cloud above everyone's heads, it was basically a mobile pub. What wasn't in doubt was we were probably the only England fans on the whole train! It was rammed full of proud exiled Scots returning to home soil in the hope they would send Prince Edward's army back down South of the Border, to think again.

But the appearance of me, this slip of a kid with a ginger mop, happy to show my allegiance to England, seemed to strike a chord with the kilt wearing tartan army. One of the group with a bottle of whisky in one hand, towered above me and clocked the rosette, and shouted to everyone within earshot "here's the first England fan I've seen!" It all seemed good natured, and before long, fellow Scots were coming up to me and giving me their loose change, 10 and 50 pence pieces started to fill my pockets, and by the time the good will had run its course, I'd collected over £4, a sizeable sum!

It was all good natured until we reached Glasgow Central Station. We got off the train, and joined the queue of fans waiting patiently for the steady line of black cabs which formed a circle within the station. When our turn came, and the back passenger door was opened, I prepared to hop in, only I never got in, there was a problem. On hearing my dad's broad Mancunian accent, the taxi driver, made the potentially fatal error of refusing to take us, because we were "ENGLISH!" Well my dad had a short fuse as it was, and it usually didn't take much to push him over the edge. After a reply along the lines of "You fuckin' what!" my dad had him by the throat through his cab window and at that moment I knew this was serious – further threats were issued as he had the now terrified driver in a head lock as my dad threatened to do all kinds of things to him. My dad's pals Alan Henson and Tommy Rooney tried to wrestle him off, and then a huge policeman turned up trying to restrain him too but he was as strong as an ox, and in the melee which ensued the policeman's hat went flying. It was all too much for me, I spontaneously burst into tears, screaming "Dad! You're going to get arrested!" The policeman managed to calm things down, and when my dad explained what had happened, the taxi driver, who was in a complete state of shock, was told to apologise for his actions! The copper then told him to take us where we wanted to go, but my dad was having none of it, he was adamant that he didn't want to take us at the first time of asking, so why should we get in now? At that point my dad had fallen out

Don't Look Back In Anger

with the whole group, and said to me "c'mon Son," and we were off, doing our own thing. As we walked outside the station, me clinging on to my dad's hand, we crossed the road and went up a huge flight of stairs into a very grand Hotel reception, where we duly checked in to a room for the evening. While in the lobby an elderly smartly dressed gentleman in a suit, overcoat and a trilby noticed us and came over.

"Hello Jimmy, what are you doing here?"

"Hello Matt, I'm taking my young boy to the game tomorrow" my dad replied.

Matt was, of course, Matt Busby, he knew my dad from business dealings, I didn't have a clue who Matt was of course, and his connections to both clubs in Manchester. The next thing he produced two grandstand tickets for the match from his pocket and gave them to my dad and with that, he ruffled the hair on my head with a friendly smile. Talk about going from one extreme to another, the emotions of the two events which had happened barely 15 minutes apart. One minute I thought my dad was going to be locked up in a Glasgow police cell, the next we'd met a legend of the game, and now had two of the best seats in the ground for my first ever International game, and I was just a bit of a kid.

The Hampden Park experience, just ten weeks after my first ever Wembley visit, was unforgettable. For the second time in my relatively short life I was to witness an atmosphere unlike anything else, albeit this was far more intimidating. I don't know how many tickets were sold to England fans that day, but it's safe to say there weren't many of us among a crowd restricted to 85,000 for ground safety reasons. I didn't know the band had played 'God Save The Queen' as the Scots completely drowned it out with the loudest boos I'd ever heard. Then I heard 'Scotland the Brave' for the first time and the hairs (albeit small ones!) on the back of my neck stood up, as the anthem was belted out with such gusto and passion, I just couldn't help but be overwhelmed by it. I recognised most of the players from both sides and of course our very own Willie Donachie was playing for Scotland that day, Asa Hartford would also have played but must have been injured presumably, while England were without Colin Bell of course, who was still out with that horrific injury sustained earlier in the season. I did get to see our club captain Mike Doyle play, as he came on as substitution for Roy McFarland. When England scored via future blue Mike Channon you could have heard a pin drop, and my muted celebration wasn't about to upset the natives, we were in the posh seats with a face value of 5 pounds. Parity was soon restored as Scotland equalised to keep the natives happy, and when a Kenny Dalglish pee roller squirmed between the legs of England keeper Ray Clemence for the softest goal he'll ever score, my enthusiasm had waned, it was an absolute howler, and it seemed to make the Scots even happier, if that was at all possible. Scotland would go on to the lift the Home International Championship as the whole of Hampden Park bounced and danced with glee, I was philosophical in defeat, and just as relieved my dad didn't get in to any further bother, I was happy just to get home with him. In the taxi on our way home from Victoria station, Scotland The Brave was still peeling in my ears, and I still had my stash of 10 pence coins safely tucked away, along with my programme and ticket stub, which I still have to this day.

5: so near, yet so far

THERE WERE PLENTY of grounds for optimism ahead of the 1976-77 season, we'd strengthened the squad; Brian Kidd had returned 'home' and with Paul Power, Gary Owen, and Peter Barnes adding youth and talent to a team packed with internationals, we were a force to be reckoned with. We were also playing European football again courtesy of our League Cup win and attendances were up, we averaged over 40,000 for home games making us the third best supported club in the country. City lived up to expectations, and to lose the league by a solitary point was a real heart breaker. Dennis Tueart had been on fire, scoring hat-tricks as if they were going out of fashion, our style of football was great to watch but the old masters Liverpool pipped us at the post, they were fast becoming the team of the decade but we'd pushed them every step of the way. We'd also done so without the services of Colin Bell, surely if he had played we'd have taken the crown?

There are always turning points in a season and specific ones which come to mind took place over the festive period that season. The game in question was at home to Liverpool; on a freezing cold night in front of a crowd of over 50,000 City had taken the lead through Joe Royle. Late in the game, with City dominating, Liverpool attacked against the run of play and a mix up between Dave Watson and Joe Corrigan (who was wearing tracksuit bottoms it was that cold) saw a back pass evade the on rushing keeper, the ball rolling agonisingly into the net at the Platt Lane End. The scousers who had braved the elements, on and off the pitch, celebrated, as we all rued the moment, and what might have been. If that ball doesn't go in, we win the league - bloody hell!

Brian Kidd couldn't score at the start of his City career but once he found the net he couldn't stop scoring and together with Dennis Tueart they provided a glut of goals which kept us in contention. The Cup competitions hadn't gone to plan, first round exits to Juventus in Europe and Aston Villa in the League Cup meant there was a lot riding on the FA Cup where we were narrowly defeated 1-0 away to Leeds in the 5th round, despite the heroics of Joe Corrigan. His change of direction to palm away a goal bound header by Allan Clarke was arguably the save of the season but Trevor Cherry would ultimately decide the tie late on, to the huge disappointment of several thousand Blues (ourselves included) who had made the short journey over the Pennines.

However the game that ultimately cost us in my opinion was a trip to the mud bath of a pitch at the Baseball Ground, home of Derby County. We had a perfectly good goal disallowed, not that it mattered, as we shipped four goals at the other end. One of the goals was scored from a penalty which couldn't be taken because the mud had churned up the penalty spot. When Joe Corrigan strode out of his goal to show the officials where X marks the spot, the referee promptly booked him! It was an unmitigated disaster to lose that heavily in that fashion to a mid-table team. The penalty was the subject of a debate in the headmaster's assembly talk at school the following week, not that it made pleasant listening or made the Blues in our school feel any better. Two draws in our last four games saw Liverpool crowned champions, our 5-0 demolition of a Spurs team on the brink of relegation was small consolation but Peter Barnes scored a goal of high quality; turning a defender inside out before selling keeper Pat Jennings a dummy and chipping the ball over his head. A recollection I have of that afternoon was watching rival fans fight on the Kippax and the chant of 'Hello, Hello, City Aggro!' could be heard sporadically through the game. When it had finished, we walked our normal route to the car, as fans ran past, trading punches with each other, and then I saw a policeman grab a fan, and promptly handcuff him to a lamp post! I had never seen anything like it! Funnily enough I never felt in danger because I was with my dad, I was just relieved that he didn't get involved in any of it, as I've no doubt he'd have been having to explain his actions to a Policeman again!

With European Football returning to City once again the following season, and the high profile signing of Southampton and England striker Mike Channon, everyone was convinced that this would be the season we'd break Liverpool's dominance. The early signs were good, and a home derby victory with Brian Kidd scoring against his former team was just what the doctor ordered. However the European campaign saw us fail at the first attempt as Zbigniew Boniek of Widzew Lodz caused huge problems as we struggled to a 2-2 draw at Maine Road. A fan invaded the pitch and tried to attack their players, which meant fences would have to be erected to stop fans encroaching on to the pitch from the seated stands, the club were also fined by UEFA and warned about the future conduct of our supporters. Whilst it is fair to say City fans weren't behind the door, I never saw our fans cause trouble on the scale of United, Leeds, Spurs or West Ham.

The FA Cup saw us back at Elland Road and this time we were victorious, despite attempts from Leeds fans to try and get the game abandoned by invading the pitch. It was quite amusing watching Joe Corrigan rugby tackle one of the young hooligans who came rushing on. My dad and I, along with his normal group of friends, were sat in the Main Stand not far from the Gelderd End as the fans continued to pour on to the playing area. A couple of them came into our stand, they didn't know we were City fans but they were intent on causing trouble with anyone. One of them came right up to the perimeter wall where they shouted obscenities, gesturing to everyone nearby to come and have a go. As soon as he got too close to one of my dad's pals he just stood up, and before the would-be hooligan could have second thoughts and back away, he received a single punch to his jaw for his troubles, the force of it lifted him off his feet and sent him hurtling backwards onto the pitch! Everyone around us stood up and applauded, we wanted to watch the match, and the minority (a sizeable one it has to be said!) wanted to spoil it for the rest.

Large groups of Leeds fans made their way to the Lowfields paddocks where thousands of City fans were packed on the terraces behind the cages in pens. The stadium announcer and police implored the City fans not to react and to stay where they were. It is to City fans' credit they did as they were told and the Leeds mob, all bravado, didn't fancy their chances of scaling the fences to get at the Blues. The referee announced that he'd wait until midnight if necessary to complete the game, he was adamant the hooligans weren't going to win. The police deployed horses in an attempt to clear the pitch, and eventually the game restarted. Going back to the car after the game we saw running battles everywhere! Two City fans were being chased as they ran towards us and almost into us, and my dad gripped one of them and asked him why he was running. The City fans pointed at a group of Leeds fans heading towards us, some of whom had temporarily paused, awaiting the outcome. My dad, teeth gritted, had an anger I'd seen before (Glasgow Central Station) and gripped the City fan and asked him "what are you frightened of? Go and batter them!" With that the two lads turned around and started running back towards the Leeds fans who had given chase, and they in turn, not sure what to make of it all, were now suddenly full of self-doubt and started backing off, these City fans had had enough, and with my dad's ringing endorsement they could turn the tables, they had renewed fire in the bellies! It was like a scene out of the Keystone Cops! I often wonder what happened and whether the Blues in question are still around, and indeed whether they may even read this one day and remember it.

City's prize for our hard earned win over in West Yorkshire was another tough away tie, this time to play Brian Clough's high flying Nottingham Forest who had taken the First Division by storm. A cavalcade of cars left New Cross Motors but we hadn't even got to the bottom of Great Ancoats Street when a heavy snow fall put paid to us going any further. Thankfully somebody had the radio on and heard the news that our match had been postponed, saving not only a wasted journey but judging by the amount of snow on the ground, a treacherous one too.

Back then, games were normally re-arranged for a day of the following week, and so the tie was re-scheduled for the Wednesday night but I had a problem. It was a school night and I'd have to miss the game, or so I thought. I asked my dad if he would write to the headmaster asking permission to leave school early. This was a bad move on my part, I'd passed my exams (the year after eleven plus was aborted) and made it to Hulme Grammar School (Oldham). There it was all about hard work to achieve excellence, they had no time for slackers, and those who didn't shape up soon fell by the wayside; taking time out of precious school hours just wasn't on the curriculum. And so after asking to leave early officially, I was summonsed to the Headmaster's office, where I was read the riot act by Sid Johnson. I didn't get the cane for it but an hour's detention was inevitable, fortunately it didn't coincide with the day of the game!

So at just past 4pm on Wednesday 31st January my dad picked me up outside the school gates and three car loads of us, including young Bernard Manning, son of the Manchester comedian, headed over the M62 and down the M1 to the City Ground, Nottingham. There was still a lot of snow around and it was bitterly cold. We were in the seats above a large paddock down the Trent side of the ground, there were 38,511 in attendance (sorry can't help it – my OCD is kicking in again!) including a good few thousand Blues. The match programme was the one which would have been sold on the Saturday, no reprinting of it with the correct date. This was to be Dennis Tueart's last appearance in a City shirt, he was off to New York Cosmos and I was devastated. Forest scored early doors and then went two up, and despite a late rally when Brian Kidd pulled a goal back for us, we'd missed out again on another piece of silverware. Once again the hooligans were up for the occasion, fans throwing each other into, and fighting in, the River Trent! We were convinced one of my dad's pals (Alan Henson) had got into trouble and been arrested. We went to the mobile police cells enquiring as to whether they had Alan in custody. They didn't and we found him, much to the relief of his sons, who were facing the prospect of going home without their dad, and having to squeeze in with us.

On the journey back up the M1 the weather was still atrocious, so we pulled in at Tibshelf services, there was no further crowd trouble, other than the fact fans were helping themselves to food free of charge! I'm not sure what had happened to the staff but some fans were in the kitchens, serving themselves and others hot food! My brother Martin spilt his Coca-Cola on his plate, so the baked beans and chips were now immersed in a cocktail of bean juice and phosphoric acid. Needless to say my dad was far from impressed, and made my brother eat it regardless.

City finished the season in 4th place. It had promised so much and yet delivered so little, although we had secured entry into the UEFA Cup for the following season. Mike Channon had struggled to live up to his reputation as one of the best strikers in England, while the loss of Dennis Tueart was a retrograde step in my opinion. The following season would be pivotal for Tony Book, and so it proved when, after a number of disappointing results leading up to Christmas, the New Year saw the return of the prodigal son, Malcolm Allison aka 'Big Mal', as head coach under Book. Malc's successful coaching methods in the Joe Mercer years had been well documented, and Chairman Peter Swales, thought it was a risk well worth taking in an effort to help Tony Book get the best out of the squad and the team. The old adage 'never go back' sprung to mind at the time, little did we know how turbulent Mal's return would prove to be.

Malcolm had an instant impact and new players were drafted in, including former Poland captain and World Cup star Kazimierz Deyna, part of an influx of foreign players arriving in the English game after the 1978 World Cup in Argentina. Our FA Cup dreams were once again shattered in the 4th round. It took us two attempts to dispatch Rotherham United in a delayed tie from the previous round. By this time I'd started a new chapter in my City life, having started to go to home games with my school mates, and pay for my own admission in the Kippax (I couldn't afford the Main Stand!) from my hard-earned paper round money. We had drawn Third Division Shrewsbury Town away at Gay Meadow, so it was another new ground on which to watch City. Bernard Manning (Jnr) and his pal Terry Burke, from Blackley, were happy to pick me up, as my dad and uncle had started to lose interest, while City's mixed fortunes started to impact on our attendances, our average crowds were down to around 30,000 – having peaked at over 40,000 in the previous two seasons. The trip down to Shropshire once again saw freezing conditions and the match was in doubt but the locals cleared the snow from the pitch, leaving a bone hard but dry playing surface underneath. We were of course bookies favourites to progress to the next round but cup football has a habit of springing surprises.

City fans had invaded the town in their thousands once again and Shrewsbury had their biggest crowd for years, with the home fans hoping to see a shock home win for the Shrews. It was a month or so before my 14th birthday, and I stood on the side paddock, with heaps of snow all around the perimeter of the pitch, and in the stands. The conditions were awful, Joe Corrigan wore leggings to cushion the blow for when he had to dive. I'm not sure whether this was where the phrase 'Typical City' was first aired, but the way we contrived to lose this game, and the embarrassment it would cause, I wouldn't be surprised. City were not at the races, our expensively assembled squad played looked as though they had never met each other before and the home side capitalised and took the lead. At one nil down the City fans packed in down the side and behind the goal, started to pepper the players on the pitch with snow balls, well they were ice balls really, as I found out for myself as frost bite set in, as I dug my hand into a frozen mass of it behind me. My next action of joining in, and throwing one myself on to the pitch, was a spontaneous thing, it didn't hit anyone, but a tap on the shoulder from a policeman telling me off for doing it had the desired effect, I'd never been told off by one before, and flashbacks to Glasgow were enough to put me off. I immediately apologised, trying to mitigate the ludicrous thought I might be arrested, while Bernard and Terry laughed at my misfortune, it was a valuable lesson learned. The second half saw the Shrews score again as City's defence went AWOL, the sense of discontent and anger was palpable among the City fans there that day, everyone was absolutely gutted. We'd gone from beating Italian giants AC Milan 3-0 at Maine Road, to this in the space of a couple of months!

The UEFA Cup quarter finals pitched us against crack German

outfit Borussia Mönchengladbach – what a great name for a team that is. Malcolm Allison had no hesitation in throwing 18 year-old, Davyhulme-born City fan Nicky Reid in for his debut, and the lad didn't let us down but a draw was never going to be enough to take to Germany, and we were well beaten 3-1 in the second leg, although our consolation goal was an absolute beauty scored by Deyna.

That summer of '79 saw Malcolm clear out all the crowd favourites; Dave Watson and Brian Kidd were moved on, but the sale of local lads Peter Barnes and Gary Owen, who reluctantly agreed to join West Bromwich Albion, were the biggest shocks, the fans were far from happy. He also brought in players with lesser ability (no disrespect to them), we had Barry Silkman, Bobby Shinton, Michael Robinson, Dragoslav Stepanovic, Stuart Lee, Steve MacKenzie, and of course Steve Daley, who we paid a mind boggling £1.4 million for (well we didn't pay for him, the bank did). So another season of turmoil ensued; we'd get the odd decent result but follow it with a bad one. Now we realistically only had domestic Cup Competitions to aim for. Beating United at home in the Derby was a high point but defeat to Sunderland in a League Cup replay in October meant that all eyes were on who we would draw in the FA Cup.

They call it the romance of the Cup; Halifax was the name of a building society where I kept my meagre savings but I'd never given the fact they had a proud football club a second thought. The Shay was a rickety old ground which had seats installed in the ground taken from our defunct Hyde Road ground that had closed in the 1920s, yes it was that old! Me and my mates joined the throngs of Blues departing Manchester Victoria for the short journey of 23 miles (for the princely sum of £1.80 return!). The ground was bursting at the seams, surely City wouldn't falter today, they just couldn't, could they?

The pitch was a mud bath but the game went ahead, although I suspect Malcolm feared the worst when he saw the state of the pitch; it wouldn't be a game of football, it would be an endurance test, and down to who adapted best to the conditions. Of course it was scripted that Halifax would somehow find a way to win the game, and they did much to our disbelief. The poor bloke selling soup from a converted hotdog stall paid the price, as he disappeared among a sea of fans, the stampede duly turned his livelihood into a scene of devastation, as his once proud stand became a flat pack. Chants of 'SOUP SOUP SOUP!' filled the West Yorkshire air as pissed off, fist-clenching City fans took out their frustration on the poor fellow, we were swimming in gallons of the stuff as it mixed in with the soil and mud beneath their feet. Blues had had enough; we were the objects of laughter, derision and ridicule nationwide once again, there were violent scenes after the game with large mobs of fans being herded together by police on horseback as they tried in vain to get us out of the town and back on the trains. At one point a horse flared up right in front of us and Brad (my lifelong pal of a red persuasion who had come along with us because he enjoyed going to City games more than going to United) squealed in pain as the horse trod on his foot, it was broken. I remember him pulling my leg quietly about the result as we had made our way back to the station so I felt that this was karma.

The final away game of the season saw us go to Derby and by now we had starting travelling to the away games on the football special trains organised by the City travel club which was run by Howard Yates, his dad Bob, and a few volunteers (including Charlie Hadfield, Geoff Perkins, Graham Coreless and our very own Ian Cheeseman!) who were all passionate City fans and did it for the love of the club. Unsurprisingly, the trip to Derby ended in defeat and a pitch invasion by the home fans (normal behaviour back then on the last day) and their efforts to goad City fans onto the pitch worked as brawls ensued. One City hooligan, with a broken leg, had somehow clambered on to the pitch and was fighting them with his crutch! The walk back to the station saw property damaged by hooligans, from buses to derelict houses having their windows smashed. This was Thatcher's Britain, it was a truly grim place to be, and football hooligans thrived in a defiant act of rebellion during an era of high unemployment and unrest (the riots of 1981 were just around the corner). Back on the train peace was restored, as any of those fans who were intent on causing trouble, did at least show some respect to a group of fans who dedicated their free time to help supporters get up and down the country.

6: a kick up the eighties

WE HADN'T MADE A particularly auspicious start to the new decade, and while a new season always brings optimism, City fans weren't daft. Malcolm had dismantled a team which had been finishing in the higher reaches of the division and replaced it with one of lesser quality and seemed destined to struggle. It didn't take long for our suspicions to be confirmed as an opening defeat away at Southampton was followed with the midweek visit to Maine Road of recently promoted Sunderland. To lose your first home game of the season is bad enough but to lose it in the way we did, by 4 goals to 0, John Hawley grabbing a hat-trick for the visitors, set the alarm bells ringing. A creditable draw in the Old Trafford derby and progress in the League Cup aside, we found ourselves rooted to the bottom of the table and after successive defeats at home to Liverpool and then again away to Leeds midweek, our Chairman Peter Swales, who was fast becoming enemy number 1 with the fans, decided enough was enough, and Big Mal had to go having drawn 4 and lost 6 of the ten league games. His replacement was swift, and another larger than life character, who had actually played alongside Malcolm in their days together at West Ham.

John Bond had always been keen to see if he could replicate the good work he had done at Norwich City on a bigger stage, and he had finally been given the chance. While his first three signings were not necessarily household names, Scots Gerry Gow, Tommy Hutchinson and Bobby MacDonald, had a vast wealth of experience between them. City fans could see the difference in the level of performance straight away and all of a sudden the players knew what was expected of them, which in turn lifted the crowd, especially the Kippax, who were once again in full voice. New songs were heard on the famous old terrace, "John Bond we love you" was about as cheesy as it gets, but the re-working of the Adam and the Ants tune "Ant Music" was very current and catchy, the chorus of which said "that football's lost its taste, so try another flavour, Man City, Oi Oi Oi!" But getting back to the serious stuff, our three new additions made a huge difference, the tenacity of Gerry Gow cannot be understated; a Glaswegian as tough as they come, he'd tackle his grandmother if she was in his way - the City song for him was predictable and to the point "Five foot eight, tackles late, Gerry Gow is f*ckin great!" and he loved it. The opposition no longer had the luxury of walking through our midfield unchallenged, they knew they had a scrap on their hands to get the better of us now. Bobby Mac was a no nonsense full back; quick, solid, and with an eye for goal, something we'd not seen from our defence in quite a while. Last, but not least, Tommy Hutch was a graceful winger and a full Scottish International back when they had a very good side, it was a joy to watch him play the game the way it should be played. Results picked up immediately, and although our three Scots were cup tied, the lift in spirits saw the rest of the team progress to the semi-finals of the League Cup, where we would face all-conquering Liverpool. Nobody gave us a chance, but when we took an early into the first leg in front of a packed Maine Road, we went into raptures, only for it to be inexplicably ruled out by referee Alf Grey. His is one of the few referees names I can remember - for all the wrong reasons! The infringement he claims he saw just didn't wash, we had been robbed, and then the scousers did what they did best back then; they shut up shop, defended deep and nicked a goal on the break. Talk about injustice, I'm still seething about it 38 years later!

The second leg at Anfield saw a mass exodus from Manchester by car, coach and train to see if we could do the impossible. In the a 1-1 draw flattered Liverpool; we had them on the ropes and once again a vital decision went against us. The walk back to Lime Street, which took the best part of an hour, was interesting. Normally the scousers would be attacking us at every junction but tonight there must have been 1,000 plus City fans walking back for the trains, and anyone who came near, soon realised the error of their ways,

Don't Look Back In Anger

and scarpered quickly when challenged. The police were actually being escorted by us! I was with my school mates Wigan (William Wardle) and Rambo (Carl Ramsbottom), they were a bit older than me and knew the score in regards to looking after themselves and always being aware of their surroundings, I was still fairly new to going to away games on a regular basis, so the experience I picked up from them was invaluable.

City's good league form continued and we also made good progress in the FA Cup, defeating Malcolm Allison's Crystal Palace in the third round (funnily enough that game still remains the only home FA Cup tie I have missed since I started watching City – I was staying over at my auntie's in Birmingham over the New Year, and went to see West Brom play Grimsby Town at the Hawthorns instead!). John Bond's old club Norwich were the next opponents to play us at Maine Road and we smashed them 6-0 on the pitch, whilst John Bond did his best to smash his back in off the pitch, falling from the directors box as he attempted to console his son Kevin as he left the field (young Bond would of course sign for us the following season). A trip to Peterborough awaited us in the next round where a Tommy Booth winner in front of nearly 28,000 fans at London Road saw City progress to the quarter finals, where we had another tough encounter, away at Everton. As I mentioned in the prologue, this was a mad day for so many reasons, but thanks to Gerry Gow and Paul Power we managed to get take it to a replay the following Wednesday.

On the Sunday morning after the match, me and my pals got the two buses down to Maine Road to join a queue which lapped the ground not once but twice! The club had 40,000 tickets to shift, and shift them they did in record time. Everybody wanted to be at the game, and with Everton getting over 10,000 tickets, many City fans were left disappointed.

It was another unforgettable night under the lights as Bobby Mac did the damage scoring twice and City got to the semi-finals for the first time since 1969. Predictably there was lots of trouble after the game, and I remember being on a match special bus which travelled back into the City centre, with its lights dimmed so any rival fans walking back, couldn't work out whether it was carrying home or away fans; the things bus drivers had to do to protect the bus from having its windows smashed and of course the safety of their passengers. Fortunately we got back into town without any issues as we contemplated a semi-final against Bobby Robson's Ipswich Town, one of the finest teams in the country, who were competing on three fronts for league, cup and UEFA Cup glory.

At the end of that month we played a rearranged home game against Leicester; it was end to end stuff and finished 3-3. Another reason it was memorable was that after the game I was running through the alleys but unfortunately me running for my bus spelt danger for some unsuspecting Leicester City supporter, who must have convinced himself I was a hooligan who had recognised he was an away fan, so at that moment decided to give me what he mistakenly thought I was after, and duly threw his scarf to the floor. My natural reaction was to shout him to tell him he'd dropped his scarf but he just ran even faster! If that Leicester fan happens to be reading this now, I'm sorry if I scared you pal.

Villa Park, Birmingham, home of Aston Villa FC, was the venue chosen for our semi-final but despite being a Kippax season ticket holder with the relevant voucher, an allocation of just over 20,000 each was never going to satisfy the huge demand for tickets. It meant a very early start and queue up at the ground to get a prized ticket, which is exactly what I did, and I managed to get one on the huge bank of terracing behind the goal known as the Holte End, which had been divided in two for the game. Most of my mates weren't so lucky and like thousands of others, travelled down ticketless, in the vain hope that they'd somehow get in. I'd got a ticket for one of several football specials which left Manchester Piccadilly bound for Witton station but as none of my pals had got a ticket, I travelled on my own. Around the ground it was bedlam, there were more ticketless Blues than those of us who had tickets. They had placards begging for '1 spare ticket please', and I realised how lucky I was. I'd heard horror stories of unsuspecting fans being relieved of their prized tickets on occasions like this, so I tucked mine away deep in my front pocket and if anyone asked if I had one, my pre-planned answer was going to be 'No, I'm looking for one myself'. I got in safely, and picked a spot half way up, I remember wearing a bubble coat which was the 'in' thing back then, but it turned out to be a boiling hot afternoon and I soon regretted the decision. I failed to spot anyone I knew, it was a surreal feeling really, but fans never had the luxury of being able to stand together, if that sounds daft, unless you travelled together or pre-arranged to meet outside the ground, it really was a case of pure luck if you were able to spot anyone you knew. The atmosphere was electric, and it was obvious that City fans had snapped up any neutral tickets which had been sold via the host club.

The game itself saw us ride our luck against an excellent side, and when extra time came after a goalless ninety minutes, you could feel the confidence of our fans and the team grow. Ipswich had played a lot of games and somewhat ironically were involved in a title run-in with Aston Villa, so the extra half hour was going to be tougher for them. When Paul Power stepped up to take that free kick we knew it would have to be a good one to beat future City goalkeeper Paul Cooper. When the ball hit the bottom right corner of the net, the pandemonium which ensued was unlike any other I had experienced. Arms, legs and bodies went everywhere, I hugged people I'd never met, I saw grown men crying with tears of joy, it was a fitting way to win any game of football, and for our young players, Tommy Caton, Nicky Reid, Ray Ranson, Steve MacKenzie and Dave Bennett, it must have been the best day of their lives. What a complete turnaround by the club, typified by our midfield warrior Gerry Gow who insisted on playing with pain-killing injections in his troublesome knees.

Saturday 9th May 1981 saw 25,000 City fans descend on London for the Centenary FA Cup Final, where our opponents Spurs were favourites. The Argentinian duo of Ardiles and Villa were their stars along with Hoddle, Archibald, Galvin, Roberts and Perryman. Yet on the day it was City who made a mockery of our underdog tag as we dominated the game and deservedly led the match after a spectacular diving header by our new hero Tommy Hutchinson. However the fickle finger of fate also decreed Tommy would then be left with the dubious honour of becoming the first player to score for both sides in a Cup Final, as a free kick by Glenn Hoddle deflected in off him, completely wrong-footing Big Joe in goal. It was an absolute killer but we somehow rallied to ensure we didn't concede again in extra time which meant Wembley would host its first ever FA Cup final replay, the following Thursday.

The following day was spent queuing with 30,000 City fans at Maine Road to claim our tickets for the replay, and a few of us were able to get tickets together in the same block of Wembley, having not been able to do so for the Saturday game. I was in my final couple of weeks of school before leaving, so wagging off for the day was neither here nor there; besides which I wasn't alone, as each class had several match going Blues in them, so back down to London it was on the special trains again, to see if we could go one better, and bring the Cup home.

Before the game even started it was clear that all was not well, as we found that Spurs fans had bought up all the spare tickets put on sale at Wembley, meaning there must have been over 50,000 of them inside the stadium. There were pockets of fighting in the lower tier, quite how they ended up among us is not clear, but it was no holds barred, and scary if I'm honest, this wasn't kids fighting, it was blokes, and the police were struggling to contain it.

The game itself was a sea-saw affair, Spurs scored, we equalised through a Steve MacKenzie volley which most of us missed because of the fighting which continued unabated. A Kevin Reeves penalty put us back in front but you could see our lads were knackered, their equaliser came from Steve Archibald and of course then there was the goal we've had rammed down our throats a thousand times since; a mazy run and fine individual effort by Ricky Villa which settled the tie. We were going home empty-handed and heartbroken. My hero Dennis Tueart, back for his second stint at the club, came on as a sub and almost scored a goal out of nothing, how fitting it would have been for him to be our Wembley saviour once again but it wasn't to be. Most Blues didn't hang around at the end, not out of lack of loyalty but we had trains to catch, and the trouble had been quite bad, it was best to get out of harm's way, lick our wounds and get home. The train was like a morgue all the way home, everyone was deflated but proud of our team none the less, I distinctly remember the train pulling into Piccadilly station at 4am, and it was school for me, and work for most of the rest I suspect. I was bleary-eyed the next day and our form teacher knew damn well where we had all been the day before, he took some kind of perverse pleasure in the fact all our efforts had ended in defeat. I couldn't bring myself to give in to him so when he asked, sarcastically, did I enjoy the match, I replied, "I didn't watch it Sir, I was too ill". Defiant to the last, I was 16 now, a young man with a burning desire to watch my club as often as I could. This sickening defeat had just made me even more determined to bounce back the following season, by which time I'd hopefully know in which direction my further education would be going.

The 1981-82 season saw some subtle changes at the club. Firstly, we reverted back to wearing the round City badge, having spent the five previous seasons wearing the Manchester Coat of Arms (my preferred badge) on the kit. Secondly, we had our first major kit sponsors SAAB and then we shocked the football world by beating rivals United to the signing of England's star centre forward Trevor Francis from Nottingham Forest. Back then it wasn't unusual for tax free payments to be made to players and managers as inducements to get them to sign for your club, and it probably wouldn't surprise you to know that this was widespread throughout football, at all levels of the game, and I am not naïve to think that City were squeaky clean in this respect. Also arriving that summer were Kevin Bond and Graham Baker.

Francis's debut for City would be away at Stoke, and once again a mass exodus of over 10,000 fans made the short trip down to the Victoria Ground to see if he could deliver the goods in his new sky blue jersey. We travelled down on the football special, and on a boiling hot afternoon twice Stoke's average attendance crammed inside to witness one of the great City debuts. Tricky Trev had pace to burn, and playing off the shoulder of their back four as soon as he got a sniff of the ball and half a chance he was off like a whippet. His two goal debut had us begging for more, it was the complete performance by arguably the best English forward playing in the league. There were plenty of reasons for optimism. The short journey back on the train was a joyous one, although my pal Beddy threw my match programme out of the window as a joke but I wasn't laughing, even then my programme was an intrinsic part of the match day experience, and we ended up in fisticuffs, much to the amazement of Pete Statham and the rest of the lads who probably didn't realise it meant that much to me. It took me years to replace it as they were scarce, due to the fact it was the game in which Trevor Francis made his debut.

The main problem we had that season was keeping Trevor fit, he barely managed half the number of matches we played, he missed both Manchester derbies and the onus fell on Kevin Reeves and Dennis Tueart to score the goals. To be fair both of them chipped in with their fair share but from being top of the league over Christmas (when Francis scored a ridiculous goal with a shot which must have been the best part of 40 yards from goal!), we slumped to 10th by the end of the season. In the League Cup our run came to an end at Second Division Barnsley. Almost 34,000 packed inside Oakwell, with 10,000 plus making the short journey over the Pennines. When Tommy Hutchinson hit the bar with a beautiful curling shot we started to wonder if it was going to be our night, then we fell for the sucker punch and were on the end of another cup shock. Rumours were abound throughout the season that City were struggling to pay Francis's huge wages and sure enough during the summer of 1982, after he starred for England in the World Cup he was transferred to Sampdoria. It was a crushing disappointment to every Blue, he'd only played 26 times for us, scoring 12 goals but the fact he was allowed to leave with the club keen to get the deal done told us everything about our financial plight.

There was even more cause for concern at the start of the following season as our new signings reflected the fact we were now shopping in the bargain basement. With all due respect to David Cross, who didn't let us down and always put a shift in, he wasn't Trevor Francis and on the terraces, despite being top after three games we knew we'd peaked and that the reality was we couldn't compete with the elite clubs. Yet few at the start of the season could have predicted the nightmare to come. In the League Cup we were drawn away at Southampton, so it was a day off college to catch the football special leaving Manchester just after midday. The weather had been shocking all over the country with torrential rain and again we didn't have the luxury of mobile phones to tell us if the game was in doubt or not. When the train made an unscheduled stop at Basingstoke, we wondered what on earth was going on. Howard Yeats had asked if the train could stop so he could ring Southampton FC from the station to ask if the game was on! The news came back that indeed it was so the train carried on to the station. The rain continued to fall, and with no protection from the weather City fans were soaked to the skin and tried to find shelter in any pubs which would accept away fans. Once we got in the open air paddock behind the goal, the rain came down even heavier and there were severe doubts again as to whether the game would go ahead but it did, and the winners of tonight's game would play United in the next round.

The paddock we were huddled together in was the one nearest the corner flag, the middle section remained empty and there were probably no more than 1,000 of us there at best. The water level at the bottom of the paddock was rising by the minute and there was a lot of arguing between the fans, police and stewards about whether we could transfer into the empty paddock next to us. Anyway, unbeknown to us, that paddock held even more water, and when the decision was taken to open the bottom gate, a huge volume of water being held back by that gate came cascading through and we were all up to our knees in it! To cap it all, Nicky Reid scored a great goal, his first one in a City shirt, only for it to be disallowed. Had it been allowed to stand the game could have taken a completely different course but in the end the home side extended their lead and ended up running out 4-0 winners. We were pissed off, piss wet through, and had a 5 hour journey home, this was now becoming the norm as a City fan, it was largely uncharted territory for most of us younger fans, but it certainly didn't put us off going again on the Saturday.

It was another Cup defeat, this time in the FA Cup by the same score away to Brighton, which proved to be the final straw for John Bond. One of the Moston Blues, Jimmy 'The Pig' Hart had hired a van from Middleton Van Hire for the trip. We all piled in the back, and I remember Arthur complaining about the fact the van had holes in it, it was on its last legs, and yet Jimmy was charging us a tenner apiece for the privilege! When confronted about the gaping holes Jimmy said it was 'air conditioned' and there was no price reduction forthcoming. We all had our cans of beer in the back of course, and frequent toilet stops were required en route. The van wouldn't go faster than 60 miles per hour, and it was bitterly cold; we were living the life! Cramped up, singing City songs, and taking the mickey out of each other. It's what we did, and I'm proud to say we never went out to cause trouble or hurt anybody, yes we were drunk on occasions and boisterous but we prided ourselves on being loyal fans who loved doing what we were doing, trawling the length and breadth of the country, in the hope we would see us win occasionally.

Brighton was awash with City fans but we were there in hope rather than expectation. The year before I had been down there with Pete Statham, Glynny, Si Draper and the rest of the crew, we hadn't even intended to go but on a Friday night out word got round that a coach was leaving town at midnight. So we checked how much money we had between us; £20 each would see us right and it was straight into the Bierkeller, dancing on tables to Soft Cell's Tainted Love, before a night journey which saw us hit Brighton at 4.30am. The place was deserted, we looked in vain for a greasy spoon café but it didn't open until 7, so we nicked a pint or two of milk from the odd doorstep (sorry!) and then managed to get into the Goldstone Ground for a quick kick about, before being cleared off by the groundsman! We conceded 4, and it pissed down all day, and we sensed that today would see more of the same and so it proved with 4 goals let in during a performance as abysmal as I've witnessed in my life. We were not happy, Arthur had smoked his big cigar but the party was definitely over, the fans wanted action, and we got it as John Bond threw the towel in. We couldn't believe how it all had turned so sour so quickly, then we remembered the lack of investment and bargain basement signings and realised that the club was in steep decline.

Our league visits to Everton and Liverpool were always interesting to say the least. Goodison Park was a tough place to go, and our pal John 'Jack' Frost, who hadn't been to an away game before, made his debut, coming down with us on the football special to Lime Street. We arrived before the turnstiles opened, and that was when the problems started. One of the Everton crew recognised a City fan Stu Hulme, who had been before and the next thing we saw Stu scale some concrete wall panels, they must have been 10 feet tall and just as me, Pete as the rest of us were about to meet our fate, a timely intervention by Merseyside Police (for once!) saved the day. After the game we all got split up, ducking and diving to avoid a kicking was the order of the day, it was a numbers game, the scousers hunted you down in packs. We managed to get on a bus back to the statues near Lime Street where the biggest mob of Everton hooligans I've ever seen were waiting. The driver was asking everyone to alight the bus but we were understandably reluctant to get off! When we did they circled the bus and a desperate situation call for desperate measures! I screamed to Jack, "Under the bus!" The driver looked through his windscreen as he saw two us slide underneath his cab to avoid the inevitable mauling. This time the mounted police came to our rescue and as we scrambled out, our Slazenger jumpers smeared with oil and grime but our City badges still intact, we ran back into the station and got back to the safety of our own football special. Talk about a tough examination for your first away game, Jack!

Liverpool away was played on Boxing Day and our train broke down so the police sent double decker buses which would transport us to Anfield where the game had already kicked off. There was one problem, and it was a big one, you could only board the bus if you had a valid match ticket, and the vast majority didn't, so out of 200 or so I bet no more than 20 of us could actually go to the game. Those that were refused entry to the buses stayed in the area and apparently there was trouble in the pubs with locals, while we got to the game at half time. When I got in, the first thing I noticed was that there were Liverpool fans in our end and of course it kept going off, I don't mind admitting I was really scared, I was on my own, and nobody was letting on to anyone, because no one knew who was who! At the end of the game we were chased around the ground, on to buses, and somehow got back to the station. It was a service train but there was another problem, the scousers were on it pretending to be friendly but you just knew it would end up being more trouble. That's the day I first met Kingy and a few blues from Gorton. Kingy had a Lacoste jacket on and the scousers wanted it but Kingy locked himself in the train driver's compartment, I think he was planning to drive us home himself! When the train set off the friendliness turned to violence; we were outnumbered and it was chaos, the scousers even battered the girl who was with us, there was claret everywhere, they got off at Edge Hill, thankfully the threat of Stanley knives being used didn't materialise but having taken a good hiding I didn't want to let them get away with it quietly so I jumped on the last one getting off, to exact a bit of retribution. However my luck ran out again as the doors didn't close and the train halted, someone had pulled the emergency chord so they got back on and I got another beating for my troubles. The train driver came down and said "is everything all right?" - the irony wasn't lost on us as we replied, "yeah we're great thanks", as we mopped up our bloody noses and examined our torn clothing. We never set out to cause trouble but back in those days it went with the territory because as an away fan trouble found you. I've stayed lifelong friends with the Blues I met that day, we might have got a good hiding but they can't take the friendships and camaraderie away from you, thankfully we all survived to tell the tale.

With John Benson in temporary charge, City had won just four games in 1983 so on the final day of the season we had to avoid defeat at home to fellow strugglers Luton to avoid relegation. Of course City did what City do best, and in front of over 42,000, we managed to find a way to lose a game we had total control of for long periods, Raddy Antic slotting home the winner in the last few minutes. The sight of David Pleat skipping over the Maine Road turf like some pantomime horse kind of summed it all up, we were a joke, and the years of chasing the dream with the bank's money had come back to haunt us. There grown men in tears again but to me it all felt part of one big adventure. Second Division football would be returning to Manchester the following season, and it was the Reds turn to gloat at our demise.

The new season saw the arrival of Billy McNeill and Jimmy Frizzell as manager and assistant manager, and to be fair Billy was a big name signing given his glittering playing and managerial career with Glasgow Celtic. The pubs and clubs of Manchester were busy discussing who we would sign but the problem was the club was absolutely skint so Billy would have to wheel and deal, bringing in the players he could, those he knew and those he could rely on. Ex-Rangers and Leeds centre forward Derek Parlane, midfield schemer Neil McNab, and Jim Tolmie were brought in for virtually no outlay. Despite the fact we would be playing our football outside the top flight, the local interest in supporting and going to watch City certainly didn't diminish, if anything it grew stronger, it felt like a show of solidarity from the light blue half of Manchester. In our local pubs, the Boat and Horses, and the Sportsman's Arms, we'd be running coaches to most away games arranged by Glynny, who was like the Pied Piper! Where he went, everyone followed, and that was usually two coach loads of us! At this point I'd made good pals with Wilky and Richard Brady, two of the Moston lads who used to be on the same bus after home games. Some of the nicknames we gave to each other always made me smile; Borneo Baz was a blue in our local so called because he used to work away a lot... in Borneo! Then there was Doughnut, Badgeman, Escher, Scivvy, Cano, Podge, Wardrobe man, Jimmy bent nose, Womble, Upside down head, and I even had my own nickname 'Rilch', after the advert about Pilchards, these were some of the more printable ones, but it was all part of the camaraderie which made the whole away day experience that much more enjoyable.

City started the season really well with our new players all chipping in, and that spurred on the fans, and the crowds got bigger with each passing game. I'd driven to Cardiff and Portsmouth taking the lads in my mam's red Vauxhall Viva (Reg no CNA 135T – how sad is it that I remember that!) We'd lost in Wales, and just avoided the trouble but won at Portsmouth where once again we had a close call when their hooligans spotted the Manchester tax disc. The threats of what they were going to do to us was a good enough reason for me to take evasive action, as I turned and sped off into the dock area, which ended up being a deep water jetty and a dead end but at least it threw the fans wanting mither off the scent!

The first real acid test was away to highflying leaders Newcastle United who, with Kevin Keegan, Peter Beardsley and Chris Waddle, had enough fire power to take them back into the big time. At the time, with various ground redevelopments having been abandoned or halted due to lack of funds, St James' Park was limited to a capacity of 33,500. As a result thousands of Geordies were locked out every home game but still insisted on turning up. It was a great show of loyalty but a pain in the arse if you happened to be a fan of the away team trying to get in! We'd driven up on the day of the game, three car loads of us, as the coaches had already been filled, so we were in effect the overspill. The fun and games had started when we parked up, as sporadic punch ups on the streets around us were taking place but it was about to get a whole lot worse. The approaches to the ground were unapproachable due to thousands of fans being gathered outside, it was way too risky to even attempt it and we knew it. In desperation more than anything, we approached a local copper to explain our plight. He took pity on our situation and before we knew it he was on the radio to his sergeant explaining how we had tickets but there wasn't a hope in hell of getting us safely to the Leazes End where our paddocks were situated. About 5 minutes later a Black Maria Police van turned up and were told to 'hop in' for a lift to our turnstile! We couldn't believe our luck! Not only had we avoided a good kicking, we were getting the best escort possible, that is, of course, until the van, trying to make its way through thousands of people, was subjected to fans banging on the side and rocking it - we kept our mouths firmly shut, one hint that there were City fans inside and that van was going over on its roof, there was absolutely no doubt about it!

The journey seemed to take forever but in reality was probably no more than 15 minutes but to our amazement, the van not only took us up to the turnstile, but was driven through a heavily policed steel gated entrance to the ground, so our tickets remained intact and we were in! No sooner had we took up our space on the terraces than it kicked off as Geordies who'd bought tickets outside off touts decided to make themselves known. Art got nicked for very little and in a frenzied atmosphere like no other, our team simply caved in to the tune of 5 goals to nil, and now we had to get back to our cars without the help of a police van. Some of the cars with Manchester plates on had been damaged and had their windows smashed, including our pals from Newton Heath. The last I remember was seeing Gilly chasing a Geordie through the petrol station for something he had said or done. It was a bad day all round and the return game at Maine Road wasn't much better; we lost 2-1 in front of well over 40,000, including a sizeable contingent from the North East. The other league leaders, Sheffield Wednesday, also won at our place by the same score watched by a similar sized crowd.

The season provided a mixture of great trips and terrible trips as we failed to win promotion back up at the first attempt. By this time I'd started my first full time job working away in Teesside, which meant horrendous scheduling problems for midweek games but that season I managed to see 44 of our 46 league games, I was extremely proud of my efforts, and I'm sure it was Marshy remembers me saying, "one day, I'll see every game in a season" and that once I did I'd carry on doing so for as long as I could.

Later on that season a few of us went up to Glasgow to take in the Scottish League Cup Final between Rangers and Celtic. I was no stranger to Hampden of course, having been there as a kid, but to see streets barricaded off just like we'd seen in Belfast on the news, from Mount Florida station up to the Rangers end of the ground, was surreal. That rivalry is like no other and we were pleasantly surprised how welcome we were made to feel by the Gers fans, who couldn't do enough to help five lads in their late teens get in to the match, so much so they found tickets for us at face value (it's illegal to sell them over the odds in Scotland we found out). We'd parked the car up in the City centre and Glynny, who was a bit of a mechanic, took the rotor arm out of my car engine, we'd heard all these stories about Glasgow being so rough and crime ridden, that we didn't want to take any chances! Rangers won a classic final 3-2 after extra time with Ally McCoist scoring a hat trick. During the game, we found the speed of their songs were different to ours, they were a lot slower and we couldn't understand many of them, which is a good job especially the ones which highlighted their religious differences. It wasn't something we could even begin to understand, besides with a name like Sean Riley I've no doubt I'd have Celtic fans asking me what I was doing in the Rangers end!

It was a great occasion to attend made all the better by seeing our adopted team win. On leaving the ground we were given some sound advice about our trip back home to England, and that was not to have any colours on show on the M8 which skirts through the East side of the City as the locals would be lying in wait on the footbridges above complete with lumps of concrete ready to be launched on unsuspecting cars and coaches. It was a sobering thought and nobody spoke a word as we passed through the concrete jungle of high rise buildings on our way back to the A74/M74, and just as the man had said, you could see the Celtic fans dangling precariously over the edge of the footbridge, trying to pinpoint Rangers fans on the move 40 feet below them. I don't think I've ever been so relieved to pass the 'Welcome to England' sign north of Carlisle and we congratulated ourselves on surviving to tell the tale.

7: back in the big time

CITY HAD FALLEN short at the end of the 1983-84 season which, considering our financial limitations, was probably the best thing that could have happened. The signing of Mick McCarthy was a key addition in the summer of 1984 after we had sold Tommy Caton to Arsenal for £500,000. Arguably the lowest point towards the end of the previous season had been our visit to Craven Cottage, where Fulham hammered us 5-1. It was a truly shocking performance by City and the few thousand of us gathered on the open terrace at the Putney End were far from happy. So much so that when their fifth goal went in a few hundred Blues left the ground, so that we could play our own game of 5 (hundred!) a side in Putney Park, which was directly behind the stand! We'd borrowed a local kid's ball and the Blues who stayed inside the ground to carry on suffering eventually gave way, turned their backs on what City were doing, and watched our game down below them peering through the wire mesh! Gordon Davies, who scored a hat-trick for them, would of course eventually sign for us.

We needed to strengthen to make sure we didn't prolong our stay in the Second Division and McNeill found a bargain in Welsh International David Phillips who he signed for just £65,000. He would prove to be a valuable asset throughout the 1984/85 season, his speciality was scoring goals from long distance and they were often spectacular!

Our opening game of 1984/85 saw us all head down to Plough Lane to play a Wimbledon side who had made a meteoric rise from non-league football; it was hard to take in the fact we were playing a league game against a side who had only entered the Football League in 1977. This was in an era before entry to the league was purely based on promotion. Clubs such as Crewe Alexandra and Rochdale were routinely re-elected despite finishing rock bottom of the Fourth Division at the expense of the top teams in the Conference. Altrincham in particular seemed to be knocked back every season in the early 80s. Anyway, Plough Lane was packed to the rafters with over 8,000 jammed inside, about half of them Blues keen to see the new signings in action. An exciting game finished 2-2 but most of us packed behind the goal had heard a commotion at half time, apparently some Chelsea 'fans' had turned up for a bit of trouble outside but our attention was soon back on the matter in hand, trying to win a physical contest on the pitch.

Our league form remained steady but largely consistent, as we stayed in touch with pace setters Oxford United and Birmingham City. In the League Cup we went to First Division West Ham in a replay and came away with a shock 2-1 victory. The next round saw us back down in London but Chelsea proved too strong, as we lost 4-1. Another trip to Carlisle was memorable for our good pal Marshy, who despite making the journey on two successive seasons never got in to the ground to see a ball kicked in anger, he was too intoxicated and spent one game in the back of our hire van, sleeping it off! Carlisle town centre was a real throwback to the 70's, it felt like everyone was stuck in some kind of time warp, when one rugged looking local came marching down the street with his full length leather jacket, we couldn't resist popping our heads out of the back of the van with a quick rendition of the signature tune to the hit 70's police programme 'The Sweeney'. The two-fingered salute in our general direction suggested he wasn't amused with the comparison.

As we got in to the business end of the season, on loan centre half Ken McNaught returned to West Brom, which triggered the welcome return of local lad Kenny Clements back into the City fold; his vast experience would hopefully help steady the ship. A lot of nerves and tension had crept into our play. I was now dating my future wife Jane and although she was a Blue, she hadn't been to a game for a few years. "There's no time like the present," I told her and the first of many games as a match-going couple was our home game against Oldham in early May. We were expected to win, we needed to win but Latics hadn't read the script, and we couldn't break the deadlock. A goalless draw was a bitterly disappointing result but worse was yet to come. Our final away game was two days later on the Bank Holiday Monday and the relatively short trip over to Nottingham to Meadow Lane where we were once again nailed on favourites to get the desperately needed three points. Notts County's average crowd of around 6,000 tripled, as another 10,000 plus Blues filled the famous old ground to capacity. What happened in that first half can only be described as Typical City, as we somehow managed to concede 3 goals! For some it was just too much to bear, as they scaled metal fences, threw objects on to the pitch, and the referee couldn't bring the players out for the second half until it was safe to do so. Billy McNeill, who was quite clearly shocked and saddened by events, pleaded for calm in the crowd, so that the game could recommence. The players rolled their sleeves up and put in a performance but despite two Paul Simpson goals, it still wasn't enough to get anything out of the match, it all rested on the final day of the season.

Saturday 11th May was upon us before we knew it and I promised Jane it would be different today, the maths were simple; providing we could at least equal Portsmouth's result we'd be guaranteed top flight football next season. So, no pressure then! The conditions were perfect, there was not a cloud in the sky, the sun was beating down and of course the fans flocked to Maine Road, over 47,000 officially but as anyone there that afternoon will testify, many more got inside the ground by any means, you simply couldn't move on the Kippax. Once you had fought your way on to the terracing and been lucky enough to find a spot, you had to stay there, nipping out of the stand for a pint or a pee wasn't an option, move and you'd lose your spot and run the risk of not getting back in!

For the first time in a few years City didn't disappoint, as we set about dismantling the visitors, complete with a rookie keeper making his full league debut. We managed to rattle in 5 goals, with a token gesture of 1 in reply. It felt too good to be true, everything had gone right for once. A pitch invasion saw what seemed half the crowd surge on to the hallowed Maine Road turf demanding the players return to accept the plaudits. The difference two years made for beleaguered chairman Peter Swales, so often on the receiving end of the protests and demands for his resignation, meant even he could enjoy the moment but I suspect he'd have just been relieved something had finally gone right and concerned that he'd need to find money from somewhere to back the manager in the top flight the following season.

It was during our after match celebrations that news filtered that a terrible tragedy was unfolding in Bradford, where the game had been abandoned after a large scale fire had engulfed the Main Stand and despite most fans having managed to somehow scale the fences and get themselves out of immediate danger on the pitch, some hadn't made it. Everyone was talking about it, and our sense of elation soon changed to a deeply sombre mood, it sounded unthinkable that this could happen and yet it was very real. What had happened at the Bradford v Lincoln game could easily have happened at so many other grounds, and it was a sobering thought, it could have so easily been any of us caught up in it. When we got home and saw the graphic scenes on TV and the scale and enormity of the disaster, you just couldn't help but be moved to tears by the horror unfolding before your eyes. 56 people had gone to a football match but wouldn't be returning home. It was hard to take in and all of a sudden the problems football faced at that time; with hooliganism on the increase and lower attendances at games, paled into insignificance. An urgent enquiry and lessons would need to be learned, this simply couldn't be allowed to happen again, but less than 3 weeks later, with the aftermath very much in the forefront of people's minds, another tragedy was about to unfold.

The largely dilapidated Heysel stadium was the venue for the 1985 European Cup Final between Liverpool and Juventus. As the TV coverage began the stadium seemed to be in chaos and so it proved. Crumbling concrete walls and terraces had played a huge part in the scale of an ongoing disaster, as 39 Juventus supporters were crushed to death after a charge by Liverpool fans. The whole unthinkable and unbelievable sequence of events were seen by the watching world at this showpiece occasion. Yet the game was

Don't Look Back In Anger

still allowed to go ahead despite players and officials being aware that people had just died, the reasoning being that abandoning the game would just lead to more unrest and violence. I was left feeling completely numbed by the whole experience. It certainly made me question myself and the potential risks I was taking not only actually getting in and out of a ground in one piece but also inside the ground as well. Football hooliganism was one thing which we were all patently aware of, and it had contributed greatly to the death of supporters in Belgium but it was quite clear that the poor state of the stadium had played a significant part, and had it been up to specification then it is entirely possible that no one would have perished. Of course the Bradford fire had nothing at all to do with hooligans, there was always the potential for a fire in that stand, indeed any stand which was mainly of wooden construction, but poorly maintained was dangerous. It was so hard to comprehend how it could happen but just as importantly, would the inevitable inquests into both disasters be enough to force clubs to take action and spend the money to make the necessary improvements and prevent it from happening again?

Our return to the top flight wasn't an easy one. New signings included Wythenshawe Blue Mark Lillis, who fulfilled his boyhood dream of playing for City, ex-Red Sammy McIlroy, who started his new career with a spectacular goal from long range on debut away to Coventry in the first game of the season and Nigel Johnson, a centre half hoping to make the step up from the lower leagues. The first Manchester Derby was at Maine Road, just under 49,000 were inside the ground, with far too many Reds inside for our liking. United, on a ten match winning run at the start of the season, walloped us 3-0 with ex-Blue Peter Barnes also playing for them - it was going to be a long haul. The highlight came on Boxing Day when a solitary goal scored by local lad Clive Wilson, and a proper backs to the wall defensive performance, gave us a narrow 1-0 victory against Liverpool at Maine Road. We very rarely beat them back then, so this win was even more special. The Full Members Cup was our only real hope of silverware, although playing in a competition nobody really cared about spread to the fans. We were struggling to attract crowds of 20,000 for league games, so attendances of 5,000-6,000 were common place, and the programme was basically a 4 page advert but we managed to qualify for the semi-final and after defeating Hull City over two legs we had a long awaited day out at Wembley to look forward to, but there was a catch. The final against Chelsea was scheduled to take place 24 hours after the Old Trafford derby, surely common sense would prevail and the derby would be re-scheduled. But United, in the middle of a title race with Liverpool and Everton, were having none of it and insisted the game go ahead as planned, probably thinking it would put us at a huge disadvantage. The Football League didn't step in and so we were told to fulfil both fixtures. This particular derby saw United slash our derby ticket allocation by half and once again there was nothing we could do about. So with our support restricted to 4,500 or so, we saw a battling performance earn us a creditable 2-2 draw. There had been the usual trouble in the vicinity of the ground leading up to kick off and after the game me and Wilky called in a favour from one of the United crew I used to work with (Lee B from Ancoats). We walked back into town, two City fans in a mob of a good few hundred United who were on the lookout for revenge, fortunately nothing happened while we were there, we thanked Lee for his help and got back to our local as we discussed the plans for getting to London the following morning.

City laid on football special trains to help fans make the journey South and as expected when we got to Wembley, our support of around 25,000 was heavily outnumbered by the Cockneys. Chelsea had a fearsome reputation back then and some City fans had to literally fight their way into the ground. So much for lessons being learned from Heysel. City were understandably fatigued from their exertions of the day before and with a quarter of the game still to go we trailed 5-1. We were just glad to get out of the poisonous atmosphere, and jump on the first special train back to Manchester. Jane and I couldn't quite believe our ears when Blues bursting with pride reported seeing City almost pull off the impossible, making the final score 5-4 to Chelsea. We couldn't believe it; perhaps we were the jinx all along?

So after a year which amounted to survival there was nothing to suggest the following season would be any different. By now English football was at its lowest ebb; clubs had been banned from all European Competitions in the wake of Heysel, hooliganism were still at large and spoiling it for everyone else, and attendances up and down the country reflected that. City were still a top six club in terms of support but what was on offer was way short of the mark, although we couldn't fault the effort or commitment of the players we had. Paul Moulden was grabbing the goals but by September Billy McNeill decided enough was enough; with no money to bring in the right quality of players we so desperately needed, he jumped ship and joined Aston Villa. The fans felt angry, let down and frustrated, Jimmy Frizzell stepped in as caretaker manager but the writing was on the wall. Peter Swales was once again vilified by the fans but there were no investors out there, nobody would touch football with a bargepole and with our club being guilty more than most of spending beyond its means, the future was bleak.

The summer signings weren't impressive: Imre Varadi was a seasoned centre forward in his day but was now in the latter stages of his career, ditto Tony Grealish who had starred in the Brighton team who had come so close to beating United in the cup final a few years earlier but although these lads put a shift in for us, it wasn't pretty to watch, and the lack of goals from the team merely compounded our frustration. We won 8 league games all season and the final game saw us go to Upton Park with survival out of our own hands. We needn't have worried, as we lost again - 2-0. At the final whistle our healthy travelling contingent waited nervously as West Ham fans staged the traditional final game pitch invasion. As thousands of them walked towards our end, the Hammers fans burst out into a song of 'Loyal Supporters!' aimed in our direction and acknowledging we'd stuck by our club. It was something no one expected and from our perspective, shaking the hands of rival fans rather than trading punches was something which will live with those of us who were there for many a year. We'd scored a paltry 36 goals all season, and Billy McNeill had the dubious honour of taking two teams down in the same season, as Villa came down with us into the Second Division.

During the summer of 1987 we managed to scrape enough money together to sign Wythenshawe-born Paul Stewart from Blackpool; we knew he was a red from his younger days but if he was prepared to pull on the sky blue shirt of Manchester City, that was good enough for us. The new arrival in the managerial hot seat was Mel Machin, a highly rated coach but not a household name by any means but we saw enough glimpses in the early season form to suggest at least he knew what he was doing. His new signings included goalkeeper Andy Dibble, strikers Tony Adcock and Trevor Morley, supplemented by a youthful looking team which included Steve Redmond, David White, Paul Lake, Ian Brightwell, Andy Hinchcliffe, Ian Scott and Paul Simpson who had all played together in our blossoming youth team that lifted the 1986 FA Youth Cup, the first in the club's history. All of a sudden going to the game was fun again; we were scoring goals and playing free-flowing, attacking football.

This was highlighted by events away to high flying Bradford City in a midweek game played in late October. A scintillating performance saw us run out 4-2 winners. For the travelling faithful, once again the away allocation had been snaffled up, well we certainly got our just desserts, it was the first time we'd won on the road in the league in 18 months! In that period we'd failed to win in 34 attempts! That's a measure of how bad we were away from home, we'd forgotten the words to 'Jingle Bells, Jingle all the way, oh what fun it is to see, City win away!' but we sang it loud and proud that night I can assure you. That's why the tongue in cheek song often sung in our direction questioning where were we, when we were shit, still gets to a few Blues, we'd been so used to being knee deep in the stuff, and still somehow managed to produce a brave smile in the face of adversity.

Saturday November 7th 1986 was another day to remember. Certainly the 19,583 inside Maine Road that day will never forget it, as lowly Huddersfield Town were the visitors to Maine Road.

Despite a strange opening to the game which could have seen us go behind, what happened next was a sight to behold, as we went on to put 10 (yes TEN!) goals into the Terriers net. When 4 became 5, and 5 became 6, and 6 became 7, no one on the Kippax or indeed any of the other stands, could believe it might happen but when we scored the ninth, we all knew it was on. The Kippax bellowed 'We want Ten! We want Ten'. So when David White went galloping into their half and dribbled round the keeper in the last minute of the game to make history, we went absolutely beserk. We might have been on the crest of a depression in terms of playing our football outside the top flight but this was a day we could shout from the roof tops, as the old song went 'Remember when, City scored Ten!'. City players actually scored 11, as former Blue Andy May netted the visitor's solitary goal from the penalty spot. We also had three hat-trick heroes (White, Stewart and Adcock) but there was only one ball between them, we were probably so skint the club probably regretted having to stump up for two more! It's just how it was then, City didn't have a pot to piss in.

Four days later we were at it again, albeit it was the Full Members Cup, so barely 5,000 of us were there to watch us smash in another 6 goals, this time Plymouth Argyle were the victims. 16 goals inside a week at Maine Road! It usually took us half a season to muster up that many; we were being spoiled, but the nation was finally sitting up and taking note, City had something going with these great young kids of ours, ably assisted by the likes of veterans Neil McNab and John Gidman.

We also found our form in the major domestic cup competitions again as we made the quarter finals of both. Our League Cup run came to end at Goodison Park against reigning league champions Everton, yet once again more than 10,000 Blues helped fill the ground to capacity. Our 4-0 home defeat in the FA Cup at home to Liverpool was harsh, but once again, the lads were roared on by over 44,000 – we believed in the team, and despite our disappointing run of form which saw us miss out on promotion, we were all of the opinion that we'd make it the following season. Our biggest problem would be how to keep all our young starlets happy, we were the definition of a selling club because we needed money in, and so it proved, as we lost our star striker, and fan favourite Paul Stewart to Spurs for a fee of £1.7 million.

While Imre Varadi would only play a bit part the following season, the fans, as a bit of fun, had nicknamed him Imre Banana. This caught on and soon fans were turning up to matches with Fyffes blow up plastic bananas in honour of our cult hero. It was meant as a laugh, and it should never be under-estimated the part City fans played in bringing fun back into football. Hooligans were being replaced by fans with a self-depreciating humour, taking plastic inflatable objects to games and having toy fights with them. It might all sound ridiculous now but it was a way of normal fans fighting back in their own way at ridiculous government schemes to issue us with identity cards. Amid this celebratory atmosphere, the business end of the 1988-89 season saw City right in the mix for a return to the big time. Over 40,000 had watched us lose 3-2 at home to eventual champions Chelsea, but second place was still achievable. On 15th April 1989 we were playing at Blackburn Rovers but although I'd qualified for one of the few tickets available (the allocation had been cut due to ground improvements), I wasn't going, as I was best man at my future brother-in-law's wedding. All the usual crew would be there including the Ostell's, the Winstanley's, the Bletchers and the Harts but I'd be relying on radio updates from the gathering throngs at the church, with everyone else coming back to the reception later that afternoon.

I'll never forget the moment when we asked the wedding car driver to switch the radio on; the games had only just kicked off but we were desperate for any information, a goal in a game, preferably our game, and a goal for us. What we all heard next turned us cold. It was FA Cup semi-final day and Liverpool were playing Nottingham Forest at Hillsborough. It was as though the football world stopped, and been put on hold, as news filtered through that there were fans injured, and fans climbing fences, trying to escape the terrace where they were housed but none of it was clear at the time. As the updates continued to arrive, it became clear that not only were there casualties, fans had died. It still makes me

Don't Look Back In Anger

emotional thinking about it. Life of course would go on and like Heysel and Bradford before it, fans had gone to a game and were not coming back. It was another extremely dark day in the history of our game and the circumstances around this latest disaster would be far reaching, and change the course of the match going fan forever, this time lessons were learned.

What the Hillsborough tragedy did do was unite rival fans on a scale which had never been seen before. Supporters of teams from John O'Groats to Lands' End and beyond, gravitated towards Anfield to pay their respects. We did too. As football tried to get to grips with the scale of the tragedy the season was completed, and City left it right to the end to guarantee a return to the First Division. We had been 3-0 up against Bournemouth on a sunny day at Maine Road and promotion looked all but sealed, yet we contrived to draw the game 3-3. We'd sign Cherries striker Ian Bishop based on his performance against us that day. Their equaliser came well into stoppage time; it was typical City, snatching a draw from the jaws of victory. The fans couldn't believe we were doing our best to throw all the hard work away once again! So now we had to needed a result in the last game of the season at Valley Parade, Bradford to secure promotion. Tickets were unbelievably scarce, but the home club had nothing but pride to play for so plenty of Blues were snapping up any spares on offer. It was a huge game, we had to avoid defeat to ensure we pipped Crystal Palace, who were playing at home to relegation threatened Birmingham, to secure automatic promotion.

With City one down, we found out Palace were winning with time ebbing away in the second half. The tension was unbearable, furthermore delays of just under half an hour in the Palace game due to crowd trouble meant they would know what was required if we didn't get the point we needed. Desperate times called for desperate measures. A lone pitch invader, with a close resemblance to Jesus Christ, went over to Paul Lake I think it was, and whispered something in his ear, probably telling him the score from Selhurst Park. It felt like the last throw of the dice, would the players find an extra gear when we needed it most, to see us over the line?

Suddenly David White found himself with the ball at his feet, we prayed for a good cross into the penalty area directly in front of us. It was the perfect ball and Trevor Morley, so often the subject of criticism if things weren't going right, made good contact with the ball, and it was only ever going to end up in the back of the net. That was the defining moment - in one toe poke of the ball Trevor made sure his name would live on in the history of our club, as the scorer of the goal that clinched promotion in 1989. The pitch invasion at the final whistle was good-natured, and in light of recent events, the gates were opened allowing fans who wanted to join those already on the pitch the chance to do so. Former manager John Bond was spotted in the crowd among the reporting press, and he received some stick from City fans for comments he had made about the club. It was a bit unfortunate really, but football being the partisan game it is, it was perhaps inevitable.

Our return to the top flight was amazing as 'Machin's Marvels' demolished United 5-1 in the Maine Road derby. We'd waited 8 years to taste a derby victory, so to do so in such style, against Alex Ferguson's multi-million pound side was about as good as it gets. We'd even managed to do it without star striker Clive Allen who was out with injury. "One, two, one two three, One two three four, five one!" was the chant to be heard, we'd taken them to the cleaners with a display bursting with pride, and as for our local lads to have played in it, well no one can ever take it away from them. But such is the fickleness of football, a few weeks later a 6-0 drubbing at the Baseball Ground, Derby in a bad run of form, saw our chairman press the panic button again and Machin was on his way.

Swales's next appointment was probably the wisest he ever made during his time in charge, with the respected former Everton manager Howard Kendall coming in from Athletic Bilbao to take over the reins. Results picked up immediately and Kendall brought in players he knew and trusted, including quite a few with connections to Everton. This raised a few eyebrows with us fans but you couldn't argue that his methods achieved results, and we became something which so many previous City teams had tried and failed to do - hard to beat. Peter Reid, Everton's captain during Kendall's glory days at Goodison, was a vital signing, and nobody could fault his appetite and tenacity for the game; he commanded respect, always leading by example. A rare away win on our travels at Aston Villa saw Reidy score the winner, the Strangeways prison riots had started on the same day, which led to some wag commenting that the riot had been caused by over exuberant City fans being detained at Her Majesty's pleasure. The return Manchester Derby that season, played in front of a crowd just over 40,000, reduced on police advice following trouble at Maine Road, was 3,000 fewer than had attended the Maine Road derby earlier in the season – and City fans were quick to snap up spares by reds disgruntled by their own team's shortcomings. A memorable goal from Ian Brightwell securing a 1-1 draw for City moments after Clayton Blackmore had given the hosts the lead.

The signing of bean pole striker Niall Quinn by Kendall proved pivotal, here was a player who couldn't make the grade in a strong Arsenal squad but was clearly good enough to play in the First Division. The final game of the season saw just under 6,000 City fans travel down to South East London where we drew 2-2 with Crystal Palace. There was a carnival atmosphere throughout the afternoon, we'd actually finished the season level on points with United in 13th and 14th place in the league respectively. The flag we had made wishing Palace good luck against United in the FA Cup final the following week had been well received by the home support. City now had solid foundations in place to build on for the next decade, or so we thought.

On a personal note, I had finally completed what I thought I'd never achieve, a 'full house'. I'd managed to get to see every league and cup game we had played in my 17th season of watching City, 46 games in all. I'd got close a couple of times and knew of other fans who'd done it. This included no fewer than three trips to the infamous home of Millwall FC, The Old Den (one in the league and two in the FA Cup) which was a feat in itself, just ask the coach drivers who were brave enough to take us there!

8: the yo-yo years

THERE WAS CAUSE for optimism at the start of the 1990/91 season. Under the stewardship of Howard Kendall people were taking Manchester City seriously, and not before time. The highly rated goalkeeper Tony Coton was signed from Watford, our very own David White had started the season on fire and couldn't stop scoring but it still felt we were one or two quality players short of being genuine contenders for a top spot and Kendall's ever increasing reliance on former Everton players was a topic of conversation among the fans, we'd become the Manchester branch of the Toffees former players association.

We were approximately a third of the way through the season; throwing away a 3-1 lead at home to United was one of the main disappointments, when we played up at Roker Park, Sunderland. We'd got a creditable 1-1 draw but on the drive back home news filtered through that Howard Kendall was going to walk out on City and return to his first love, Everton Football Club. To say we were distraught was an understatement. After all the years of being mocked and being the laughing stock, we finally had a credible manager, a candidate for the England job no less, and now we were about to lose him!. Of course you hope the rumours and speculation are just that but not at City, it was never that simple. We'd had a period of stability and craved more of the same but once again we were being denied by forces beyond the fans' control. Of course Kendall's reputation was now forever tarnished where City fans were concerned, he was duly christened 'Judas', as Blues vented their spleen on radio phone-ins which had now become a staple of the post-match journey home. I remember writing at length to Howard; I wanted to tell him how strongly I felt about it, how it was wrong for him to go back for a second time to Everton, how he'd regret the day he walked out on a club which was begging to be made great again, in short I told him he had the opportunity to become a legendary manager for the sky blue side of Manchester.

To be fair to Peter Reid, while he had been brought in by Howard he was his own man and while his appointment in succession to his erstwhile boss was seen as the cheap option by many, he motivated the squad and lifted City to a grandstand finish which saw us finish the season fifth, one place ahead of United in the league for the first time in well over a decade, with Niall Quinn having a tremendous season. In the Derby County home game, not only did he score, but as an emergency replacement keeper after Tony Coton had been sent off, he saved a Dean Saunders penalty, and we won the match. The bloke could do nothing wrong, and City fans had a hero to worship once again, along with home grown fleet-footed striker David White, who scored for fun, and no more so than in a midweek game at Villa Park when he helped himself to four goals as we routed Aston Villa 5-1 on their own patch. Our final home game victory over Sunderland saw the Wearsiders relegated at the same time, it was an emotional occasion, with the visiting fans turning up in huge numbers clinging to the faint hope of survival, much as we had done in seasons gone by.

Our big summer signing in 1991 came in the form of Wimbledon's lightning quick centre half Keith Curle. He cost £2.5 million but you had to pay the big bucks for the quality, the problem was we couldn't attract enough quality players to the club to take us further. If the truth be known, we never really knew the true state of the finances of the club, we certainly were nowhere near United in terms of spending power even if during this period we actually spent more on players. Academy players Michael Hughes and Michael Sheron were making inroads into the first team and once again we achieved a highly creditable 5th place finish, although the disappointment of going out of both cup competitions away to Second Division Middlesbrough was a bitter pill to swallow.

The fans remained in high spirits, and stuck with the team, even when we uncharacteristically shipped four goals away at Sheffield United. Their Kop, situated at the Shoreham Street end of Bramall Lane, were in buoyant mood that day, and knowing they had won the game, their full repertoire of songs were in full flow. The obvious one aimed at their city rivals 'We Hate Wednesday!' was heard, to which City fans quickly responded with 'We Hate Saturday!' at least we'd not lost our sense of humour!

The following season saw the start of the newly formed Premier League which, however you slice it, was a deliberate move by the big clubs to capitalise on revenues from the new product sold to the world by Sky TV at the expense of the rest of the Football League. We spent big again, Wimbledon defender Terry Phelan arriving for £3m. Wimbledon must have loved us, we'd given them £5 million for two players! We also signed Ricky Holden from Oldham, an honest grafter but was he really going to help take us to the next level? Steve McMahon was a great servant to us in the twilight of his career but he wasn't getting any younger but then we had Garry Flitcroft coming through the ranks as a replacement. Then we signed Kare Ingebrigsten from Norway; with all due respect, was he really cut out for the rough and tumble of England's premier division? At least Kare showed us glimpses of what he could do, scoring a hat-trick at home to Leicester City in the FA Cup the following season. We ended up finishing a disappointing 9th in the 'whole new ball game' which was made all the more sickening by you-know-who winning their first league title in 26 years.

Tottenham Hotspur were two words which stuck in the craw of every City supporter that season. We played them 4 times and managed to lose all 4 and 3 of them were at Maine Road! Out of those 4 defeats, the hardest one to take was the FA Cup Quarter Final at Maine Road. It was all set up nicely; a home quarter final and a chance to make amends for the pain some of us still suffered since our final defeat to them in 1981. It was the official opening of the brand new Umbro Stand which had replaced the old Platt Lane benches. Although the structure looked big enough, it was woefully under capacity with seating for no more than 5,000. It was yet another City cock up, someone had sold us a pup!

We had to relocate it into it because 7,000 Spurs fans were

being housed in the North Stand where we normally sat. That day was also my 28th birthday, although we had never won on my birthday, certainly as long as I've been watching them anyway! But today would be different, the Match of the Day cameras where there to beam it live to the nation, expectancy was high, this was Reidy's first real chance to prove to the country that he had what it takes and lead us on to FA Cup glory!

When Mike Sheron headed us in front only a few minutes into the game, we were in dreamland but Spurs soon redressed the balance and with Nayim scoring a hat-trick, they simple tore us apart. When their 4th goal went in, the anger and frustration of our fans spilled over on to the pitch, mainly from the newly opened stand, and before long there was a full scale pitch invasion. At first I honestly believed it was in protest over the way we'd thrown it all away once again but it soon turned into something completely different, as large groups of fans converged on the away end. I couldn't believe it was happening to my club and on my birthday; the shame, disgrace and embarrassment of it all! I hadn't gone on the pitch that day, I had no intention to do so but I still took the stinging criticism from the nation's media and rival fans personally. Some of our fans just weren't man enough to take defeat on the chin and the trouble which followed was just the final straw - had it really come down to this? When the police horses finally cleared the pitch of spectators, City actually pulled a goal bag, a magnificent solo run and finish by our costly defender Terry Phelan. We should have been talking about the game and the goals but the headlines would be about how City had failed to control the crowd and, more worryingly, how the majority of fans had been able to get on the pitch from a brand new state of the art facility.

Chairman Peter Swales had intimated there would be £6 million available for Peter Reid to sign new players. When the season started however the only new addition was a Dutch player we'd never heard of called Alfons Groenendijk; we couldn't spell it, let alone sing it! The fans were ill with it all, we'd had enough, Reidy was being asked to find bargain buys from the European Leagues because the money he'd been promised didn't materialise, because it never existed. We played Everton second game of the season, having scraped a 1-1 draw at home to Leeds on the Saturday. We made a banner to display in the City end asking the chairman where the £6 million had gone. The fans chanted throughout the game in protest at the lack of transfer activity and 5 games into the season Peter Reid was out of work.

Such was the animosity from fans towards Swales that he appointed former journalist John Maddock (not to be confused with City author and statistician John Maddocks) to deal with the replacement of the new manager. We'd never heard of this guy and while he certainly wasn't camera shy, he didn't impress us, although to be fair to the bloke he was in an impossible situation. The fans were demanding Swales resign and hand the club over to former player Francis Lee, as the 'Forward with Franny' campaign gathered momentum. Maddock announced he was travelling by car '3 and half hours south' to meet up with our new man, and we all hoped and prayed it was the highly-rated Gerry Francis, even though that's not enough time to London by car! It was enough time to get to Oxford however and so it transpired that the relatively unknown Brian Horton was handed the opportunity of a lifetime to manage Manchester City FC. Of course none of us saw it that way at the time and the press, who were revelling in the haphazard, slipshod way the Club was being run, wasted no time in getting the thoughts of the fans. One interview always stands out for me, when a reporter announced to an elderly fan at the ground that we'd acquired the services of Brian Horton. "Brian who?" asked the fan, then after pondering for a moment he said "is he a golfer?". You had to laugh, or you would have cried! Of course Brian was anything but the novice he was portrayed to be, he was a vastly experienced football man who had enjoyed a long playing career, and was an astute manager, albeit in the lower echelons of the Football League. To his credit, he understood the reservations about him but all that he asked was that we judge him on performances and results. Sure enough, we now had an exciting brand of football to watch again and with players like Paul Walsh, Peter Beagrie, Nicky Summerbee, and a German player by the name of Uwe Rösler, he managed to keep us in the Premiership.

During the second half of the season, and after a protracted boardroom battle, Franny Lee eventually took over. I actually attended the last shareholders meeting that Peter Swales attended before he relinquished control. He was a frail old man who looked broken and while most of us there that day had gone to voice our opinions and make our feelings known, you simply had to show some compassion. The club he had spent half his life trying to build into one of the powerhouses of English football was slowly but surely killing him. He'd tried to hang on as long as he could but the stresses and strains of trying to compete with the big guns had been a step too far, and we were in grave danger of being left behind for good.

The new regime of Francis Lee and former City player Colin Barlow, took over at the beginning of February 1995. Of course Brian Horton wasn't Franny's man so that made his job even more tenuous. A shock cup defeat away at Cardiff in the FA Cup was a day to forget, and another throwback to the bad old days off the pitch, with a lot of crowd trouble inside and outside the ground, it was more reminiscent of an England versus Wales battlefield.

The following season under Brian saw us lose more than we won but the quality of football at times was as good as anything we'd seen for some time; memorable victories at home to Spurs, (5-2) and a away at champions elect Blackburn Rovers (3-2) with their star striker Alan Shearer saying 'what I'd like to know is where have Manchester City been all season' were superb. On the flip side a 4-0 thrashing at Crystal Palace in a mid-week League Cup tie remained one of the very low points, especially as it took plenty of us most of the day to get there on the jammed packed motorways, having to get out of our car on the M25 for unauthorised toilet stops because there was nothing else you could do. So while Brian had protected our Premiership status, Franny was always going to bring his own man in to do the job, and that man would be Alan Ball...

9: ball, lee and division three

THE 1995-96 SEASON was one of the most turbulent in the history of our club. Everyone had pinned their hopes on our new owners, complete with the completion of the new Kippax Stand, returning the glory days back to Moss Side. Alan Ball was Francis Lee's pal from his England playing days and Franny was convinced that if anyone could sort out Manchester City, then Alan Ball was that man. The wider world of football, including most City supporters, begged to differ. Alan's playing career was not in question; he'd been there, seen it, done it, got the tee shirt from domestic honours to a World Cup Winners' medal, he was one of the most decorated players of the sixties and seventies but the burning question was, could he manage? More importantly, could he manage a club like ours where the number of quality players could be counted on the fingers of one hand.

The first 11 league games of that fateful season only confirmed what most of us suspected; it was as close to an unmitigated disaster as you could imagine as a football fan. We'd won none, drawn 2 and lost 9, scoring 3 goals and conceded 21. As Phill Gatenby recalls in the introduction to this book, Liverpool put 10 past us in the space of 4 days. We'd gone from watching nice football under Horton to a team who didn't know each other, let alone which system they were playing, under Ball. Young Steve Lomas ran his heart out for the cause but far too many others didn't and signings like Gerry Creaney and Carl Griffiths were, with all due respect to those players, woefully short of what was required to survive in the all singing, all dancing Premier League. The Oxo cube/laughing stock jokes were linked to City again, and it was painful to endure. In complete contrast, the City supporting Gallagher Brothers were conquering the world with Oasis, their hit tune 'Wonderwall' became a new chant for City fans, "and after all, you're my Alan

Ball", yet the harsh facts of the matter are that he wasn't the right man to propel City forward, and the man he had been brought in to replace had a better pedigree in terms of wheeling and dealing and man-management of his players in the Premier league, because he had gained invaluable experience of doing it lower down the football pyramid.

The panic buy of Nigel Clough, whose best playing days were clearly behind him, highlighted our predicament. We'd been triumphant about securing the services of Geo Kinkladze, but while he provided moments of individual brilliance (the mazy individual run and dribble at home to Southampton being a case in point) it was going to take more than that to ensure our survival. Players were brought in on a trial basis; in March we were losing at Stamford Bridge and a substitute came on by the name of Guiseppe Mazzerelli, a Swiss born defender on loan from Zurich who we'd never heard of before and after 2 substitute appearances, he disappeared without trace, and we never heard of him again! It was symptomatic of a club where there was no structure or plan and no hierarchy of control and all this transmitted on to the pitch where the players were trying but they ultimately knew it was destined to fail, you can't start a season as badly as we did, and expect to 'get away' with it.

We lost three times to the Reds that season, just to rub salt into the wounds, but if ever a game summed up the joke we'd become at everyone's else's expense, it was the final home game against Liverpool. It seemed obvious to all of us inside Maine Road that the scousers weren't busting a gut to beat us, they had nothing to play for, but we still contrived to be drawing a game we should have been winning and when the instruction came from *our* bench for the lads to go and play keep ball by the corner flag because of a wrong score line being communicated to them, well quite frankly, we deserved to go down for that alone. It was embarrassing and when our players went off that day, we knew we'd not see the likes of Curle, Quinn and Coton again because they were the high wage earners and we simply couldn't afford them. This of course meant our relegation wouldn't be a quick fix because we wouldn't have the calibre of players to claw our way back out of the Second Division again, so if we thought that season was tough, then we were all in for an even bigger shock - City were about to go on a magical mystery tour of towns and grounds that would take us down to the third level of English football, it was uncharted territory for Blues and it would take some adjustment.

Remarkably, Alan Ball survived three games into the new season and ironically it was away at Stoke, one of the clubs he'd managed before, that the grim reaper finally brought the axe down. The cruelty of football and football fans in particular knows no bounds — at this game the chant of "you're getting sacked in the morning" was being sung by both sets of supporters! The truth of the matter was Alan Ball was on borrowed time from the moment he agreed to take the job. Francis Lee had arrived as the knight in shining armour to save the club but in reality he never had the cash. While I'm sure he had the very best of intentions, the truth was he found himself saddled with a club which had suffered mismanagement for years, and was already struggling to pay off existing debts, let alone raise the large amount of capital required not only to bring quality players in but to replace and build the new Kippax, hence the rush job and 'cheap' build of a new stand which housed less than half of the stand it was built to replace.

New signing Paul Dickov had only been at the club two minutes and he was already working with a new manager in the guise of former United player and Crystal Palace boss Steve Coppell. Steve's reign at the club lasted all of a month before he resigned! You couldn't make it up! In between all the mayhem we were losing more games than we were winning, we were still a box office attraction both home and away, but the Manchester City story was entering a new phase of 'just when you think it can't get any worse' and while it made for fascinating entertainment for the rest of the football world, it was agony if you were a Blue.

Permanent and temporary managers continued to troop in and out of the Platt Lane training complex; Asa Hartford was followed by Phil Neal. The run of results were alarming as we slipped further and further down the league, while the board searched desperately for a 'big name' replacement. The next manager to fall for the poison chalice was Frank Clark, who had been relatively successful at Nottingham Forest. The choice was seen by many at the time as a sensible one as the general consensus seemed to be that he would bring much needed stability to the club. Results in the second half of the season seemed to back that up, and the addition of Kevin Horlock was certainly a good one. The acid test for Clark's tenure would be the following season as we looked to build on the solid foundations we thought were in place.

The close season saw Clark spend a club record £3 million on former soldier and Portsmouth front man Lee Bradbury. Expectations were sky high and a pre-season friendly at Burnley saw the new man look like the answer to our striking issues. The season opener, at home to Portsmouth, complete with Liam Gallagher gesturing to the travelling Pompey following before kick-off, saw an entertaining 2-2 draw in front of a capacity Maine Road crowd while our first away game gave us the honour of being the first league side to visit Sunderland's brand new 54,000 capacity Stadium of Light. Tony Vaughan got his marching orders, and despite the efforts of Kinkladze, we lost the game 3-1.

Tranmere Rovers were the next team to visit Maine Road, and in what proved to be a recurring theme, the opposition took one look at a packed ground and probably thought, this could be the biggest game they ever played in, and it showed, as our opponents lifted their game, and we struggled to cope with the weight of expectation. The game was drawn and the following week we lost 2-1 to Charlton. Lee Bradbury was struggling to hit any kind of form, the goals had deserted him, and the rumours which quickly spread around the terraces saw the deadpan humour return, 'he couldn't hit a barn door, are we sure we didn't sign Lee Badbuy?'

Nottingham Forest away saw one of our best performances in an otherwise dismal campaign, an under fire Ged Brannan striking twice in a surprise 3-1 win, our first of the season. Next up saw a trip up to Gigg Lane, home of Bury FC for a televised game. Over 11,000 packed inside the famous old stadium, with half the crowd having travelled up the A56 from town, the locals were no doubt rubbing their hands at the prospect of putting one over one of the Manchester clubs. Their manager, Stan Ternent, was a respected coach and what he had already achieved at Bury by getting them up to the Second Division meant he was already a legend in the town. We missed a penalty, Bury scored, and David Morley, a rookie centre half who was making his league debut, scored a vital equaliser for us but make no mistake, Bury were the better side and if we didn't realise the size of the task beforehand, we certainly did now.

Norwich City came to Maine Road a week later, and won by 2-1 but there was a positive as Lee Bradbury scored his first league goal for City, we were hoping it would open the floodgates, and when he scored again the following week as we finally won a home game, in some style it has to be said, by demolishing Swindon Town 6-0, we started to believe.

The month of October soon kicked any of those unfounded beliefs straight into touch, as we lost 3 of 5 games. The only goal we scored in those games, by young academy player Chris Greenacre, saw us at least win that game, although it is interesting to note that, despite our dreadful form, and it being a midweek game against one of the less fashionable clubs in the league, there were over 27,000 fans inside Maine Road. There was almost a reverse psychology going on here; logic would suggest that if a club is doing well, then more fans will want to watch their team and crowds go up. Conversely, if a club is struggling, or has fallen on hard times, then it would be normal to expect attendances to fall accordingly, but this certainly wasn't the case at City. Our support was not only remaining constant, our attendances were going *up*! It was one of the strangest phenomenas in football, while our neighbours across the road were sweeping all before them domestically, and on the cusp of Champions League glory, here were poor little City at the complete opposite end of the football spectrum, with everyone feeling sorry for our plight and yet we were filling Maine Road every other week. I've never been prouder of that fact, to say that so many of us were there when we were shit, and nobody can ever take that away from us. Success may be defined by trophies in the cabinet but you cannot measure the quality of a club's support in the same way, it is easy to follow a successful team but a true measure of any club's support is what those fans do when times are tough, and we passed that particular test with flying colours, in my opinion.

November was another dreadful month, a solitary win in six games played, our win at home to Bradford came courtesy of a Tony Vaughan goal before just under 30,000 sufferers. The 3-1 defeat down the road at Edgeley Park, home of Stockport County, was another nail in our coffin. We were 3-0 down inside half an hour, we were being ripped apart, and watching on in disbelief, could we actually fall any further than this? Our fans were kicking off with each other, with some demanding to be let out of the ground; it wasn't pretty but the frustrations were understandable, I identified with them. The County fans were in dreamland, they lived in a town where most locals were either Blue or Red, this was their day and they were going to make the most of it. Just to crown off a great afternoon, my car had been vandalised during the game – it never rains but it pours! Having any form of team identification in the form of scarves or stickers always left you open to the small minded minority, the defeat felt far more damaging than the wing mirror which was hanging on by a thread. By now there were protests against Francis Lee before, during and after games. The six games played in December yielded another four defeats and two wins and this form carried on into the New Year. The visit of Bury to Maine Road on Valentine's Day proved to be the end of Clark's time in charge. The Shakers winning goal that day was scored by mad City fan Paul Butler, it could only happen to us.

Joe Royle, who had been approached by and turned down City previously, was the man tasked to come in and sort out this sorry mess, Willie Donachie would be his assistant. Both players knew the club well from their time with us and they had a great deal of affection for the club. One of Joe's first decisions wasn't a popular one; he had seen enough of Kinkladze to think that while his natural skill and ability wasn't in question, he could also drift out of games, and his hero-like status among fans wasn't helping to build the togetherness and spirit which was desperately required to keep us up.

We still managed to lose more games than we won for the rest of the season, a comical own goal from our recent signing Jamie Pollock saw us lose two points which we couldn't afford against QPR and it call came down to Stoke away where even a victory wouldn't guarantee our survival in the second tier of English football. City did the business that day, one of our other new signings Shaun Goater looked like the type of goalscorer required, as we smashed in five goals to Stoke's two but it was academic as Portsmouth (ironically managed again by Alan Ball, who had performed miracles to create their great escape) and Stoke's local rivals Port Vale both won, meaning we were both relegated into the third tier of English football, in our case for the first time in our history.

Photographs of heartbroken City fans sat slumped in their seats as the realisation dawned upon everyone connected with the club were fodder for the nation's tabloids. The reality outside the stadium was rather different, as we crouched to avoid a hail of bricks raining down on us from the Stoke fans above. Football still had its problems off the pitch but we had our own right at that moment – how to get back to our transport in one piece. Changes were afoot at boardroom level as Francis Lee had been forced to step aside, he was replaced by former French Connection supremo David Bernstein (the high street clothing chain not the violent 1970s film) while Dennis Tueart was also promoted on to the board.

Our first home game in the Third Division saw us brush Blackpool aside in a convincing 3-0 victory. The game was a sell-out and demand for tickets exceeded supply. City were still big business, despite our fall from grace. Our early season form, apart from a 3-0 reverse at Fulham, was certainly far more encouraging. Our new local derby for the season was Macclesfield Town and in September we travelled to the compact Moss Rose ground, where 6, 381 of us crammed in to see what many thought would never happen, Macclesfield Town, enjoying their third season in the

Football League, were playing at home in the league to Manchester City. Just let that sink in for a minute, it really did happen! Security was tight but fans desperate enough to get in will always find a way, and forged tickets were doing the rounds and turnstile operators were being bribed by City fans desperate to get in. It took a Shaun Goater goal to decide the game and it was a feeling of relief, rather than jubilation, as we came out of the ground that afternoon. One thing was for sure, all our opponents were determined to make sure that we didn't walk out of this division, we'd have to earn the right to do so.

After a couple of successive defeats, away to Lincoln City, and at home to Reading, Joe and Willie had already made contingency plans to bring in a bit of steel to shore up the defence. The player in question was a stocky centre half who resembled a tank and he'd had his fair share of problems on and off the pitch, so it was a calculated gamble when we paid £50,000 to secure the services of Andy Morrison from Huddersfield Town. His impact was immediate, scoring on his debut at home to Colchester United, and he was an immediate fans' favourite. He looked fearsome because he was, and while he wasn't the tallest defender around, he was surprisingly agile for such a big bloke.

A succession of drawn games saw us lose touch with the chasing pack and in November we achieved another notable first, beating Halifax Town at home in the FIRST round of the FA Cup! December then saw us play in the AUTO WINDSCREEN SHIELD CUP, a 2-1 defeat at home to Mansfield with a largely reserve team selected by Joe Royle. The Club knew that fans weren't interested and only two stands were opened for the match. I was one of a crowd of just 3,007 that bothered to turn up, of course this bore no reflection to our league gates but the media were quick to seize upon the opportunity; an empty Maine Road being shown alongside a full Old Trafford as United hosted Bayern Munich in the Champions League the following evening. It was a timely reminder to us that some of the media were only too happy to stick the boot in while we were down.

A defeat at Bootham Crescent, home of York City, just before

Christmas, saw us down to 12th, our lowest-ever league position in 118 years. Craig Russell had scored our goal and looked like our best player before being substituted. It was the only time I remember our fans giving Joe and Willie any stick, because we couldn't understand the logic behind taking him off, it felt like we had given the initiative back to the home side, and the Minstermen duly made the most it. We trudged back to the car knowing that it would take a monumental effort from now until the end of the season if we were to be in contention for a play-off place and that is exactly what happened, it pleases me to say! Starting with a hard fought 1-0 win at Wrexham on Boxing Day (which technically was in Europe, with it being in Wales) we went on to win 15 of our remaining games, culminating in a 4-0 home victory at to now relegated York City. We had some unsung heroes; the Whitley brothers Jim and Jeff, Terry Cooke, Gareth Taylor, Michael Brown, Danny Tiatto, Danny Allsop, as well as the other regulars we knew we could rely on. Our young goalkeeper Nicky Weaver typified the spirit in the team as did Shaun Goater and former Arsenal striker Paul Dickov.

One of the few games we failed to win was a 0-0 draw at home to Northampton Town, the date of the game coincided with mine and Don's birthday. Geoff Durbin, who was on City's commercial team at the time, was able to offer the Prestwich and Whitefield Branch an executive box in the Umbro Stand for the game at a knockdown price, and we snapped up the offer. A few of the branch regulars, Keith Roberts, Paul Holt, Kev White, Brian Livesey, Darbo and Neil McCaslin clubbed together, with our better halves, to enjoy a bit of corporate hospitality. Well the City catering and bar staff didn't know what they were letting themselves in for; when the waiter came to take the drink order, he had mistakenly thought Darbo had ordered two beers, when in fact he meant two crates! 96 bottles! Boy did we need them, as we probably witnessed the worst of all the games played in our unbeaten run. After the game, our party went on, and some would be potential overseas investors were certainly a bit surprised to hear a box full of very drunken City supporters chanting 'Who the f*ckin 'ell are you!'

as they walked across the Maine Road pitch in what they thought was a now deserted stadium. Nothing like a friendly Manchester welcome from some of the club's hard core vocal support, is there? The club ushered us off the premises as quickly as they could, so the party carried on in the Parkside!

The play off semi-final saw us drawn against Wigan Athletic and in a tense first leg at the last ever competitive game to be played at Springfield Park, City recovered from a horror start, conceding a soft goal within a minute, to secure a draw. The second leg was decided with a Shaun Goater goal, it went in off his body, Wigan fans will claim it was handball but if we did get the rub of the green, then it was for the first time in a long time.

So imagine the scenario, your local rivals have just won the treble, including snatching the Champions League with two goals in injury time and we had arguably the most important game in our history as we would travelled down to Wembley to face Gillingham in the play-off final. Tickets were in huge demand and with the Kent club taking up their full allocation, City fans who couldn't get their hands on one of the 40,000 or so we'd shifted, were down in Kent quickly making friends and paying way over the odds for a ticket for the game.

Managed by Tony Pulis, the Gills were a decent side, and we certainly couldn't underestimate them, although we'd drawn 0-0 at home and beaten them 2-0 away in the league that season. Playing in our change kit of dark blue and yellow stripes, it seemed as if half of the City of Manchester had descended on North London to see if City could complete the great escape. With so much at stake, it was hardly surprising neither side was giving too much away. We didn't seem to be firing on all cylinders and so when, with 9 minutes to go, the Gills drew first blood through Asaba it looked as if half a season's blood and sweat to pull us back into the reckoning was going to prove ultimately pointless. Then with with 3 minutes left Bob Taylor made it two and if anyone had any doubts it wasn't all over, well Gillingham had confirmed it now, hadn't they?

Blues that couldn't stand anymore of it headed for the exits, I couldn't tell you how many left as I was sat there with my head in my hands thinking, well at least Scunthorpe away is another new ground next season. It was just the final kick in the teeth we didn't need but Kevin Horlock had different ideas, as he kept his cool and slotted in what we all thought was a consolation in the 90th minute. 'Typical City' was the cry, they'd done it to us again, given us false hope, when it was too late. When 5 minutes additional time were signalled, I don't think many of us truly believed we could score again but when all seemed lost, that man Paul Dickov, the hardest working centre forward in the game, well he had to be because of his size, had an opportunity to shoot on goal, and with literally the last kick of the game, found a gap and his shot hit the roof of the net. In that instant we all knew fate was on our side, we were back from the brink, whatever you want to call it, our players had refused to give in, and now we had the upper hand, that equaliser had galvanised our team and fans, we were as one, Meanwhile outside the ground, City fans were streaming back *in* to the stadium, as news filtered through of the unlikeliest of comebacks.

Extra time saw both sides seem content to take it to penalties, Nicky Weaver made the save which saw us win it, and our side of Wembley went absolutely mad, it was mass hysteria on and off the pitch. My abiding moment of our penalties was the one taken by Richard Edghill; the lad had battled with injuries and dips in form but he always showed for the team and when he kissed the City badge after scoring his penalty, you knew he meant it, Richard would have no hesitation in spilling blue blood for the cause. Defeat that day was simply unthinkable and yet we had come within seconds of it but we had escaped what could have been years in football oblivion. We'd certainly done it the hard way but the strains of Blue Moon heard in the early evening as City fans wandered back to their cars, coaches, trains and planes, told you all you needed to know.

City's homecoming after Wembley was relatively low key, the players and management had a celebration meal within the confines of the Midland Hotel but word got round and before you knew it the road and surrounding streets were full of expectant Blues singing and celebrating. The players appeared briefly, almost apologetically, on the balcony to acknowledge the fans (although Flynny somehow managed to blag into the hotel, and appeared on the balcony complete with his customary disguise – a huge head from a cabbage patch doll!).

The hard work started here, we had only just got on the road to recovery and now we desperately needed to trim the squad, and bring better quality players to the club. Mark Kennedy, a winger with real talent, was the big money acquisition, and one of the elder statesmen who had served Joe so well at previous clubs, Richard Jobson, came in to strengthen the back four, along with no nonsense full back Danny Granville.

Once again season tickets were snapped up in record time, with plenty more joining the queue. Despite an opening day defeat at home to Wolves, and a draw away at Fulham, there was every reason for optimism. We looked a different proposition now, and if any doubted it just ask the Sheffield United fans who made the trip over the Pennines to Maine Road as we hit them for 6. The following week we had our first local derby of the season, away at Bolton. Tickets were like gold dust and plenty of Blues were in and around the ground that day. What we saw was a goal fit to win any match, let alone a derby. The scorer, our new Irish hero 'Super' Mark Kennedy scored his second goal for the club and one he won't forget in a hurry, a powerful, swerving shot which flew into the top of the net from distance, it had quality written all over it, and we knew that in him we had a weapon in our armoury that was going to hurt the opposition all season. His crosses into the box were a defender's nightmare and there would be plenty to 'Feed the Goat' that season!

We had a slight blip in form at the end of September, losing away narrowly to Ipswich and Norwich and the end of November early December saw three successive defeats but that aside we were winning the vast majority of our fixtures and we were on course for back to back promotions. Robert Taylor was brought in from Gillingham to further strengthen our attacking options, along with centre half Spencer Prior. As the season reached its climax, a couple of draws cost us the chance to go back up as champions but in a tense final home game against Birmingham City a goal from 'Super' Bobby Taylor was enough to secure those vital 3 points, and all eyes were focused on our last game of the season, away at Blackburn.

Our official allocation of 7,500 tickets were swallowed up in no time and with nothing riding on the game for the home team, City fans found ways and means of buying tickets all around the ground. Those that couldn't get one found a small hill between two stands where they could see some of the game. If the players were in any doubt as to what it meant to the fans and the club, then the roads approaching the ground told them all they needed to know. City fans had gathered in their thousands and could be seen at every vantage point as the team bus slowly made its way to the ground. It's difficult to say how many Blues actually got in that day but I wouldn't be surprised if it was twice the official number. The mathematics were simple; provided we avoided defeat, then we'd be guaranteed top flight football, a defeat however would let Ipswich leapfrog.

If fate had dealt us a bad hand throughout the years, then it was certainly kind to us that afternoon. With a wall of noise and fans on all four sides of the ground roaring them on, we went in a goal down at half time, which was bad enough but Blackburn also managed to hit Nicky Weaver's woodwork on no fewer than *four* occasions! Can you imagine the mental torture we were experiencing off the pitch. Had Blackburn scored any or all of these, it would not have flattered them. The longer the game went on, the more we rode our luck and when Shaun 'Feed the Goat' Goater (who else?) popped up to score an equaliser we barely deserved, the sleepy Lancashire town erupted. A bizarre own goal then saw us take the lead and great finishes by Kennedy (who ran straight over to the gaffer to embrace him) and Wembley hero Paul Dickov secured the unlikeliest 4-1 victory away from home I've ever seen. The pitch invasion was good natured, and full credit to the Rovers fans, it can't be easy to see your own patch taken over, but they accepted it with good grace, as the jubilant scenes and the chant of 'City are back!' told the country in no uncertain terms this sleeping giant of a club had awakened once again.

Outside the ground fans gathered with cans of beer for company, drinking in the special moment, the sweet taste of success was back, and we were lapping it up! A few us ended up sneaking in the main reception area inside the Main Stand and the next thing we knew City player Lee Crooks was there, swigging from a bottle of champagne. We cheekily asked for a little taste, and he duly obliged (cheers Lee!), before security politely asked us to leave. We'd had our very own champagne moment so we didn't complain, and did as we were told. On our way back into Manchester via Regent Road, Salford, the local Reds were straight out of the pubs to give us their very own welcoming party, shouting abuse and throwing stones at our cars and coaches, this is how it rolls in Manchester but along with the counting clock at the Stretford End denoting the number of our 'trophy free' years, we knew that despite their claims to the contrary that we mean nothing to them, we know we do, and I for one always clung to the hope that like the old saying goes 'every dog has its day'. Today was our day, we had our credibility back once again, and they didn't like it one little bit.

For the new season we obviously needed to strengthen a squad which had lost only 11 league games out of the last 73 played, to help us achieve back to back promotions. Joe brought in tough tackling Alfie Haaland from Leeds, Richard Dunne, Paulo Wanchope, Laurent Charvet, Steve Howey and somewhat surprisingly George Weah. Our Premier League campaign started in South London against the team which had pipped us to the First Division title, Charlton Athletic. The manner of our 4-0 defeat certainly brought us back down to earth with a bump; if this was going to set the tone for the season, we were in trouble. Our new signing Haaland wasn't impressed either, and bumping into a few Blues in a petrol station after the game, he promptly coughed up a few quid to get them back home at his expense. It was a nice gesture and demonstrated to us that at least the fans mattered to him.

Maine Road was packed to the rafters for our Premier League return, complete with the aptly named Gene Kelly temporary stands, one located either side of the Kippax, to take the capacity up to around 35,000. Sunderland were the visitors, and we bounced back in style beating them 4-2 with a hat-trick on his home debut for the wonderfully talented, if sometimes erratic, Paulo Wanchope. A surprise 2-1 win at Elland Road was an early season highlight, the first Manchester Derby for four seasons saw them nick it by a solitary goal at Maine Road. I was in the family stand that day taking my nephew Michael to his first ever derby. As Beckham's free kick went in, a couple of their Neanderthals jumped up in our section, it was the family stand remember, scaring the kids in the process, my nephew couldn't understand why 'City' fans were celebrating a goal for the opposition! This didn't go down well with the City dads among us and a couple of them wasted no time at all in taking the law into their own hands and 'escorting' the offenders out of the stand. A run of six successive league defeats was extremely damaging as we tried to establish ourselves but the horrendous run of form was ended in style, as we thumped Everton 5-0 at home, by now Weah had been and gone after a fall out with the manager, the Goat was back in and Darren Huckerby was signed over the Christmas period, but damaging home defeats suggested we had our work cut out to stay.

Despite a creditable draw at Old Trafford in the return derby, it wasn't enough. That game will always be remembered for Roy Keane 'doing' Haaland in an apparent revenge attack after the Norwegian taunted Keane following an injury the Irishman sustained the season before at Leeds. Keane was given a straight red and Haaland never fully recovered, eventually retiring from football. Whenever bad blood between the players has boiled over in the derbies, we've always ended up coming off worse, remember Best on Pardoe, Buchan on Bell! Imagine the furore if that had been the other way round.

Our defeat at Ipswich in the penultimate game of the season confirmed our return to the First Division with the last home game of the season, a 2-1 defeat to Chelsea, proving academic. We'd only managed to win eight games all season and lost an alarming 20. We'd been found wanting although the subsequent dismissal of Joe Royle felt a bit premature. Given what he had achieved for us many felt he should have got a second chance to put things right. It all went sour with Joe due to contractual issues which was a great shame as both he and Willie Donachie had put City back on the map and the fans appreciated that.

10: end of an era

KEVIN KEEGAN REPLACED big Joe and the appointment was met with widespread approval. His passion and enthusiasm for the game was bound to rub off on the club, and his ability to attract players to City would be vital as we attempted to bounce back at the first attempt. The signings of Stuart Pearce, Ali Bernabia and Eyal Berkovic would prove pivotal as we became the nation's great entertainers once again.

The football was breathtaking at times and with Shaun Wright Phillips now established in the first team, it was one of the most enjoyable seasons watching City. Teams were simply brushed aside with Ali and Eyal pulling the strings. Great early season performances included a trip to Hillsborough where we hit Sheffield Wednesday for six. Millwall away was to prove rather trickier, not least because after consultation with police and in light of crowd trouble in previous fixtures, both clubs agreed not to allocate tickets to each other. We still managed to book tickets via Ticketmaster for the away game but these were subsequently cancelled because we didn't meet their criteria as home supporters. We'd negotiated three games before where no fans were officially present; Luton twice, and United when they were rebuilding a stand at Old Trafford, but this was a true test of our endurance. One of our friends who had a South East postcode bought us tickets for the game, we now had to work out how to get in and out alive!

A plan was hatched to disguise ourselves as Millwall fans so we popped along to their souvenir shop and bought hats, scarves and lapel badges and even managed to park at the ground thanks to Mike Owen who had blagged his way into the press box working for a newspaper reporting on the game. We joined in with the Millwall chants throughout the game to blend in, and seeing and hearing nothing when we scored was such an eerie feeling but we couldn't blow our cover. Darren Huckerby's celebration, clapping an empty stand where our fans should have been, made us smile inside. With the game heading for a draw after a couple of dodgy decisions, our young prodigy Shaun Wright-Philips drifted into a forward position before hitting the ball from distance, and imagine his and our delight when the ball hit the back of the net for his first ever senior goal for the Club. It was so quiet, you could hear a pin drop, just the sound of the ball as it rolled along the inside of the netting. Not many of us were in their ground that night, perhaps 40 or 50 of us dotted in ones and twos, but I wouldn't have swapped it for the world, plus it kept my unbroken run of attending games going, I couldn't have been happier!

City wrapped up the Second Division Championship (now confusingly known as the First Division) in style, scoring 108 league goals and accumulating 99 points. We thrashed Premiership side Ipswich Town 4-1 at Portman Road in the FA Cup before losing narrowly to Newcastle United, roared on by 7,000 Blues, in an emotional return to Tyneside for Keegan.

One of the reasons it was so important to win promotion was that the 2002-03 season was our 80th and final year playing at Maine Road before re-locating to the City of Manchester Stadium, over on the east side of the City. The high profile signings of Nicholas Anelka, Peter Schmiechel, and Marc Vivien Foe were statements of intent and these players would go on to prove their worth throughout the season. The last ever Maine Road derby saw us triumph 3-1, with the former United keeper becoming one of an elite band of players to have played and won on both sides of the Manchester divide.

However we found goals harder to come by and Keegan splashed out a further £6 million to secure the services of Robbie Fowler from Leeds, although there were serious questions about his fitness, and this transfer proved to be the turning point for our chairman David Bernstein who had pleaded with the board not to sanction the deal due to his concern over the player's fitness. The best away performance of the season undoubtedly came at Anfield in our last away game of the season, where we secured a rare 2-1 victory thanks to two goals from Anelka, as well as two world class saves from Schmiechel in goal.

So it was on the last ever competitive game to be played at my second home for the last 28 years of my life; Maine Road, Moss Side, Manchester, M14 7WN. The date was Sunday, May 11th 2003 and the visitors were Southampton. We'd spent the morning walking around the surrounding streets, taking photographs, having a drink in our favourite pubs; the Denmark and the Gardeners Arms. It all felt surreal to think that after that day we'd *never* come back here to watch our team. It was a sobering thought, and while the move to a brand new state of the art stadium was obviously exciting, I don't mind admitting I felt a bit of trepidation. What if we don't like it, could they keep Maine Road open just in case?

Just a few short of 35,000 squeezed into the famous old ground for one more time, we contrived to lose the game 1-0, and got piss wet through as we went for a drink in the Whitworth after the match. It was just 'Typical City' in so many ways. My mind cast back to players I'd watched there who had since passed away; Tommy Caton and Kaziu Deyna most notably but within a month or so the tragic death of Marc Vivien Foe, the last City player to score at Maine Road with his brace against Sunderland, would be added to the list. I'd made so many friends there down the years, I knew some of them would be lifelong mates. Manchester City was a community club, we were proud of our diversity, everyone was welcome, regardless of race, colour or creed. That's what made being a City fan feel so special. Then there were characters such as the late Helen Turner, with her beehive style hair and her bell, which you would hear periodically throughout the game, and if the fans didn't hear it, the Kippax would sing 'Helen, Helen ring yer bell!' We had a social club, one of the first of its kind in the country, which gave you a sense of belonging, we had the Junior Blues, the envy of clubs everywhere, and the idea spread to others based on its success at City. We had the biggest floodlights in Manchester, our rivals from across the City would tease, well in the dark days at least they would light up the sky and it was good to know we had something trivial to throw back in their faces.

Don't Look Back In Anger

We had black footballers such as Stan Horne, Roger Palmer, Dave Bennett, Alex Williams, Clive Wilson, most of them local lads born within a stone's throw of those large floodlight pylons I was joking about. At City if you were good enough, you were in the team, it was simple as that. We had celebrity fans from the great LS Lowry, to England test match fast bowler and Ashes hero back in 1981 – Bob Willis. We had comedians Bernard Manning, Eddie Large and Les Dawson who were all Blues. I could go on and on, but hopefully you get my drift, City was a people's Club, and we all wanted to be a part of it.

City continues to be a way of life for generations of fans and long may it continue. A lot has changed since we left Maine Road, and the success we never thought we'd see has finally come our way. I've been extremely proud and privileged to follow the Club for 45 years now and all being well I'd like to get another 45 years in, good health permitting.

11: thirty not out

THE POPULAR CHANT '30 years and we're still here' is a declaration of our undying allegiance to the City cause, despite having endured three decades of living in the shadows, with no trophies, no Cup Finals, five relegations and enough managers to fill a double decker bus. As I'm sure I mentioned previously Marshy, one of the match going crew from back in the 80's, distinctly remembers me saying "I won't miss another game" but of course that is easier said than done.

When I attended the home match against Barnsley on Saturday 22nd April 1989 it never occurred to me that I'd spend the next 30 years of my life on a one man mission prepared to go to any length to ensure I went to every competitive City game, be that home, away, or abroad, forever more. The one exception in those 30 seasons was the CSKA Moscow game played behind 'closed doors' (or before a select group of CSKA ultras!) otherwise I've been ever-present. It sounds ludicrous, because it is ludicrous but yet I did exactly that. It actually frightens me to think about it; Was I ill? Do I need counselling? And how the hell has my wife put up with this obsession of mine? I'll try to expand on how it snowballed into a lifelong obsession that has seen me attend in the region of 1,500 consecutive games (or 1,258 matches before the Moscow debacle) which, given the capricious nature of football re-scheduling to suit TV, bad weather, periods of national crisis and the vagaries of personal circumstances and the reliability of transport is some feat. Even if I do say so myself!

The 1989/90 season was the first where I managed to see every game but there was a close call; the away leg of our midweek League Cup tie against Brentford. I'd travelled down on the football special with my pals as usual but the train parked up at Willesden and got stuck there courtesy of a planned engine change

Don't Look Back In Anger

that was delayed by a good couple of hours. When it was obvious we would miss kick off, some Blues took their lives into their own hands and jumped off the train and ran down the line, disappearing into a nearby industrial estate. The Transport Police were on board our train in no time desperate for names and descriptions, all we wanted was the replacement diesel engine and a driver! We finally made it to Brentford station and ran to the ground, getting in just before half time. We lost the game 2-1, at the time they were our jinx team having dumped us out of the FA Cup there the previous season (3-1) but it obviously didn't impact on our league form, as we promptly went into the Manchester Derby and smashed the Reds 5-1!

The next challenge that season was how to get into Kenilworth Road for our league game with Luton Town. They had banned all visiting fans from attending their ground so it was a case of 'who you knew' to get you in with the home support. Fortunately the late City vice-chairman Freddie Pye was a close friend of the family so he arranged for tickets for us to get in, this involved a lot of trust as had we abused the privilege it would have come back on him but Freddie knew he could rely on us, and for two consecutive seasons he sorted the tickets and we passed the test with flying colours. At the same fixture the following season, I distinctly remember pockets of City fans all around the ground that had been smuggled in by Luton fans against the banning order, and occasional chants of 'Blues are here, Blues are there' gave everyone a good laugh.

In the early 90's we played Torquay United in a mid-week home Rumbelows Cup tie at Maine Road. Not a problem under normal circumstances, as I only worked up the road in Stalybridge, but I'd flown out to Sardinia on a job so on the day of the game the rush was on to get back. But there was a problem, after flying from Cagliari to Rome, I was told the Manchester flight was full, and knowing I only had a few hours to spare before kick-off, I grabbed any flight I could, so I ended up flying to Gatwick and getting the train back up to Manchester via London. I made it to Maine Road with an hour to spare, the relief was tangible, the 0-0 score line incidental, I'd kept my record intact.

Don't Look Back In Anger

In the 1995-96 season we didn't receive any tickets for the derby game due to ground reconstruction work at Old Trafford restricting capacity. I wrote to United sending them photocopies of all my away match tickets showing them my unbroken run of games, and their secretary Ken Merrett (who I understand was a Blue) posted out two complimentary tickets to me a week before the game, which was a brilliant gesture, and because I already had two tickets sorted via Freddie, it meant four of us could get into the game. Before kick-off former United player Paddy Crerand spotted me. He knew my family and joked about how I had managed to get in! After the game started the bloke sat next to me, with a Northern Irish accent, decided to take me to task about my allegiance, saying I shouldn't be in the ground. I was livid but knowing I had everything to lose and nothing to gain by making a scene I played it cool and said to him, "look, I was born a few miles up the road from here, and I'm here to watch the game, and I know where you sit, and I have a lot of friends in the city, so if I were you, I'd keep quiet and watch the game", it worked a treat and he didn't bother me again. Quinny missed a sitter, and at half time the Main Stand bar was packed with Blues, obviously they had all called in favours from their Red pals, so we certainly weren't on our own that day. We ended up losing the game 1-0 but at least we'd got the game under our belts.

In the last decade it has been increasingly tougher to keep the record going, my work involves a daily commute to Sheffield so every midweek home game in effect becomes an away game, and I've had my fair share of traffic problems, vehicle issues, and bad weather to contend with.

My work takes me over to Antwerp on occasions and I've had to arrange cover on three separate visits so that I could fly back on the day to make the relevant fixtures. Two of these involved midweek games at Stoke City and the other was a Champions League home fixture against PSG. This was the most difficult one to negotiate because Brussels Airport had had a terror attack two weeks before and on the day of the game travelling back for the match, Antwerp Railway station had been closed due to a terror threat, so the airport had to put in place temporary measures due to the bomb damage, meaning there were delays getting in to the terminal building and to cap it all the control tower had called a sudden strike! With less than three hours to kick off I was sat on the floor resigned to missing the game, my wife Jane was tweeting the airport saying the airline had to get me back, they were replying to her saying they were doing their best. As if by magic our flight did get out, and we landed in Manchester 50 minutes before kick-off. With a PSG fan and two Blues tagging along I instructed our cab driver to follow my directions cutting through Victoria Park and Longsight to get to the ground. We made it just as the game was about to kick off, and the sense of achievement and elation was unlike anything – I really can't put it into words other than to say the bigger the obstacles which are put in your way, the higher you jump to overcome them.

There have been some great trips abroad. In the Faroe Islands the whole island ran out of beer! Then there were some that were not so great, including being ambushed in Moscow on our first visit to CSKA. There have also been tough decisions to make; I've attended games at difficult times during family bereavements and I had to turn down being best man at my pal's wedding so I could get to Coventry away. It's taken a lot of precision planning, good health, and in the main good jobs with understanding employers, to keep it all going but most of all the understanding of my best pal and the love of my life – my wife. She was there when we got in at Millwall when we were banned, she watched all the dross we had to endure, she is old school City and she has been my inspiration. Without her backing, I'd never have been able to do a fraction of what I was able to do; so to Jane Riley, and the many Blues out there I've had the pleasure of meeting and making friends with, I thank you all. The camaraderie of the fans was what kept us all going in the dark days, and we should never lose sight of that, it makes the success we are now privileged to see all the sweeter.

A mention in despatches if may to a few of the fellow diehards over the decades – the Johnsons, the Gregorys, the Pages, the Seftons, the Seerys, Trav, the Pierces, Sykesy, Jocky, Gary Griffiths,

Don't Look Back In Anger

Charlie Hadfield, Ian Cheeseman, Debs, Buxton, the Nolans, the Roberts, the Liveseys, the Holts, Glynny, Si Draper, the Ostells, the Winstanleys, the Prices, Ash, John, Tom Ritchie, the Wallaces, the Wilkinsons, Phil Dooley, John Dalton, Mark Payne, Wigan, the Sloans, the Stathams, Pat Godfrey, the Foys, the McGoverns, Stephen Holt (Inspirals and Winchester! Plus Lee and his lad), the Grimshaw twins, Sean Smith, Graham Corless, the Moreheads, Gilly, the Carnforths, Andy Moore, Mike Owen, Darren Wood, the Swindells, Bragger and Phil, the Bradys, the Fishers, the Barbers, the Browns, the Murrays, Dave Parr, Tim Ryan, Bedders, Dave D, Stephen Riley, Adam Cooper, the Hanrahans, the Dignums, the Sudworths, the Simpsons, the Frasers, the Dunkinsons, the Singletons, the Brocklehursts, Shez, Olly, the Boyles (where are you now Kelvin and Mark?), Jags, Mucky, the Moss's, Derbo, the Whites, the Swifts, the Cookes, Gary Yates, Martyn Ball, the Noons, Mike Davies, Winners, Paul Canes, Steve Lane, Al, the McGranes, the Temples, Ankers, the Harts, Clinchy, Brogey, Ozzy, the Hensons, the Martins, Andy Bell, the Bolgers, the Brines, the Clancys, the Issacs, Andy Sinclair, Andy Tasker, the Knowles, the Leydens, Jeff, the Tappers, the Winwards, Oggy, the Nicksons, the Needhams, the Cottons, the Hays, the McGuiness family, the Millars, Halifax Steve, Anne Marie, the Floyds, the Naylors, the Walkers, the Veritys, Dante, the Lowes, the MacMahons, the Sutcliffes, Glinks, the Todds, the Gows, the Crossleys, the McGuirks, the Bletchers, the Cheethams, the Horrocks, the Channons, the Kierans, the Harpers, the Valentines, the Berrys, the Muirs, the Bodens, the Baxendales, the Grindles, the Shaws, the Siddalls, the Fletchers, the Peeks, the Plants, the Cavanaghs, the Dicksons, the Jacksons, the McLellands, the Parlanes, the Currans, the Kings, the Svenssons, the Hinces, the Wilsons, the Mullenders, the Brennans, the Palmers, the Matears, the Storeys, the Scallys, the Mitchells, the Ibbetsons, the Faulkners, the Cosserons, the Fowles family, the Gowers, the Burrs, the Hockins, Mick and Debs, Ian, the Hulses, Bosh, Mark, the James's, the Cummins's, Botty, Kev, Neil, Nick, Boydy, Baz – there are so many more. I could fill a book with them all, so apologies in advance for all those I haven't named this time around, you will appear in the sequel, I promise!

And last not least, all those Blues who are no longer with us, keep smiling up there in sky blue heaven.

Thank you one and all!

afterword

WELL WE HOPE YOU liked the stories and contributions from all the different fans. It was great putting it all together even though I probably did everyone's head in as I kept mithering the life out of people to get the chapters in on time. It's not all plain sailing this writing lark! Now some of the games we have written about you might have seen from a different perspective, you might not have seen any trouble at the games mentioned or you might have seen trouble at different grounds that the contributors didn't see. Wrong place, wrong time and all that jazz. It is amazing what we took for the norm back then and in a way that inspired the title of the book as there is no point looking back and moaning; let's look forward to a very bright future.

Feel free to email me on don-price@live.co.uk if there is any part of the book you want to discuss or want more information about. I can also be contacted on Facebook under the name 'Don Cath Price'. Writing the memorial chapter was very emotional and I was not too sure if it was going to work in the context of this book but I contacted a few people and they gave me a big thumbs up plus once they read it they thought it was excellent. As far as I am aware something like that has never been done in a football book so again I would love your views on the chapter.

If you could leave a review on Facebook I would be chuffed to bits. Talking about reviews if you could spare the time to leave a review on Amazon as well I would be very grateful (so would Sean) and all the others who have played a part in putting the book together. I would also encourage any of you who has ever thought about writing a book to take the plunge. We all have got a story in us, getting it out is the hard part and again if you are planning to write a book and want any advice please give me a shout on either email or Facebook or contact the publishers, Empire Publications at enquiries@empire-uk.com

Okay then that's all from me, I am going to get a hot chocolate as soon as I send this off to the publisher. So once again many thanks to all who contributed and to everyone who took the time and trouble to read the book.